Design Makes a Difference

Shipbuilding in Baltimore

1795-1835

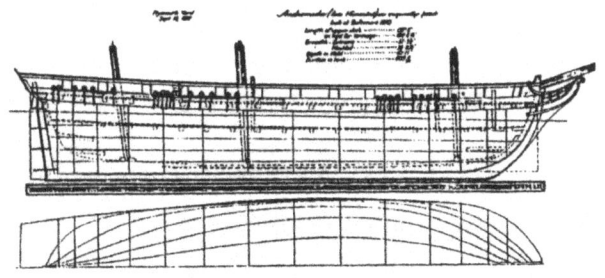

Toni Ahrens

HERITAGE BOOKS
2011

HERITAGE BOOKS
AN IMPRINT OF HERITAGE BOOKS, INC.

Books, CDs, and more—Worldwide

For our listing of thousands of titles see our website
at
www.HeritageBooks.com

Published 2011 by
HERITAGE BOOKS, INC.
Publishing Division
100 Railroad Ave. #104
Westminster, Maryland 21157

Copyright © 1998 Toni Ahrens

All rights reserved. No part of this book may be reproduced or transmitted in any form or by any means, electronic or mechanical, including photocopying, recording or by any information storage and retrieval system without written permission from the author, except for the inclusion of brief quotations in a review.

International Standard Book Numbers
Paperbound: 978-0-7884-1001-7
Clothbound: 978-0-7884-8689-0

Table of Contents

Introduction vii

I. The Birth of a Maritime Nation 1

II. Baltimore, Town of Traders 39

III. Baltimore's Vessels 65

IV. The Shipbuilders 93

Conclusion 115

Appendix 1: Commercial Vessels
    Built in Baltimore 1795-1835 117

Appendix 2: Shipbuilder Production 1795-1835 154

Appendix 3: Documents Relating to the *Hannibal* 164

Endnotes 167

Sources Consulted 183

Index 195

List of Illustrations

Graph	1.1	National Ship Construction	23
Graph	1.2	Urban Populations 1790-1840	36
Map	a	Port Warden's Map, 1799	40a
Map	b	Port Warden's Map, 1828	40b
Photo	2a	Former Site of Price's Shipyard	40c
Photo	2b	Former Residence of William Price	40c
Photo	2c	Former Site of Kemp & Gardner Shipyard	40d
Photo	2d	Rear View of Price Residence	40d
Table	2.1	Early Baltimore Shipyard Production	42
Table	2.2	Carriage of Foreign Trade	49
Table	2.3	U.S. Merchant Marine Tonnage 1790-1840	50
Table	2.4	Vessel Construction 1797-1834	51
Table	2.5a	Total U.S. Merchant Vessels Built & Documented by Type 1797-1840	52
Table	2.5b	Baltimore Merchant Vessels Built & Documented by Type 1797-1840	52
Table	2.6	Population Expansion Comparison: Baltimore vs Maryland	54
Table	2.7	Population Comparison: U.S. vs Baltimore	55
Table	2.8	Slave vs. Free Black Population	56
Table	2.9	Slaveholding Shipbuilders 1790-1830	61
Graph	2.10	Slaveholding Shipbuilders 1790-1830	61
Table	2.11	Other Fells Point Slaveholders	62
Graph	3.1	Fells Point Vessels: Statistical Recap	67
Graph	3.2	Fells Point Vessels: Type & Average Tonnages	68
Illus.	3.3	The *Hannibal*: Drawings	85
Illus.	3.4	The *Hannibal*: Hull View	87
Chart	4.1	Shipbuilders: Career Longevity	95

I wish to thank those who guided me along my way, those who assisted me in my research, and, most of all, my husband, Rudi Lamy, who gave me the support that made it possible. For technical assistance, I would like to thank my computer expert, Gary Ahrens, photographer, Don Andberg, and mapmaker, Jeff Zimmerman, who reproduced some of the 200-year-old documents that had become illegible over time.

Introduction

In late 1796 Baltimore Town and Fells Point became Baltimore City continuing a period of phenomenal commercial expansion begun about 1750. "[T]he community's connection with the West Indies trade actuated its spectacular rise....Baltimore's rapid growth resulted from its capitalizing upon this expanding market."[1] My premise proposes Baltimore's shipbuilding industry as the primary driver of this growth, which lasted until the mid-eighteen thirties when manufacturing and the industrial revolution began changing the nature of the city.

Behind the city's early and "spectacular rise" were the people who built Baltimore's commercial fleet, who responded to their customers' needs by designing and building vessels that enhanced the opportunities presented by a world in chaos. The relationship between the socio-political restructuring that was occurring worldwide and the vessels that drove the commerce of Baltimore is one that has not as yet been studied. This will be the first attempt to describe Baltimore's maritime industry and its relationship to the success of the transportation and commercial revolution that blossomed in Baltimore. Studies of Philadelphia, Charleston, and Boston indicate that as each began their decline, another began its prosperity, with New York ultimately ascending as though destined for primacy. Baltimore, as America's first post-colonial city, presents an unique window into the process of urban expansion in a democratic milieu.

Migration to the Baltimore area of the Chesapeake Bay began about 1750 as the area switched its main export crop from tobacco to grain:

> Demands for large deep-water anchorages and warehousing facilities arose only when wheat and flour challenged tobacco in value and acreage planted. Annapolis was unable to capture the bulk

Design Makes a Difference

of that business because of its limited anchorage, small loading area, and its lack of fresh water feeding into the harbor needed to combat the worms (toredo navalis) weakening the bottoms of wooden vessels. That port, additionally, lacked Baltimore's close proximity to the wheat-growing areas in the central and western counties of Maryland.[2]

Baltimore Town's population exploded from about 200 in 1750 to 5,934 in 1776, and fourteen years later had risen to 12,838. It then doubled by 1800 to 26,000, moving Baltimore from fourth to third place in ranking of U. S. cities, a position it retained until 1830 when Boston's population of 85,600 again exceeded Baltimore's 80,600.[3]

This commercial and maritime expansion had continued unabated during the Revolution when privateers sought shelter from English patrols. Shippers found a cozy harbor in the Patapsco River at the end of the bay and, when retired from sea, discovered economic niches as well. According to their skills, they became shopkeepers, merchants, and artisans as shipbuilding and the number of shipyards increased. Prosperity bred specialization, of course, but technological specialization was most important. The enterprise that allowed this small city, in spite of its late start, to enter the competitive climate of Atlantic trade and be relatively successful was as much due to the sharp built design of the schooners that sailed from her wharves as it was to the cargoes those vessels carried. The commercial alliance composed of local farmers and manufacturers, and Baltimore's merchants, mariners, and shipbuilders, relying on these speedy vessels, gave them the comparative advantage which underpinned Baltimore's success in the period from 1795 to 1835.

Baltimore remained a smaller port than both New York and Philadelphia, but it did not fit their pattern of development. Nor did it fade away like Charleston or stagnate like Boston. Furthermore, industry grew in Baltimore as it did in Philadelphia and New York, by enhancing rather than replacing commerce. Of course packet scheduling gave the port of New York a competitive edge, but Baltimore remained a contender because of ship design. Only gradually, as steam technology mitigated the benefits of design, did

Design Makes a Difference

Baltimore's fast-sailing schooners begin to falter in the metropolitan race among America's Atlantic seaports.

This interport rivalry was no secret to contemporaries or historians. In his classic *The Rise of the Port of New York*, Robert G. Albion spoke of its even larger ramification: "The completion of the Erie Canal aroused the rivals from their lethargy....The rivalry of the seaports thus became a major factor in the development of the nation's transportation systems." Baltimore fared well in his opinion, "more successful" than Philadelphia and with "surprisingly rapid" growth. "Its chief asset in this rivalry was the fact that it lay closer to the West than any of the other ports and that it had an excellent approach up the Potomac valley to Cumberland on the western border of Maryland"[4] These statements define Albion's perspective; basically he argued that natural advantages, even with technological help such as the Erie Canal, are not by themselves the key ingredients to commercial success. More important, he concludes, is the enterprise behind the use of these factors.

Albion's comparative study of factors that affected New York's commercial success covered a wide range of elements. He considered ten Atlantic seaports, examining physical features such as depth of water, channels, ice, fog, and shelter and distance from open sea, and concluded: "[N]ature had distributed her advantages among the ports with a fairly even hand. The northern ports had ice and fog; the southern had sandbars. All had fairly adequate shelter. The two ports most handicapped in the matter of sea lanes had the best natural connections with the West."[5] His conclusions reduced geography to a predisposing condition, rather than a major contributor to a port's success or failure.

New York's edge developed after 1818, Albion theorizes, with the beginning of the packet lines, first with sailing ships, later using steam power:

> [I]t may be possible to demonstrate that New York's rise as a seaport was caused more by its capitalization of its sea routes than by the building of the Erie Canal...At that critical period of port rivalry, these sailing packets did much to cause the

Design Makes a Difference

channels of trade with Europe to flow toward New York rather than to Boston or Philadelphia.... Whether under sail or steam, most of the crack liners of the world have made New York their western terminus ever since that initial venture.[6]

Regular scheduling of freight and passenger runs decreased the cost of transport enough to give New York an advantage over all of the other American seaports.

Charleston's boom had occurred even earlier than New York's, from 1730 to 1820. George C. Rogers, Jr. believed that the winds and the currents which favored sailing vessels were responsible for the vitality of the city. Charleston was a typical colonial port because it lay on the terminus of the sea lanes that began in England and passed through the West Indies to reach Carolina's shores. Then, after refitting and repairs, the ships completed the circle, returning to England heavily laden with colonial staples. This passage became so routine by 1766 that the British Post Office designated it for mail transport.

The development of these fairly regular shipping schedules foreshadowed the packet system that later developed in New York. But in Charleston, Rogers saw a direct relationship between the technology of the ships and the success of the port: "Charleston's golden age coincided with the last century of the age of sailing vessels."[7] Absent in Charleston after 1820 was the vision of using innovation to maintain their competitive position. Charleston's boom turned into a bust:

> The change from sail to steam left Charleston behind, far from the main east-west Atlantic Ocean routes... When New York began regular weekly packet crossings, she could give service which Charleston's great merchants....could not give. When the Erie Canal was completed in 1825 just as South Carolina's efforts were failing, there was no stopping her [New York].[8]

Design Makes a Difference

Since Rogers saw the decline of Charleston as well under way by 1820, it is obvious that the most important factor of the three mentioned above was the scheduling of the vessels sailing out of New York. The Erie Canal did not become a factor until the late 1820's and steam was not a major source of power until just prior to the Civil War.

This pattern of an early successful colonial development followed by later decline characterized Boston and Philadelphia as well as Charleston. Boston had begun trading with the West Indies in the early eighteenth century, especially in the lucrative triangular trade pattern of shipping African slaves to the West Indies and North American continent and rum, cotton, tobacco, rice, indigo, sugar and other raw materials to the European markets. Boston shippers also mined the coastal trade between the West Indies and North America's seaports. America's geography, its long coastline strung out along the Atlantic, encouraged water transport and New England's settlement quickly became dependent on locally built water craft, making shipbuilding New England's most important industry: "By the time of the Revolution more than half the vessels involved in the Atlantic trade were American-built, and ships themselves ranked fifth in value among American exports..."[9]

But such early success carried the seeds of Boston's own destruction. Early settlement and maritime enterprise, depending as they did on the vessels of New England, were limited to the resources that kept the shipyards productive. Boston's growth peaked in 1760, and subsequent immigrants to American shores turned to other ports. Why? Because the hinterland support necessary to the city's success had evaporated: "...by the mid-eighteenth century it was virtually stripped of its timber. The available farmland was occupied; there was little in New England to attract immigrants."[10] Boston stagnated during the generation before the Revolution as maritime prosperity moved south.

"The largest port in America by 1760, Philadelphia was the leading financial, political, and intellectual center of Revolutionary America. Although the city's foreign trade declined rapidly after 1815, Philadelphia was the foremost industrial city in the United States during the first half of the nineteenth century..."[11]

Design Makes a Difference

Philadelphia's early growth was a measure of the energy of its citizens, and its international trade grew out of the fertile valleys west and south of the city which produced bread for the world. As long as Philadelphia's freight costs remained competitive, trading was active and profitable; but when this was no longer the case, Philadelphia followed the general pattern of moving away from trade and toward manufacturing.

* * *

Turning now to Baltimore as a case study: Chapter One of "Design Makes a Difference" will investigate the various economic and political changes that occurred nationally and internationally in the late eighteenth and early nineteenth centuries and detail how these changes affected the city's growth. National factors include the reorganization of the former colonial and aristocratic mercantile order into an independent and more democratic, capitalistic one; the transition of a labor system based on slavery or apprenticeship into a free labor market; and new Constitutional and Congressional legislation regulating commerce and shipbuilding.

Baltimore's shipyards of the 1790's exemplified the entrepreneurial environment of this developing capitalism. The commercial activities of the 1790's and early 1800's followed from the political attitudes of the 1780's and their legal repercussions.

After 1787, Baltimore's businessmen faced a fractious world. Alliances among the European nations shifted constantly which caused chaos in the trans-Atlantic markets until the end of the Napoleonic era in 1815. Politically, the new United States had problems with them as well as their common enemies, such as the Barbary pirates. Some of these problems were handled with diplomacy, some with bribery, and some with war.

Great Britain and France were almost continuously at war from 1792 to 1815. The dangerous instability resulting from the French Revolution, both at home and abroad, created problems in the West Indies as well as on the continent, sending refugees to seek haven in America's seaports. Slavery and the slave trade also became major issues at the turn of the eighteenth century. Although the United

Design Makes a Difference

States postponed more than token action on this subject, France was forced to admit defeat at the hands of the black rebels in San Domingo and both Great Britain and the United States outlawed slave trading after 1808. Great Britain continued her colonial expansion during this period, resulting in control of India by 1814, for example, and began enlarging her navy into a force which would rule the open seas for the next century.

Such political unrest disturbed the delicate balance of commerce across the Atlantic. In particular, the eruptions in the West Indies and the coercive trade policies of Napoleon toward British restrictions on the grain trade had serious repercussions for Baltimore's merchants. America's reaction covered the spectrum from total withdrawal in 1807 to total involvement in the War of 1812. All of these events affected the fortunes of the merchants and shipbuilders in American ports. Shipbuilding records during this period indicate the interactions between the international turmoil and one of America's major industries and will shed light on the effects each had on the other during these continuing crises.

Chapter Two then refocuses this broad picture of international commerce into the smaller and sharper one of Baltimore's urban development. Here, geographic considerations emphasized three factors: Baltimore's port location on the Chesapeake Bay with its national and international implications; its commercial ascendancy over Annapolis, a less successful city which maintained, nevertheless, its political primacy; and finally, the site of the city as a North/South demarcation point where both free and slave labor contributed to its commercial success. Of course, other elements -- such as immigration, the effects of economic conditions on labor, housing and its relationship to family businesses and social stratification patterns -- contributed to Baltimore's dramatic growth and will be discussed. Social hierarchy was particularly important in Baltimore at this period because mobility was based, for the most part, on economic success in a high-risk atmosphere.

All of these factors influenced the way that the city of Baltimore expanded from a sleepy little eighteenth century village to the feisty privateer's nest of the War of 1812 and afterward into the commercial center that it became. But the core of this chapter will

Design Makes a Difference

concern itself with the maritime economy of Baltimore between 1795 and 1835, a city that flourished because of the ingenuity of its merchants. Whether in times of peace or war, Baltimore's vessels moved in and out of the Chesapeake Bay, steadily expanding the commercial base of the city and changing its hinterland economy.

Although vessels had been built in Baltimore during colonial times, few primary records of these shipyards exist before 1797. Federal law first affected Baltimore's shipbuilders in that year, when the 1792 law which required that Master Carpenters in charge of shipyards file a certificate describing the vessel prior to its registration, was finally implemented. These certificates gave a comprehensive picture of the commercial vessels built in the city, particularly at Fells Point, the center of such activities, for they describe the builders as well as their products. I have correlated ship design, construction, output, and the technology of the Master Carpenters from these records from 1797 to 1835 and related them to the fluctuating economic conditions of the era.[12] This chapter will also examine the financing, forms of labor used, and kinds of ship built, leaving the actual ship design, technology, and style for the following chapter.

The use of slaves in industry has been controversial and little known about. In its largest and regional perspective, there is little agreement. Richard C. Wade addresses the role of Southern urban slavery in his *Slavery in the Cities: The South 1820-1860*. Not only does he maintain that the adaptation of slave labor to an urban environment was unsuccessful during the period preceding the Civil War, but that it would have become dysfunctional on its own account had the war not intervened. Claudia Dale Goldin, in her *Urban Slavery in the American South 1820-1860*, disagrees and concludes that the institution of slavery had become particularly workable in the urban environment of Antebellum America. Slaves were not only employed in Baltimore in the period 1795-1835, but a significant number of them were concentrated in the commercial section of Fells Point, where they staffed maritime businesses. The Fells Point shipbuilding industry thus affords an opportunity to compare the use of slave and free labor. Surprisingly, little work has been done on slavery in Baltimore and, with few exceptions, almost all slave

Design Makes a Difference

history in Maryland is concerned with plantation slavery. Historians have assumed that urban slavery in Baltimore consisted mostly of small household work forces that contributed little to the general economy of the city. I have used census records, city directories, and tax records between 1790 and 1830 to identify which shipbuilders used slaves and which used free laborers and the evidence shows a wide spectrum in the use of slave labor in shipbuilding. The spectrum ran from one very prominent shipbuilder, William Price, who used slave labor exclusively and profitably throughout the life of his shipyard, from 1794 to 1835, through other shipbuilders such as Thomas Kemp, a Quaker, who probably did not use slave labor at all. Many in-between examples - such as George Gardner - employed both free and slave labor. These in-betweens were where the problems discussed by Frederick Douglass in his autobiography occurred and stand in contrast to the lack of problems in slave- and free-only yards.

The rivalry between Annapolis and Baltimore presents different issues based upon the distinction between rural and urban power bases. Annapolis' commerce during colonial times focused on tobacco production and shipment and was subject to the vagaries of mercantilistic control and subjugation. This affected the political structure, with the transfer from colony to state occurring smoothly in Annapolis two decades before Baltimore became a city. After a long and difficult battle, Baltimore Town was able to convince the State government to allow incorporation and officially merged with Fells Point to become the City of Baltimore in 1796. The new city then immediately became the first major Republican seaport.

One early result of this power struggle was the establishment of a Federal Navy Yard near Washington, where Annapolis landowners lobbied for its location, rather than at Baltimore. This made Baltimore the only major seaport on the Atlantic that did not have a federal shipyard such as those built in Boston, Philadelphia, New York, and even Norfolk, and had dire consequences for Baltimore's maritime industry.

The geographic location of the port of Baltimore made it particularly profitable to engage in coastal and island trade and this proclivity affected the type of vessel that was built in the city. Sharp,

Design Makes a Difference

fast vessels that carried small loads to nearby markets were the stock in trade of Baltimore shipbuilders. The efficiency of this type of vessel made it particularly suited to privateering activity and the vessels built in Baltimore were particularly effective in the Quasi-War and the War of 1812, harassing foreign vessels, taking valuable prizes, and keeping necessary goods flowing in and out of Atlantic ports despite blockades. Although this subject has been well covered by Jerome R. Garitee in *The Republic's Private Navy*, mention will be made of Baltimore's and Fells Point's shipbuilders' important roles in both of these conflicts.

The War of 1812 spurred the construction of commercial vessels in Baltimore to great heights, which the Carpenter Certificates illustrate. This tremendous expansion was the backbone of the Baltimore privateer fleets. In contrast, periods of financial instability, such as the Panic of 1819 and commercial depression that followed, reveal general economic conditions and ship construction during periods of stress. Overall economic stability, or lack of it, in a port city, dependent as it was on the goods that cleared its docks each year, also had a ripple effect on the smaller support industries of the maritime community, the sail makers, ropewalks, chandlers, and others. For these more marginal groups, many of whom have not left records, the Carpenter Certificates present an incomparable record of a vital early American commercial complex.

Chapter Three will discuss ship design and construction and detail how these spurred the type of commerce that was so successful in early Baltimore. Viewed in these terms, Baltimore's development fell into two sequential periods, from 1795 to 1815 and from 1815 to 1835. The first one was a generation of conflict, shifting affiliations, and high-risk profits. The coastal and Island trade was emphasized, privateering was common, and many fortunes were made. But most importantly, speed underpinned everything, and Baltimore's fast-sailing schooners became famous and in great demand. In fact, the city's shipyards supplied vessels not only locally but to other ports as well. In addition, location played an important role: Baltimore's yards were closer to the head of the Chesapeake Bay than to its mouth, about five days sail away, and thus well protected from attack and blockade. The one major effort that was made to assail

Design Makes a Difference

Baltimore was stopped by the citizen's militia at North Point and by the failure of the British to take Fort McHenry in 1814. Washington, D.C., New York, and Philadelphia were extremely vulnerable and their yards were at greater risk. Perhaps this freedom of movement is the reason that such a huge percentage of the prizes taken during the War of 1812 were seized by Baltimore ships.

The second period, following the war, was less spectacular; in fact, from a commercial standpoint, it was grim. British goods flooded all American seaports and by 1819 the financial stability in the United States had become so desperate that the ensuing panic touched off a short, devastating flurry of bankruptcies followed by a long commercial depression. Productive commerce in Baltimore waned, industrialization increased, and Baltimore's shipbuilders found markets in Boston, New York, New Orleans and other American ports. The record of the buyers' names in the Carpenter's Certificates illustrates the extent of Baltimore's commercial network, the high regard of its shipbuilders, and their search for new markets as their overseas commerce stagnated.

But once again, entrepreneurial ingenuity raised its head: the return of peacetime shipping encouraged technological innovations, resulting in larger ships which carried greater volume. Some of Baltimore's shipbuilders built these new vessels but most continued to build the city's trademark, light and fast schooners. More than increased size was involved, of course; the types of vessels built changed and new people appeared to build them. Barques came into fashion in the 1830's, for example and schooners began to carry three masts instead of the usual two. These changes are reflected in the Carpenter Certificates, as well as the most significant shift of all: the use of steam to replace sail. This technological advance permitted more consistent timetables and was important to packet boat scheduling. Steam also enabled vessels to travel upstream on the inland rivers and waterways that had just begun to develop on the eve of the war, and which now proved a major factor in trade to and from the new settlements opening up in the West.

But canal connections to the interior wrought the most important immediate effect on the seaports. New York took the dramatic and early lead by building the Erie Canal which states like Maryland

Design Makes a Difference

were never able to overcome. Whereas New York extended its European markets westward into the interior through the Erie Canal, Baltimore was left with the coastal and Island trade, both of which were less important now. New York thus developed its position as an entrepôt between the European and western markets, and replaced Charleston as the chief shipper of Southern cotton while Baltimore's coastal trade correspondingly grew less and less as the plantation economy in the Islands waned after the abolition of slavery in 1833. Caribbean commodities continued to be shipped through Baltimore, of course, although at nowhere near their previous levels. By 1840, a new age was dawning for Baltimore as its economic base tilted away from commerce toward industry.

A final Chapter Four will focus on the three major shipyards of Baltimore during their heyday, the lives of the shipbuilders, their interactions, and their relationship to the greater Baltimore business and social community are observed.

Social history can enrich understanding of the economics of this period because its society cannot be separated from its economy. Especially then, a time of monetary scarcity when credit wholly depended upon a man's good name and business ability, such social credibility often made the difference between success and failure. Privately-owned corporations did not exist in the shipbuilding industry, joint-stock companies were very rare, particularly at the beginning of the period, and even partnerships were uncommon. Most shipbuilding was done by one man or a man and his family. Personal histories in this era, therefore, assume a greater dimension in overall economic study, particularly in a community as close-knit as Fells Point.

Additional sources, both primary and secondary have been consulted. Baltimore County Court records provide data on land ownership and transfer, personal estates and inventories, and legal proceedings. Early business records preserved at the Maryland Historical Society also shed light on Baltimore's former commercial activity.

Chapter One

The Birth of a Maritime Nation

United States commerce was at a standstill in May 1789 when Baltimore's businessmen petitioned Congress for legislative relief. The end of the American Revolution had disrupted all of the usual trade channels and postwar demand for finished goods was high. Lack of capital, organization, and support for domestic manufactures forced the importation of even middling quality wares; most of these were British, transported in British bottoms. In addition, the disorganization of the tariff policies of the several states under the Articles of Confederation had created much confusion and resolved none of the issues. The need for a coherent maritime policy was overwhelming and became an important catalyst in the movement toward federation: "The commercial situation in the American states was directly responsible for the creation of the Constitution and the federal government established by it."[1] This early recognition of the relevance of trade to the success of the nation led to policy decisions that encouraged shipbuilding along with international commerce, a combination which led to permanent, long-term prosperity for the United States.

Baltimoreans had at its very inception expressed their hope and faith in the new government:

> The happy period having now arrived when the United States are placed in a new situation; when the adoption of the General Government gives one sovereign Legislature the sole and exclusive power of laying duties upon imports; your petitioners rejoice at the prospect this affords them, that

Design Makes a Difference

> America, freed from the commercial shackles which have so long bound her, will see and pursue her true interest, becoming independent in fact as well as in name...[2]

This was a clear statement by early Americans of their perception of the alliance of politics and economics, and their need to reach beyond the mercantile economy that had been imposed by Great Britain.

Mercantilism had encouraged trade policies designed to create a positive balance of payments to the mother country through market restrictions in the colonies. Raw materials, for example, were produced in America for shipment to England, finished products returned; in most cases an economic balance was achieved. Often overlooked is the fact that this system was as much concerned with the shipping of the goods as it was with production and consumption. British law reflected this proclivity and American merchants and shipbuilders benefited substantially. "During the mercantilist period, the key factor for the colonists was that the navigation laws considered them Englishmen and their ships, English ships. In promoting English trade, Parliament promoted colonial trade. In promoting English shipping, Parliament promoted colonial shipping."[3] British regulation of shipping had begun in the middle of the seventeenth century, as the Baltimore petitioners mention in their request, and resulted in strong, positive maritime growth for Great Britain by the late eighteenth century. American commercial and shipbuilding interests had associated industry regulation with prosperity for over one hundred years, an attitude that led them to the halls of Constitutional government at the earliest opportunity.

The commercial downturn which had so adversely affected the shipbuilding industry in the 1780's also prompted the shipbuilders of Baltimore Town to petition Congress: "[F]or want of national protection and encouragement, our shipping, that great source of strength and riches, has fallen into decay, and involved thousands in the utmost distress."[4] American shipyards had been busy since Colonial times and had never been without eager markets for their vessels. Only after the onset of the American Revolution and the withdrawal of the British colonial aegis was there a problem, and that problem escalated between 1783 and 1789, reaching crisis proportions by the end of the decade. Baltimore's concerned shipbuilders had appealed to Congress less than three weeks after a letter to the House of Representatives by the shipbuilders and mechanics of Charleston and New York, and several weeks before Philadelphia and Boston, indicating the national scope of the problems in an industry unused to such distress.

The resolution of the shipbuilders' dilemma involved a pragmatic combination of national legislation, international political and economic factors, and local ingenuity, all aimed at reducing transport costs to achieve a competitive advantage. For Baltimore, for example, that meant building ships that maximized speed and minimized distance: "the basis for trade, whether international or interregional, lies in comparative cost differences which are not neutralized by transport cost;" the importance of cost factors in the equation of profitable shipping cannot be underestimated: "trade consists of the impermanent commerce which originates solely in the temporary technological superiority gained by the nation making the industrial breakthrough."[5] Baltimore's schooners were inexpensive to build, easily manned by small crews, and, most importantly, speedy enough to provide considerable cost advantage to shippers. But before this competitive edge can be appreciated in the context of Baltimore's success as a rising seaport, it is essential to understand the political underpinnings of the emerging United States and their place in the international scene as the nineteenth century began.

Congress under the Articles of the Confederation had no delegated power to regulate international or even interstate commerce. The individual states, from 1783 to 1789, had been deciding policy individually, leading to diversity and confusion, with the one common factor being a retaliatory posture toward England stemming from the British order in council in 1783 which banned America's trade with the British West Indies. This severely dampened the new nation's postwar revitalization. The period between 1783 and 1789 was financially unstable: credit contracted, interest rates rose to as high as twenty-five to thirty percent, specie was extremely scarce, and bankruptcies soared. The dry goods trade suffered, and business fell off by fifty percent. Imports into Pennsylvania from Great Britain,

Design Makes a Difference

for example, fell from £700,000 in 1783 to about £200,000 in each of the years 1786 to 1788. This downturn resulted in decreased demand for trade vessels in Philadelphia: "During the inflationary boom of 1783 and 1784, an annual average of forty-two vessels, with a mean tonnage of 4,890 tons, slid off the stocks and into the Delaware. But in 1786 only thirteen ships, with a total tonnage of 905 tons, were produced -- the lowest level since 1745."[6] These hard times were a direct result of the British order in council of 1783 and, in their determination to damage American shipping, the British did not foresee the harm that would come about both to English commercial interests and to the British West Indies. As an example, it is estimated that fifteen thousand slaves perished from starvation in the West Indies between 1780 and 1787.[7] Of course, the actions of the British council provoked immediate response from the various states.

Maryland, for example, had imposed a tonnage fee early in 1783 of two shillings per ton, with a slight advantage in tonnage given to local ships; after the 1783 order, this fee was raised on British ships to five shillings per ton. Import and export duties in Maryland were reduced for locally-built vessels in 1784, amounting to "one-third of the duty on exports and one-eighth to one-half on imports."[8] This type of subsidy was common, laws being passed to favor local shippers and shipyards in New Hampshire, Massachusetts, Rhode Island, Connecticut, New York, New Jersey, Pennsylvania, and Virginia.

In addition to discriminating duties, legislation was passed to protect the shipbuilding industry. As an important model for later federal legislation, Pennsylvania passed a protective tariff act in 1783, revised in 1785, which levied duties on maritime manufactures, specifically, a ten percent duty on ready-make sail and comparable duties on tarred cordage, yarn, and fixed rigging, and white rope. Raw hemp and flax could be imported duty-free and foreign carpentry works for ships were charged a duty of 7½ percent. In addition to these incentives, bounties were paid by the various states for the production of naval stores; hemp and flax were the most common. Sail, cordage, tar, pitch, and turpentine production had been encouraged from colonial times and both quantity and quality were supervised by governmental authorities.[9]

And yet Maryland, and particularly Baltimore, shippers took more direct measures to combat the negative results of the ban on British West Indian trade:

> The Americans, however, smuggled produce into the West Indies, or after entering the British islands for repairs, conveniently sold their cargoes to pay for those repairs... Between 1783 and 1785 there were over two hundred twenty-five clearances from Baltimore for the West Indies with many vessels returning with colonial products for reshipment to Europe. The majority cleared for the French, Dutch, and Spanish islands, but British islands were also visited.[10]

In other words, higher risks did not quash established markets, rather the challenges of the Island trade encouraged a new, adventurous entrepreneurial class that accepted the high stakes. The survivors were those who won more than they lost, learning along the way how to better their odds. Baltimore exemplified this new attitude, and stood in contrast to the older colonial cities such as Boston and Philadelphia which had flowered under the mercantile umbrella.

British mercantile policies had even broader implications than simply commercial and shipping regulation. American colonial production had also been controlled, with support for specific staple goods and discouragement, or outright ban, on some finished goods. Maryland and Virginia, for example, grew and dried tobacco which was shipped directly to England for processing and re-export. British factors, suppliers of colonial farmers, imported cheap cotton cloth for slave garments, along with tools, household goods, tea, spices, and other items. Tobacco, although primary, was not the sole product exported by Virginia and Maryland; semi-processed iron ore was also shipped out, in fact, it was used as ballast with tobacco. Iron deposits were found on the western shores of both colonies early in the eighteenth century and, by 1753, iron ore was in such demand in

Design Makes a Difference

England that Parliament set up a bounty for all shipments from the colonies. Under the mercantile system, encouragement of the iron industry returned positive gains to Britain, but as domestic processing matured and the Revolution approached, the benefits of local iron production became a definite plus for the rebellious colonies as well. "[B]y the eve of the Revolution the colonies produced more pig and bar iron than the mother country, and about one-seventh of the total world output."[11] In Baltimore, for example, the Principio Iron Works operated north of the city and, in 1727, purchased Whetstone Point, just south of the city proper. The company was owned by a group of British iron workers, makers of pig and bar iron and for many years, this local mine was their major source of ore. During the Revolution, this company was taken over and its output "became part of the war effort," and, following the war Maryland sold the company's land at auction.[12]

In other colonies, the cycle was more complicated. New England, with subsistence agriculture, relied principally on her fishing fleets and forests to provide commercial staples. New England traders found a ready market for their fish and lumber in the British West Indies, exchanging cod and wood products, including ships, for sugar. Refineries in New England turned the sugar into rum and the rum was shipped to England. Parliament supported this cycle by tacitly refusing to listen to London's complaining shipbuilders and sugar distillers who petitioned them for relief. Any legislative interference in the American commercial pattern would have disrupted the flow of colonial trade and, consequently, have resulted in both fewer English vessels and fewer English seamen. The English merchant marine, which included the American colonial as well as European fleet, was the backbone of the English navy, a ready-made reserve for both vessels and men and Great Britain, being constantly hard-pressed for both, did nothing to diminish New England's trading patterns.[13] After the American merchant marine was severed from the British Empire, impressment of seamen from American vessels functioned as replacement for the former colonial reserve force.

The mercantile system was flexible enough to remain productive for over two centuries, as long as global demand held up prices. As

Design Makes a Difference

market fluctuations occurred, however, and prices fell, for example, on tobacco, the American colonies, by necessity, became more innovative and colonial production more diversified. Local vessel production resulted in considerable cost advantage and this saving, combined with an increasing range of exports and expanding markets, began to erode the mercantilist dependency. Shipment of goods in American bottoms was in part responsible for the political autonomy that evolved in Atlantic seaports; economic alternatives fostered self-reliance and bolstered self-confidence.

The least expensive method of transporting goods along the American seaboard was by water, and the colonists were quick to begin both coastal trade and the construction of coastal vessels. One step beyond coastal trade was the Island trade and trading patterns and vessel efficiency insured that American vessels could transport goods to and from the Islands much cheaper than British, a prime example of the efficiency of the mercantile system. "That the West Indian carrying trade was exclusively colonial was a function of geography; the merchants of London and Liverpool could not compete at that great distance with the merchants of Baltimore and Norfolk."[14] In addition to proximity, however, vessel size was important. Transatlantic voyages demanded large ships both to withstand the rough Atlantic seas and to carry enough freight to offset costs. Coastal and Island trade was more efficient in smaller vessels that carried diversified cargoes, thus encouraging local shippers. As British control over foreign shores expanded, local trading networks expanded profitably, and regional systems operated to their own best advantage as well as that of Britain's. Such enterprise in the American colonies was compatible with the mercantile system since British shipbuilders, along with most of Europe's, were suffering from a severe lumber shortage. American vessels soon filled an important niche in the system. Colonial shipyards constructed about one-third of the British commercial fleet as well, with a value of approximately £2,500,000. Altogether, America's annual output amounted to 40,000 tons, half of which was sold overseas in colonial times.[15]

Baltimore was the best example of this type of expansion. As the markets in the West Indies expanded and grain demand increased,

Design Makes a Difference

Philadelphia merchants moved west to better control the movement of grain from western Pennsylvania, Maryland and Delaware. Shipment of this grain directly out of Baltimore became more economical than trans-shipment through Philadelphia and by the 1740's Baltimore Town began the expansion which led to its eventual establishment as a city in 1795. Baltimore's growth received another boost in the 1760's as European commodity markets in southern Europe opened to offset poor harvests and significant population increase.

As expected, business was adversely affected throughout the colonies by the American Revolution. Wartime shortages were especially difficult when almost all goods were imported. Since trade with other colonial possessions could not be halted, British ships continued to cross the Atlantic, presenting rich targets for enterprising American raiders. The lack of a sufficient professional American Navy prepared the way for the issuance of Letters of Marque and Reprisal, officially sanctioned powers to attack ships of belligerent nations. Baltimore's effective use of the system of privateering during the Revolution, combined with the suspension of repayment of loans to British agents, resulted in a significant influx of capital. The response to these new business conditions established cooperation between merchant shippers and shipbuilders that was to become the foundation of Baltimore's commercial success for the next four decades.

Even more disastrous than Revolutionary disruptions, however, were the trade policies of both Britain and the American states following independence. The suspension in the global flow of trade was as harmful to Britain as it was to America, although the results were neither as sudden nor as visible on the European side of the Atlantic. "Indeed, since the nation's [United States] financial system depended heavily on import tariffs as a source of revenue, and America's imports came primarily from Britain, the United States' economic health required uninterrupted trade with the former mother country."[16] The minimal and sporadic enforcement of the trade ban was evidence of Britain's tacit acceptance of their dependence on American vessels as suppliers to the West Indies.

Design Makes a Difference

America's independence was more political than economic. The despised Navigation Acts and the mercantile system were swept away, but they left a vacuum that restricted attempts to organize trade between Europe and the American states. Any hope of a smoothly functioning, cooperative system in the Island trade was dissolved in 1783. Although some opportunity remained in the French, Dutch, and Spanish islands, these tenuous ties would soon be shattered as well, particularly by the French Navigation Act of 1793 which "preserved the colonial and coastwise carrying trades for French ships and restricted the foreign trade to vessels of France and the country of destination."[17]

In addition to interference in West Indian commerce, European bias had built up antagonism toward American-built vessels:

> [A]lthough the arrêt of France, of December, 1787, grants that vessels built in the United States, and sold in France, or purchased by Frenchmen, shall be exempted from all duties, on proof that they were built in the United States,' yet your petitioners build few vessels for that nation. That an edict of Spain, of January, 1786, lays a heavy duty on American-built ships, purchased by their subjects; and, also, prohibits them from trading to their colonies, although the duty is paid, and they are owned by the subjects of Spain...[18]

Sales of ships were down to one-third of pre-revolutionary tonnage, said the Philadelphians, and that city's petitioners joined the other Atlantic ports in reporting that times were hard for both shipyards and shippers. Such was the situation when Baltimore Town's shipbuilders sought relief from Congress in 1789.

Under the new Constitution, with colonial mercantilism a thing of the past, both the lost advantages and the new-found opportunities challenged the American Congress. In searching for ways to handle the problems that arose in the void, the House and Senate were attentive to the needs of the petitioners. Regulation of interstate and international commerce was the most urgent responsibility of the new government, as well as their main source of revenue, so matters moved along rapidly. As happened often in early American lawmaking, the legal form followed English precedent; in fact the petition of the shipbuilders cited English law to give weight to their request. The first two statutes were in place before the end of July 1789, and they were to provide a solid base for future American commercial legislation.

The program begun by Congress in that year consisted of two major parts, one to raise revenue through duties and port dues, the other to organize the shipbuilding industry. Actually, the two aspects worked hand in hand since the basis for preferential legislation was American production and ownership. The first customs legislation gave American-built vessels a ten percent discount on import duties.[19] This was revised the following year to replace the discount of American vessels with a surcharge on foreign built and owned vessels of ten percent. The Registry Act of September 1789 defined an American vessel as one which was:

> built within the United States, and belonging wholly to a citizen or citizens thereof, or not built within the said States, but on the sixteenth day of May, one thousand seven hundred and eighty-nine, belonging, and thereafter continuing to belong wholly to a citizen or citizens thereof, and of which the master is a citizen of the United States, and no other, may be registered, in a manner hereinafter provided, and being so registered shall be deemed and taken to be, and denominated, a ship or vessel of the United States, and entitled to the benefits granted by any law of the United States, to ships or vessels of the descriptions aforesaid.[20]

This preference for native construction, registration, ownership, and command gave American merchants, mariners, carriers, and shipbuilders a fellowship that forged a solid American merchant marine establishment, a valuable asset to a young nation with no naval protection.

Design Makes a Difference

Other legislation passed in the same year encouraged American vessels to seek foreign markets. Tea duties, based on type, ranged from 6¢-20¢ per pound for American vessels, shipped directly; 8¢-26¢per pound for tea shipped from Europe in American vessels; and 15¢-45¢ per pound for tea imported in foreign ships. In addition to import duties, port dues were assessed and American vessels were again given considerable advantage. The dues enacted were 6¢ per ton, once a year for American vessels, and 50¢ per ton for foreign-built and foreign-owned vessels, due at each entry into an American port.[21] American tonnage entering foreign ports in 1789 is estimated at 53%, by 1796 it had grown to 94%, and ranged between 94-82% until 1812. American tonnage entering American ports was 76% in 1815, 92% in 1819, and ranged between 91-85% until 1830 when it began to drop somewhat to 77% in 1831 and 71% in 1832.[22]

Once ship registry, duties, and tonnage were established, Congress was able to revise these regulations as the need arose. In 1792, a registry law was passed for ships built after 1789. Section 8 of this bill required that a certificate be filed at the local Customs Office by the Master Carpenter in charge of construction of any ship or vessel built after March 1793. He was required to state: "she was built by him, or under his direction, and specifying the place where, the time when, and the person or persons for whom, and describing her built[sic], number of decks and masts, length, breadth, depth, tonnage and such other circumstances, as are usually descriptive of the identity of a ship or vessel..."[23] This act was followed by another in February 18, 1793 which further supported American shipbuilders by limiting American registry to ships built in the United States; this law is still in effect today and continues to protect and favor American shipbuilding.

By 1793, therefore, the pieces were in place and American merchants began an extremely profitable decade which meant that business was also good for shipyards. The years 1795 and 1796 were boom years for American shipbuilders with about 100,000 gross tons built each year. Prices were high and the number of yards multiplied. Record of the Carpenter Certificates are found dating from 1797 and, by the beginning of the nineteenth century, regularly document production at Baltimore's shipyards. There was a decline

Design Makes a Difference

in shipbuilding nationwide in 1797 and 1798, but activity accelerated in 1800 and 1801 and remained high in the periods 1804 to 1806, and 1809 to 1811. Nationally, between 1789 and 1815, the most productive year was 1811 with 146,691 tons and the least was 1814 with 29,751 tons.[24]

The shipbuilding industry in America had been successful since the seventeenth century, in part because the mercantile system existed as much to stimulate the carriage of goods as the actual interchange itself. After all, the favorable cost of vessels was intrinsic to the economics of the transport. "The perceived need to control and thereby to profit from the shipment of goods - as contrasted with the goods themselves - was an early and continuing feature of mercantilism."[25] The economics of mercantilism thus dictated that cost of transport in American vessels contributed to the profitability of colonial trade. American products had considerably more value in the West Indies than they would ever have in Europe and England recognized that transport in the smaller, lighter vessels of American ports, moving between the Islands and North America was much more efficient and less costly than could be achieved in the ocean-going bottoms sailing out of Liverpool and London.

The two main commodities that Maryland found expedient to export in this manner were grain and iron, both of which were needed throughout the islands. In addition, finished products such as hardware, bricks, barrels, flour, dried meats and other foodstuffs found a ready market on the plantations of the Islands. The maximum return on investment was realized in small, locally owned vessels whose cargoes would not be beyond the means of the small island communities to absorb. Coffee and sugar made the return voyage and were processed locally or accumulated for transshipment to European ports. The ready market for grain encouraged increased production in western Maryland and Pennsylvania from the middle of the eighteenth century and the larger crops altered former trade patterns, particularly favoring the growth of Baltimore. The best vessel for transporting the goods was soon discovered to be the schooner, a design that was improved over the years in the hands of the competent shipbuilders in Maryland, particularly in Fells Point and Baltimore.

Design Makes a Difference

American shipyards were major employers of artisans and skilled craftsmen, along with the journeymen and apprentices who were learning their trades. Some were newly arrived from Europe, looking for opportunities to start their own yards, others were retired seamen whose knowledge of ships came from an intimate awareness of how a ship should perform. Many hoped an apprenticeship would give them a trade sufficient to provide for a family, and still others built ships because they had no choice. Maryland was the border state, the merging point of North and South, with slave laborers alongside the free. There is not a great deal of information pertaining to industrial slavery, particularly skilled labor, but there were slaves who built ships in Baltimore, and their contributions were considerable. At least one of the shipyards in Fells Point employed slave labor exclusively. The vessels built there were admired for both design and durability and the yard was in constant production for over thirty-five years. The lean years in the 1780's preceded the establishment of this yard, but many shipbuilders in business prior to the Constitution were not still building ships in 1790. The uncertain economic climate of this period was severe enough to strain capital reserves beyond the breaking point and many in Baltimore did not survive. The particulars of Baltimore's responses to the stresses of business in the later years of the eighteenth century, particularly the oscillations in the maritime segment of the economy, will be discussed further in following chapters.

The most direct cause of global fluctuations in production was the French Revolution, which began a period of severe instability that was to last until Napoleon's defeat in 1815. For the most part, this unstable era was one of great prosperity for American merchants and shipbuilders as American vessels became more and more responsible for the neutral carrying trade between American and European ports. "Reexports from the United States thus grew at a staggering rate, from less than $1 million to almost $60 million between 1790 and 1807."[26]

As the French Revolution spread to the Americas, it provided a sorely needed boost to Island trade. While French colonies, after 1793, were prohibited from trade with non-French ships, this could not be enforced on rebelling colonies such as San Domingo, whose

Design Makes a Difference

war for independence from France had begun in 1791. Britain's blockade hindered most French vessels from crossing the Atlantic and the French West Indies were severely distressed, with starvation of thousands of slaves reported after 1793. Many of the San Dominguan businessmen had long-term ties with firms in cities such as Baltimore and Philadelphia and, while they fought for their freedom, they preserved their trading partnerships and North American contacts. Some Baltimoreans assisted the rebels; perhaps they still retained some revolutionary fervor, perhaps they were simply attempting to preserve commercial relationships. American policy regarding the revolution in San Domingo was confusing: for the most part, official American policy was neutrality, but trade, particularly of arms and ammunition, was not effectively regulated and had substantial impact on events on the island. In addition, during the last years of the eighteenth century, when American naval patrols were stationed throughout the West Indies, there was confusion between official and actual policy regarding Rigaud and Toussaint, the two rebels who vied with France for control of the island. This confusion was not confined to the Island conflict, but reached into Franco-American relations at every level.

In April of 1793, Citizen Edmond Genét began his American trip to Philadelphia from Charleston, visiting America's ports and appealing for assistance to France. He recruited adventurers to harass Spanish and British possessions, disbursing letters of marque to lend authority to the privateers recruited.[27] President Washington received Genét coolly, making a point of America's neutrality, while the Secretary of War, Henry Knox warned Maryland's Governor against military expeditions reputed to be emanating from Baltimore, and stated:

> that the President of the United States deems the setting out of any military expeditions from any of the ports of the United States as unlawful and therefore to be prevented...Authentic information has been received that there are at the time two French privateers setting out at Baltimore, the one

a brig, two-masted 14 guns, and the other a Virginia pilot boat.[28]

Knox explained to the Governor that Citizen Genêt had informed Washington that "accomplices" of the rebels of San Domingo had fashioned "military expeditions" that violated the neutral position of the United States, an unlawful conspiracy that must be stopped. A commission led by John Kilty was immediately sent by the Governor to Baltimore to investigate. From these two incidents Genêt came to support America's neutrality in regards to the San Dominguan rebellion, as well as its neutrality in assisting France against Britain and Spain.

One important political development grew out of this episode: President Washington may have violated the French-American Alliance of 1778 which "sanctioned French use of American ports to conduct privateering raids on Spanish and British shipping in the West Indies."[29] But rapidly changing circumstances made it difficult at that time to separate the official French from the rebelling French, and even as the French government of Genêt was overthrown in 1793, relieved Washington of the immediate urgency created by Genêt's presence. Yet he realized that this was temporary for the interruption in the French government did not lead to the revision of French policy regarding the United States and, as the pressure increased, the futility of neutrality became apparent.

The 1790's, then, were tumultuous for the Atlantic community, with French intrigue and British machination keeping the American attempts at neutrality in constant jeopardy. In 1791, San Domingo rebelled against France. Two years later France declared war on Britain, Holland, and Spain and, as mentioned above, restricted trade with the French West Indies, inhibiting American commercial networks in the Islands. The Treaty of Alliance of 1778 between the United States and France was strained by the attempts of France to embroil the United States in anti-British activities, and the efforts of President George Washington to remain neutral. In an effort to authenticate American neutrality, the President appointed John Jay to negotiate a reconciliation with Great Britain.

Design Makes a Difference

The Jay Treaty of 1795 pleased no one and, in fact, served to further alienate France and the United States. French vessels, spurred on by Napoleon's economic policies, increased their interference in American commerce, and France issued another Arrêt. "[I]n the fall of 1796... French reprisals came swiftly as French agents in the West Indies, particularly Victor Hughes, authorized the capture and sale of American ships and cargoes. In metropolitan France, increased retaliation brought confiscation of American Maritime trade under the authority of several government decrees."[30] John Adams, succeeding Washington in 1797, carried on the American policy of neutrality, but was even less successful as the instability in the French government increased.

Americans, reacting to the hostilities in Europe, established pro-British or pro-French factions and the press heightened these attitudes. When the American public became aware of French attempts to extort $250,000 in what became known as the XYZ Affair, hostilities became almost inevitable.

The complexity of the neutrality problem cannot be overstated and was influenced by several factors: the importance of trade to the American economy and the dependence of that trade on the good will of Great Britain; the Treaty of Alliance of 1778 with the French nation, and its status as perpetual; the French Revolution and the ensuing instability of the French governments; and the division in American politics between those favoring one European faction or the other. The disputes which occurred in the United States between the beginning of negotiations and the final settlement of the Jay Treaty exacerbated that political disunity, while also alarming and angering the French. Each of these problems became even more dangerous as American economic balance became threatened by the continuing attacks on its trading vessels. The perilous position of the nation, however, was appreciated by Congress and increased military and naval expenditures were approved in the event the committee was unsuccessful.

The interaction between politics, legislation, and international commerce fused, and only the refusal of the President to request a declaration from Congress kept the United States from formal hostilities with France. But the French were occupied with more

Design Makes a Difference

important issues and preferred to maintain an undeclared status, leaving them free to harass American vessels or ignore them, whichever best suited their purpose at a particular time. American merchants filled an important niche in keeping the French West Indies supplied with foodstuffs and other necessities. American vessels trading in the West Indies had grown to about six hundred by 1796, offering myriad targets for French privateers.[31] This Quasi-War remained unresolved until 1801 and placed demands on American merchants and their vessels, emphasizing the need for speed and maneuverability of vessels, as well as experienced seamen who could trade with the right hand, and, when necessary, fire cannon with the left. The privateering merchants and their crews who had accomplished so much in the American Revolution were again busy in American ports. Without naval protection, these hardy sailors increased the Island trade, expanded commerce with Europe, and entered the seas that led to the Orient. The United States was on the way to becoming a world power and the merchant vessels of the Atlantic seaboard were the avant-garde.

Benjamin Stoddert, a Georgetown merchant and President of the Bank of Columbia, was Secretary of the Navy during the Quasi-War from 1798 to 1801. His attitudes reflected the general ambivalence of the American public at that time when confronted with the question of professional militarism. For a nation that was investing most of its capital in maritime ventures, this became an important issue in a world at war. "The reason for the war was, after all, not only to protect American merchant vessels, but also the financial underpinnings of the entire commercial establishment."[32] Merchants in the Atlantic ports were getting high returns on the money they invested in wartime trading. In the mid 1790's, everyone needed the goods that they transported and there was not a viable neutral alternative to the American vessels. By the end of the decade, however, the British pressure on the French Atlantic fleet was relaxed and the French accelerated their forays against American vessels. As it became more difficult for American merchants to realize the profits needed to remain in business, they began to take steps to reduce their risks, arming their vessels with guns, as well as procuring the letters of marque and reprisal that legalized

17

privateering. Subscription ships were also financed by contributions of the merchants in various cities and these were built at their expense and offered to the government in return for interest payments on the money invested in ship construction and fitting out. A federal law of April 27, 1798 allowed the President to accept these vessels, twelve in number, and arm them for use against the French. The privateers and subscription ships sailed out of ports like Baltimore, New York, and Charleston. These activities represented the maritime version of the local militia, their response was organized and directed privately; for example, the captains of the subscription ships were appointed locally and answered to their home ports rather than usual naval channels.

At the same time, official United States naval action was being organized. On June 18, 1798, Stoddert was appointed the first Secretary of the Navy and his authority was moved from the War Department to the new Navy Department. The first problem facing Stoddert was an extreme shortage of vessels, a result of the popular feeling in the nation that standing professional armies, and navies, were of too little value and too much expense to be worthwhile. In 1794, a practical President Washington had recommended and Congress had passed, an act calling for the construction of six frigates. Of these six, three were ordered completed in 1796, and in fact, were finished in 1798. "In 1797 the American government could do nothing to stop the French raids. It had no navy. Except for a few small revenue cutters, each manned by crews of six men, it did not have a single national vessel in commission."[33] The *United States*, *Constellation*, and *Constitution* were the nucleus of the infant navy and in July of 1798 were joined by the first prize of the war, the *Croyable*, taken off the New Jersey coast by a small merchant packet, the *Delaware*. Also appropriated under the authority of the Navy Department were the ten Revenue Marine cutters, whose use Congress had authorized in the Naval Act of 1 July 1797 and who were officially taken into the Navy Department in February 1799. Prior to the frigates being put to sea, these cutters had been: "outgunned, outsized, and outmanned by even small privateers."[34] Congress was soon made aware of the inadequacy of the country's maritime defenses and appropriated funds to expand the navy,

𝔇esign 𝔐akes a 𝔇ifference

providing for the construction of ten more cutters, ranging in crew size from 34 men to the more usual 70 men. In all, "...while forty-two men-of-war answered the secretary's orders in the course of the Quasi-War, the maximum strength of the navy was thirty-two ships, operational in June, 1800."[35]

As the size of the Navy increased, so did the demands on the new Secretary who was faced with the task of arming, supplying, and providing crews and officers for these vessels. Naval strategy was not clearly defined and there was no precedent to guide either the Navy Department or its new officers. Many of these vessels, both naval and private sailed with less than full crews; the *Patapsco*, one of two subscription ships built in Baltimore, was so urgently needed that she was ordered to sea with carpenters still aboard as well as a short crew.

Stoddert's plan was to create a navy that would outlast the immediate emergency, and he expected the frigates to form its nucleus. This narrow vision restricted his appreciation of the positive value of the small, fast vessels that were so active in the Caribbean during the Quasi-War. After the war, he recommended to Congress that the smaller vessels, such as the subscription ships, be sold off and the frigates retained. Congress agreed and naval strength was cut back, again echoing the debate over professional defense forces, and the leading specialist believed that Stoddert's "October 1799 recommendation to Adams that the navy needed no more small vessels, was based on a fear that funding for the addition of such ships would come at the expense of the battleship program."[36] This may well have been the case since the election of Thomas Jefferson in 1800 brought an anti-navy faction into power and naval forces were, in fact, drastically reduced beginning in 1801 and culminating in final peacetime reorganization by the Congressional Act of March 3, 1803. All that were retained were thirteen frigates and, of these, only six were kept active, and these with reduced crews. Also discharged were all the navy constructors and designers and many officers and enlisted men. The frigates that had been deactivated were improperly stored and "[a]s a result, most of the vessels laid up deteriorated rapidly; the frigates not placed in service once in four years soon decayed and finally became wholly

Design Makes a Difference

unserviceable."[37] Robert Smith, the second Secretary of the Navy, appointed in 1801, assumed command of a woefully inadequate force.

Peace with France in 1801 did not diminish the need for maritime protection. Trade expansion in the last two decades of the eighteenth century had sent American ships into the Mediterranean and problems that had been festering for some time came to a head in the early 1800's. As early as August 1784, the *Maryland Gazette* reported a sighting on 30 July of a Barbary cruiser seeking prizes in the Atlantic sea lanes at latitude 39N, longitude 25W, and warned captains to watch out for her.[38] From this period on, the Continental Congress and then the U.S. Federal Government had agreed to demands for payment of tribute. In fact, this was not an unusual accommodation, "[T]hrough the latter half of the eighteenth century every major seafaring nation paid them [the Barbary states] an annual tribute to avoid having its commerce plundered."[39] Jefferson, however, balked at continuing tribute payments, perhaps from his own convictions, perhaps as an extension of America's pride and policy against bribery begun in the XYZ Affair. In any event, the Tripolitan pasha declared war on America in 1801. After consulting his Cabinet, Jefferson sent a fleet of frigates to protect American vessels. It was soon discovered that smaller schooners were much more effective. Since the navy had none, privateers were again authorized and these vessels remained the nation's first line of defense until 1803. By this date, a naval force had been assembled and, led by Lieutenant Stephen Decatur, blockaded Tripoli harbor and forced a peace settlement in 1805.[40]

Decatur's victory in 1805 was not the only triumph of the year; Napoleon's navy, along with that of his Spanish allies, was finally and totally crushed at Trafalgar by the British Royal Navy. This victory was to begin a period of uncontested maritime global dominance by the British Navy. Intensified skirmishes between American and British vessels would lead to the War of 1812, a confrontation which would be fought principally on the high seas. Prior to open warfare, however, political and economic strategies were attempted by President Jefferson.

Design Makes a Difference

The opportunities offered to investors by the lucrative neutral carrying trade absorbed most American capital into the early years of the nineteenth century. The problem of minimal domestic manufactures that had existed in 1789 had not been ameliorated by any sizable investment in American production facilities:

> As a result of the profitability of trade, the maritime and commercial investment so dominated the economic life of the nation between 1790 and 1807 that it absorbed most of the risk capital. One effect of this was that prior to 1807 very little capital flowed into manufacturing, and what few efforts did occur were largely financed from the profits of maritime trade.[41]

Industries in the early nineteenth century tended to be peripheral to commerce: shipbuilding and wharf expansion went on at a steady pace; or to provide enhanced standards of living for the new wealth: construction of mansions and museums by urban merchants, for example. This narrow spectrum of investment was soon to expand, however, as international forces coalesced, forcing the Jefferson administration to react.

Jay's Treaty had been unsuccessful in resolving Anglo-American issues; foremost of these was the impressment of seamen. Harsh conditions drove English sailors from their navy and toward American vessels. Naval actions such as the battle at Trafalgar, as well as heavy demands for patrol vessels to enforce blockades put pressure on the British navy to restock low manpower reserves, so interference with American vessels intensified as hostilities between France and Great Britain escalated. "The Royal Navy resorted to stopping American ships and forcibly removing British deserters, British-born naturalized American seamen, and other unlucky sailors suspected of being British. It is estimated that six to eight thousand Americans were drafted in this manner between 1803 and 1812."[42]

In addition to impressment, both France and Britain increased their attacks on the neutral trading vessels of the United States. After the defeat at Trafalgar, Napoleon retaliated with commercial sanctions, attempting to depress Britain's economy through trade restrictions. He developed the Continental System, and by the Berlin Decree in 1806, forbade the importation of British goods into all of the European countries within his sphere of influence. London reacted to this mandate by issuing an order in council in November 1807 which effectively closed Europe to American neutral carriers; this order decreed that neutrals might enter Napoleonic ports only after stopping first in Great Britain. Napoleon responded to this action with the Milan Decree, which stated that any vessel which had stopped at a British port was subject to confiscation by French naval ships or privateers. With such conflicting edicts, both belligerents felt justified in seizing American vessels and taking them before Admiralty courts for confiscation. To contain financial losses and escape political complications, Jefferson, acting in as moderate a manner as possible reinstated the Non-Importation Act. This act had been passed a year before in protest over impressment, then suspended. As it proved woefully inadequate, another statute, the Embargo Act, was passed. Where the first law had prohibited importation of select products from Britain, the second prohibited importation of all British products. Some Americans agreed with this course of action and, in a letter to the House of Representatives date 11 January 1808, the Committee of Commerce and Manufactures of Philadelphia stated:

> The embargo was laid as being the safest course: it was considered as the best means that could be resorted to, for the protection of our citizens, and for the preservation of our vessels and merchandise...Should the embargo be rigidly persevered in, the advantages to be derived from its adoption will amply repay all the sacrifices made to obtain them. New and important treasures, heretofore neglected, will be brought to light, and, what is more important, into use. The United States, regenerated by their own energies, will acquire a confidence in, and a reliance on, their own resources, without which it is in vain to

endeavor to give effectual and commanding protection to the rights of the citizens and those of the republic. The embargo, by teaching foreign nations the value of American commerce and productions, will inspire them with dispositions to practice justice. They depend on this country for articles of first necessity, and for raw materials to supply their manufactories. The embargo will have no considerable influence in breaking those municipal fetters which circumscribe the motions and liberty of commerce.[43]

Needless to say, this long-term view, while close to accurate, brought no immediate solace to commercial investors. The Embargo, along with the Non-Intercourse Act of 1808 which reopened trade with all nations but France and Great Britain, were counter-productive and American exports fell by 80% in 1808. To understand directly how global events affected maritime trade, national shipbuilding statistics are useful.[44]

Graph 1.1

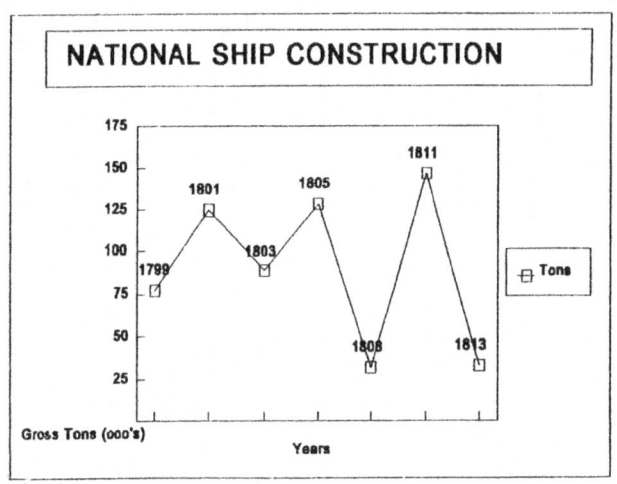

Design Makes a Difference

These same statistics indicate the strong demand for vessels in more normal times. Overall, however, maritime conditions deteriorated rapidly between 1805 and 1812. With both Great Britain and France preying on American vessels and Admiralty Courts in London and Paris anxious to confiscate cargoes, it became increasingly difficult for merchants to procure adequate returns on their investments. Roughly $5 million in risk capital, which had formerly been concentrated in maritime ventures shifted to domestic industry in the first half-year after the embargo, causing catastrophic decline in maritime employment: "...shipowners lost their source of income; sailors lost their livelihood; shipbuilders offered an unwanted product; and shipment of exports, largely farm produce, ceased. An estimated fifty-five thousand seagoing jobs evaporated, as did one hundred thousand others in related industries."[45] The depression not only hurt seamen, but also distressed farmers and fishermen who could no longer ship their produce overseas. Vessels sat in port, loaded with goods that could go nowhere: "The petitioners represent that they have on hand a large quantity of dry and pickled fish, which, unless exported before the summer heats, will be liable to perish."[46]

Goods that were to be transshipped through American seaports were subject to an import tax, with privilege of "drawback" upon their being exported within a year. When the embargo hindered this export, petitioners pleaded for relief, but were refused: "To grant the prayer of the petitioners would be (as the committee view this subject) to destroy the drawback system, and to compel the United States to *refund considerable sums of money* to persons who have heretofore shipped merchandise after it had lost its privilege of drawback."[47] The third ward of the city of New York drew up a petition to the House and submitted it in February 1809. This petition declared the willingness of the petitioners to defend their country "not only against subjugation from abroad, but against usurpation and despotism at home." The subscribers then go on to enumerate the violations of their constitutional rights that occur in the enforcement of the embargo, with particular emphasis on the necessity to transport all supplies to the island of Manhattan by boat:

Design Makes a Difference

> We presume New York is the only city on earth, where, according to a public and formal law, the people may be starved at the mere will of a single individual....No law could give the President power to issue instructions for taking our lives by military execution without offence, accusation, proof, trial, or sentence, upon the collector's mere belief of our intention to violate the embargo....It cannot long be concealed, that, in this and the neighboring States, the act has excited a spirit which is rapidly uniting all real friends of the country in a common sentiment of disapprobation....We solemnly forewarn our Government of the dangers which may ensue from an attempt to array its powers against the rights of the citizens...[48]

The embargo was neither effective nor popular with American investors. There followed a major shift in capital, resulting in approximately $5,000,000 being moved from commercial investment into manufacturing. It was permanent as well as intense, and, "it set in motion the complex events which would destroy the attractiveness of the sea as a source of livelihood for most Americans and would offer to investors greater profits and less risk than found in shipping."[49] The golden age of the trader was fading fast. From farm to seaport, the tide which mounted against the embargo would finally cascade into the War of 1812.

What was the real cause of the War of 1812? Answers range from impressment on the open seas to Indian warfare on the open plains, but what was pertinent to the shipbuilding community was the affrontry that occurred on the Atlantic Ocean and in the Caribbean to American vessels. They were boarded and searched for contraband to the point of harassment, they were depleted of crews, and they were deprived of the freedom to carry on the trade that kept America an economically successful nation. Negotiations prior to the declaration of war resulted in Great Britain agreeing to abandon the practice of searching neutral vessels for contraband, but unfortunately that information did not reach the United States in time to prevent war, if in fact it would have, since the British emphatically refused to desist from impressment of seamen on these same neutral vessels. Laws to protect American seamen were ineffective when British sailors who had become naturalized Americans could be taken off American vessels at the whim of British captains. In an attempt to evaluate the extent of the problem, Congress requested the custom houses to report the number of naturalized citizens who registered as seamen and the records submitted to Congress in 1809 show that between 1796 and 1808, 449 men were listed officially. It was noted that these returns were less than complete but that the amount was close to the true count. The problem became most troublesome, however, because of the large number of British deserters who entered American ports and subsequently served on American vessels: "It has been estimated that between one-half and one-third of America's merchant fleet was manned by foreign, mostly British, seamen. Without the deserters America's trade would have been crippled. The quarrel over impressment involved economics as well as national honor."[50] The United States really did not have much quarrel with the British reclaiming their deserters, that was understood; the problem became aggravated, however, by the lack of discretion on the part of British captains who were apt to sweep naturalized British and native-born Americans along with their own deserters. When Americans taken aboard British ships refused to serve, they were punished, some even hung, and this was too great an affrontry for American seamen (and the American public) to accept, or for the national government to disregard. The *Chesapeake* affair in 1807 was a flagrant example of the impotence of the United States: an American vessel was stopped in American waters by the British *Leopard* which sailed away with four men (three were American citizens), one of whom they hung, leaving behind a crippled *Chesapeake* with three dead and eighteen wounded. President Jefferson's response to this outrage was the Embargo, which brought about more problems than it resolved.[51] The adamant refusal of the British to cease impressment was the primary factor, both economically and practically, pushing the maritime community toward war. Other groups had their own agendas and surely these

Design Makes a Difference

different perspectives combined to exert influence on the President and Congress to declare war, but to the maritime community, the ability to protect the seamen on American vessels was necessary to keep commerce flowing smoothly and profitably.

The gap between the naval forces of the United States and the British Royal Navy was so immense that comparison is almost impossible:

> Britain's navy, which she was constantly augmenting, numbered over 700 ships of all types and some 150,000 men. Between 124 and 150 of the vessels -- the estimates differ -- were ships of the line and well over 100 were frigates. The American navy totaled between 16 and 20 ships -- the estimates of it differ, too -- and a personnel of but 4,000 men. Its largest vessels were frigates.[52]

The upside to this dreary imbalance is that Britain's naval forces were spread out around the world with minimal concentration in American waters. The United States' coastline was long and irregular; the small, shallow-draft ships that composed most of the American fleet could enter ports where the Royal Navy could not follow, thus maintaining a blockade of the seacoast was difficult at best, almost impossible in areas like the Chesapeake Bay. The advantage of smaller vessels and the lack of adequate naval strength encouraged the employment of privateers and armed traders. Being outside of naval influence and control, these private vessels were less predictable; being financial enterprises, both officers and crews were a little bolder than regular naval personnel, thus more successful overall.

Jerome R. Garitee's exhaustive study of privateering in the War of 1812 reaches several important conclusions. Using Baltimore as his primary example, he points out that the structure of privateering was well in place, having been practiced in the Chesapeake since the French and Indian War: "There was little doubt in June of 1812 that the Baltimoreans knew how to finance, build, and handle sea-going vessels, understanding the system fully....Facets such as documentation, articles of agreement, prize court procedures, and distribution schemes followed existing models."[53] American schooners, a great number of which sailed from Baltimore, were effective: "In a very short time Baltimore schooners inspired British cries of outrage, increases in insurance rates, and pleas for convoy escorts even in home waters, something other European nations using privateers against England never accomplished."[54] Aside from harassing the enemy, the privateers also produced national income by converting prize proceeds to custom duties; destroying unprizeworthy British vessels at sea; and, most importantly:

> British losses to American private armed vessels are difficult to ascertain, but *Niles Weekly Register's* running prize list encouraged its editor to estimate that at least 1,750 vessels, plus 750 that were recaptured, were taken from Britain by American vessels. The total figure, including Newfoundland fishing vessels and small West Indian craft, was probably from 1,300 to 2,500....Even a maritime establishment as large as Britain's in 1815 could not ignore such figures nor enjoy the prospect of greater losses at sea if the war were extended another year or more.[55]

This was truly the zenith of the private armed schooners as they maneuvered over the Atlantic waves, placing the British Royal Navy in an untenable position. The maritime community in the United States contributed greatly toward the survival of not only the American merchant marine, but to the incredible victory over vastly superior forces. A major part of that triumph belongs to the shipyards that perfected the efficient schooners which formed the heart of the private army.

The Treaty of Ghent which ended the war in 1815 rang down the curtain on the pre-modern era; in its place was a world of opportunity for many, disaster for some, and change for all. The Baltimore schooner, successful as she had been, began her descent into oblivion. Peace brought new conditions to the sea lanes, and

Design Makes a Difference

new methods of transportation which would rival and then replace these graceful sailing vessels.

After 1818, with the Black Ball Line in New York for example, enterprising businessmen established packet lines which connected to Europe, with scheduled departures and arrivals for both passengers and freight. This innovation was to prove so popular that it, along with effective financial organization, was to elevate New York to primacy among American seaports, causing complex alterations in the North American Atlantic economy. The value of regular transport between North America and Europe had been recognized much earlier: in December of 1783, the *Maryland Gazette*, referring to the French king, reported: "his majesty has thought proper to order the establishment of packets, which are to sail at stated times from Port Louis to New York and to return to the same port."[56] This packet service was to be for mail and passengers only, so as not to interfere with the usual freight transferals. The constant warfare in the Atlantic, however, made it impossible to implement regular scheduling since the best way for a ship to cross the Atlantic, aside from joining a convoy, was by undisclosed route and unspecified time. The new era of peace not only allowed open and regular crossings but also encouraged more substantial shipments of goods in larger and larger ships. Risk of loss by force was diminished, although by no means eliminated, and the advantage of speed was displaced by the reliability of regular sailing times. What was true for sailing vessels remained valid for the steam-powered vessels that followed: "Whether under sail or steam, most of the crack liners of the world have made New York their western terminus ever since that initial venture."[57]

The earliest packet liners were small sailing vessels, averaging between three and four hundred tons. "Gradually, over a period of more than thirty years, the tonnage of the packets steadily crept upwards, passing the 600-ton mark in 1826, 700 tons in 1834, and 1000 tons in 1838."[58] As these sailing ships grew in size, they were able to afford commodious accommodations for their passengers; travellers cabins and lounges were built on deck, which also housed: "the 'barnyard'...to provide for the table of the cabin passengers--with a cowpen and with pigs, sheep, and poultry crowded into the jolly

Design Makes a Difference

boat lashed over the main hatch."[59] The average trip took between thirty and forty days, with passengers betting on arrival dates; two ships made the crossing in 16 days and one passage, the slowest, lasted eighty-nine days. Of course, the ships brought news, particularly business news, and fleets of small vessels scurried out to meet incoming ship and gather the latest European tidings for publication in the many newspapers. "Some of the papers co-operated to support a single news boat and thus reduce the expense, but generally one enterprising competitor would have a boat of its own and the resultant keen rivalry brought the overseas tidings even faster to the waiting public."[60]

Markets for grain and cotton were sensitive to European circumstances and advance knowledge gave buyers and sellers a financial edge:

> That was one of the advantages of packet ownership. The incoming liner bearing news of financial moment often sent a mate ashore on Long Island with instructions to carry such information to the owners privately. The packet, meanwhile, would dawdle along toward Sandy Hook to give ample time for profits to be made by the advance information.[61]

These packets carried the more affluent passengers, while other, less luxurious vessels transported the great number of European immigrants who began to flock to America's shores, and particularly New York City, after 1815.

Other cities attempted to compete with New York, but fell short. Thomas P. Cope, a Philadelphian, started a line from that city to Liverpool in 1821, which was moderately successful, but never emulated New York's success. Boston, with little to export eastbound, did not achieve even that much prosperity. Baltimore attempted a line to Liverpool; Charleston and other cotton ports, as well as some European cities, also ventured into the business, but none of these efforts effectively competed with New York City. It is probable that New York's western markets were prime contributors

Design Makes a Difference

to its success. The Erie Canal, which opened in 1825, economically moved grain from the west and the steady increase in shipments shows the importance of this traffic:

> In 1820, Baltimore led with 577,000 barrels [of flour exported], followed by Philadelphia with 400,000, and then New York with 267,000. By 1823, when part of the canal was already open, New York had passed Philadelphia but Baltimore was still in the lead. In 1827, however, the western flour put New York in first place, with a score of 625,000, followed by Baltimore at 572,000, and Philadelphia at 351,000. New York's lead increased steadily after this.[62]

Other factors also influenced New York's preeminence in this period. In Charleston, for example, the westward movement of cotton production to Alabama and Mississippi made it more expedient to ship cotton down the Mississippi River to New Orleans, and thence to New York, where it was warehoused before being marketed in Europe. This regular shipment eastward was facilitated by the packet lines, with their ears for news and market fluctuations increasing profit margins. Technology also played a part in Charleston's decline, as steamboats began to ply the Mississippi. Canals, which might have made viable connections to the western markets, were unsuccessful, as were railroads which were tried later on. Labor, predominantly slave in Charleston, was repressed and consequently not competitive with free labor, a fatal flaw in the productivity of the South. All in all, New York was able to leap ahead, leaving many ports as far behind as Charleston.

In Philadelphia, there was a major shift in capital investment during this period, a move from commerce to manufacturing. Prior to 1820, the city had focused its capital on trade ventures and land-the traditional investments for the colonial economy which it had not yet outgrown. After 1820, however, internal improvements affected both markets and labor supplies; canals and railroads turned western farmers into exporters and consumers.

Design Makes a Difference

> The forging of the transportation network and massive migration from the countryside, in connection with the expansion of credit and imposition of erratic but protective tariffs, solved major problems for urban entrepreneurs. In combination such developments supplied access to regional and distant markets, provided a relatively cheap, if still inadequate, labor pool, and offered more credit.[63]

Investment of capital in the production of consumer goods for local and regional consumption reduced the importance of export to foreign markets, as well as the need to import European-made goods, thus curtailing to some extent, international commerce. As economy of scale in the United States became effective, quality of goods improved, and prices became more competitive. Also, in the postwar atmosphere with nationalistic feelings high, Americans were more inclined to buy American-made goods than they had been.

For these reasons, commerce after 1815 was erratic at best, and the opportunities that had been readily available in the twenty years prior were not to be found. The neutral carrying trade that had kept American merchant vessels moving over the seas during wartime was no longer needed. Direct trade replaced transshipment which meant that, for maximum efficiency, trade goods should move from point of manufacture or origin to point of consumption in one shipment. Moving goods from Great Britain to the eastern U. S. seaports was commercially feasible; moving them again to the newly expanding markets in the American West added freight charges that few consumers could afford. For the most part, it was more practical to produce locally, regionally, or at most nationally. Imported goods were only affordable to the wealthy. In the antebellum period, this meant that wealthy Southern planters could afford European clothing, while Western farmers must make do with American-produced cloth and locally made garments.

In the first five years after the war, Europe resumed the usual prewar trading pattern; huge shipments of stockpiled dry goods were

Design Makes a Difference

dumped on the docks of the Atlantic seaports, with liberal credit terms, of course. The market could not support such an influx of goods and trading houses began to suffer. Bankruptcies became common and, by 1818, there was a major depression in commercial firms up and down the coast. The glut of goods was responsible for some of the problems, but also contributing to the imbalance was the competition that arose from American production.

The American economy had begun accelerating immediately after Independence; it moved slowly, however, because capital was more productively invested in commerce than in manufacturing. As commercial investment became more hazardous and entrepreneurs were pushed to look for safer havens for their capital, local production began to flourish. Begun under the Embargo Act in 1808, demand for manufactured goods during the War of 1812 increasingly affected investment direction: troops needed supplies, for example, and other nations could not be relied upon to provide the American Army and Navy with clothing, blankets, and arms.

Southern cotton was shipped to the Northeast where the manufacture of cloth, begun in the late eighteenth century, was maturing into a profitable industry: "The third period of textile manufactures in this country began with the introduction in 1814 of the first successful power loom at Waltham, Mass[achusetts]. This brought weaving, as well as spinning, into the factories,...."[64] The development of this industry was beset with problems between 1815 and 1825, but stabilized during the 1830's. Among other difficulties, it had to overcome an initial lack of investment capital and efficient machinery, as well as inexperienced labor and inferior raw materials. Eventually the economies of scale realized by factory production allowed one man to produce between 90 and 160 yards in a day as compared to a housewife's daily production of about four yards, reducing the cost of ordinary shirting material from 42 cents to 7½ cents per yard.[65] This leap in efficiency and productivity resulted in effective competition with Great Britain, and increased exports of finished goods from the United States, breaking into the cycle that had carried raw cotton to Europe for manufacturing.

Wool production began later than cotton, but was well under way by the War of 1812, when it expanded to fill wartime demand. By

1816, $12,000,000 was invested nationally in woolen mills, with an estimated annual production of $19,000,000. These mills, like the cotton factories, were located in the Northeast; there were, for example, twenty-five mills in Connecticut by the end of the war. Postwar fortunes reflect the general economic picture: immediately following the war, foreign competition dealt a crucial blow to the industry and marginal companies were forced out of business. Those that were able to survive began to recover in 1818 and 1819, with appreciable growth by 1820. "Most woolen companies earned money between 1820 and 1825, but their losses were serious the following year and their situation remained precarious in 1827."[66] Again in the late 1820's Europe had overproduced and flooded American markets. Profits returned in the 1830's and the industry, as well as the economy in general, stabilized in the following decade.[67]

While these industries were in their formative stages, Congress nourished their growth with protective legislation. In 1815, the Reciprocity Act which allowed foreign vessels the same terms of entry in American ports that American vessels were allowed in theirs, was formalized by a treaty with Great Britain on July 3. This treaty covered Great Britain as well as her European possessions. The Tariff of 1816 taxed imported woolens, cottons, especially cheaper ones, iron, leather, paper, hats, and sugar.[68] As indicated above, American manufactures of woolen goods were suffering postwar declines in 1816 and they, along with other industries, demanded legislative support to reduce foreign competition.

Manufacturing was not the only enterprise that needed relief during this period. The Navigation Act of 1817 reflected worsening conditions for American commerce and closed coastal and inland waterway trade to foreign ships; this legislation has, over the intervening years, been responsible for much American commercial success, with internal trade expanding as foreign trade contracted. The Act of 1817 also prohibited the importation of goods in foreign ships, except those of the country of origin with, however, provision being made for reciprocity. Congress went further in support of the American merchant marine, passing an increase in tonnage dues in American ports of $2 per ton. In 1818, U. S. ports were closed to British ships originating in British colonies where American ships were not welcome and a requirement was passed for a bond of double the value of the cargo, guaranteeing that foreign owners would not land American goods in ports closed to American vessels. While this economic warfare was in progress, American vessels were still prohibited from trade with the British West Indies; in fact, this detrimental prohibition lasted until 1830.

British trade restrictions and competition were not the only economic problems during this period; difficulties with France also prompted Congressional action. In 1820, an $18 per ton duty was placed on French vessels; this remained in effect for three years, until both France and the U. S. agreed to "reduced discrimination."[69] Eighteen twenty-three also saw the proclamation of the Monroe Doctrine, a watershed document which declared that colonization of the Western Hemisphere by European nations would not be tolerated; that, further, European nations were not to interfere in American affairs politically; and in return, the United States would not interfere in European affairs, including those of the European colonies already in existence in the Western Hemisphere.

Trade legislation continued: in 1824, discriminating duties and tonnage charges were removed, reciprocally, on direct trade with Netherlands, Prussia, Hamburg, Bremen, Lubeck, Oldenberg, Sardinia, and Russia, with Columbia being included later. In 1828, this treaty was extended to include indirect as well as direct trade, and in 1830, a special reciprocal act reopened trade with the British West Indies. It is important to remember that these laws were reactions to world economic pressures, on the one hand, and influential factors which stimulated economic results, on the other.

Throughout this period, America was expanding westward as well as in the older urban areas. This was especially true after 1820, with about 2.3 million new farms opening up in the antebellum period, between 1820 and 1850. "The population in urban places grew 3.3 times faster than the rural population between 1790 and 1850...In 1800 about 84 percent of the work force was in agriculture. In 1840 only 63 percent and in 1870 just 52 percent worked on farms."[70] What this meant to Baltimore shipbuilders and those in the other expanding Atlantic seaports during the period of this study, in concrete terms, is illustrated on Graph 1.2.[71]

Design Makes a Difference

The phenomenal growth in both city and country opened more markets than the older, mercantile system could support, with the result that industrialization, particularly technologically, was necessary to provide ample supply to fuel the growing demand. America's major problem, from the beginning of settlement, had been shortage of labor, and the Industrial Revolution, as it moved into American industry was to mitigate this problem, creating expanding markets as the labor supply swelled. Trade patterns reflected this economic development with the merchant marine adapting to the various demands placed on the emerging American economy.

Graph 1.2

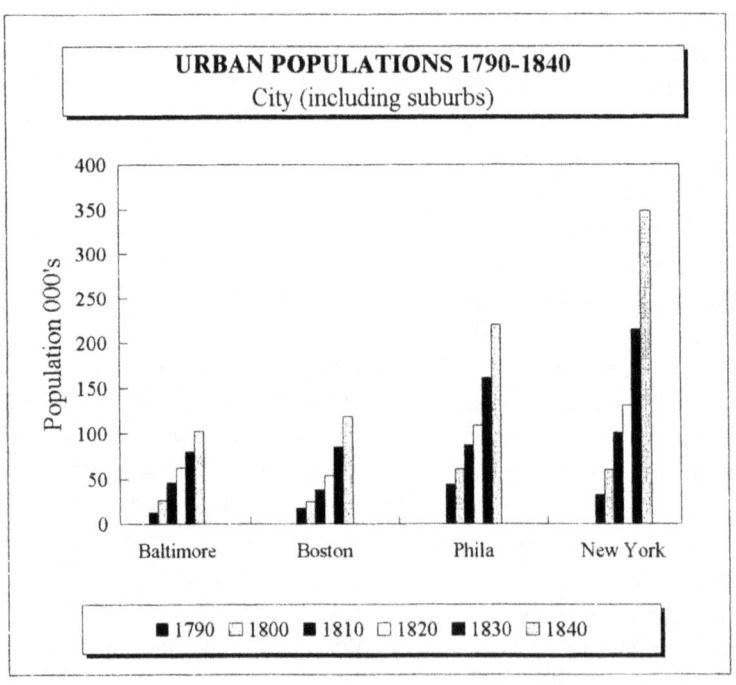

Other factors also affected commerce. Privateers put out of business at the end of the War of 1812 looked to other maritime activities when commercial patterns shifted. The racy schooners that had carried many of the Atlantic cargoes could no longer find traditional freight and turned instead to arms and slaves, both of which were in demand in the southern latitudes of the Western Hemisphere. Slave trading had been outlawed by almost all Western nations by 1808, including the United States, but because of the wars between 1790 and 1815, little was done to control this traffic. Once peace prevailed, however, British naval vessels began to patrol the Atlantic, searching out these ships, particularly along the American and African coasts. The result was a virtual barricade of slave shipments by the late 1840's.[72] In addition to these infamous goods, some delicate cargoes were booked, of course, such as fresh produce that required minimum travel time, but by and large, the schooners were put to dubious uses.

Colonial enterprise had concentrated almost exclusively on transport of goods. This trend was supported by a complex support system centering on shipbuilding. In addition to the actual construction of ships, there were attendant maritime supplies that kept production active: maritime supplies were needed by the merchant marine, as were the stores of food and clothing used by the mariners. American seaports had been founded to fill these demands, growing along with the trade that was so important to a new nation, dependent on her maritime activities. The successful expansion of the capital base in the United States in the early nineteenth century led to a reduction of foreign imports and an increase of exports, both nationally and internationally. Throughout this period, American vessels moved the cargoes from the Atlantic coastal cities where goods were imported and manufactured, to the growing base of consumers who flowed ever further westward. This early expansion of the United States, relying as it did on the maritime health of its seaports, affected the growth patterns of these eastern ports, and a study of the shipbuilding industry in one such city, Baltimore, illustrates the economic evolution of the period.

Chapter Two

Baltimore, Town of Traders

Baltimore's entry into the world grain market created opportunities for its merchants in both the eastern and western hemisphere from the beginning of the French Revolution in 1789 until peace descended on the world in 1815. The period between the end of the American Revolution in 1783 and the beginning of the French Revolution was one of turmoil for both farmers and merchants as the United States attempted to overcome the economic void brought about by their separation from the British common market. The national problems mentioned in the previous chapter were felt as keenly in Baltimore as they were throughout the nation, if not more so. The Baltimorean's response to the difficulties was simple and direct. They did more of what they did best: buy up grain from the nearby farms at the lowest price they could negotiate, transport it as cheaply as possible to whoever needed it the most and could pay the highest price. The least expensive and most reliable mode of transportation for this grain was the fleet of trading vessels supplied by the Baltimore shipbuilders.

Although there were attempts to shift capital investment away from commerce and toward manufacturing from the time the Constitution was approved, by 1795 there was as yet insufficient development in this direction. For the next two decades and more, the nation would continue to rely on commerce for the majority of its economic growth as well as its finished goods,[1] and it is on this level that we must first discuss the early formation of the city of Baltimore.

In the mid eighteenth century Philadelphia families began sending their sons south into Maryland to deal with the wheat farmers and flour millers who were increasingly marketing their goods in the West Indies and Europe. These early families, the Tenants, McKims, Hollingsworths, Smiths, Calhouns, Ellicotts, and Hollins, were able to realize considerable profits trading from Baltimore, and they provided a ready market for the shipbuilding and subsidiary industries that flourished on the Patapsco River, centering on the deep harbor at Fells Point. Baltimore Town was founded in 1729 and, as it grew, economic power shifted, polarizing Annapolis and Baltimore, the two extremes of the State; politics and economics began a struggle that has endured to the present. For some years, Baltimore Town petitioned the State Assembly to authorize the merger of the town and Fells Point into a city, but the State was reluctant to allow that much factional power to accrue so far from Annapolis. In addition, the citizens of Fells Point were averse to surrendering their independence by being absorbed into a larger entity. Eventually this union was realized: on 31 December 1796 Baltimore Town and Fells Point became Baltimore City.

The importance of the industrial activity of the Fells Point waterfront was recognized earlier than this, however, and Port Wardens were appointed in 1783 to oversee the development of the wharves and businesses that blossomed along the busy shores, as shown on Map 2.1.[2] Fells Point was established by a shipbuilder and land speculator, Edward Fell, who readily appreciated the value of the waterfront location. He purchased the tract and the plat map was laid out by him before 1763 [see Map 2.2]. His death in 1766 left the promotion of the new community to his wife, Ann, the executrix of his estate. who actively sought to develop the site. She placed newspaper advertisements announcing terms: for those short on capital, the lots were leased on a ground rent basis, with provision being made to construct dwellings and businesses within a certain period, usually two years, or the lease was forfeit. As the economy expanded, the population was eager and able to invest in both personal and business site development, so Fells Point grew at a rapid pace.

Baltimore, a haven for privateers during the American Revolution, continued the tradition as long as European conflicts provided opportunities. Vessels built and crewed in Baltimore

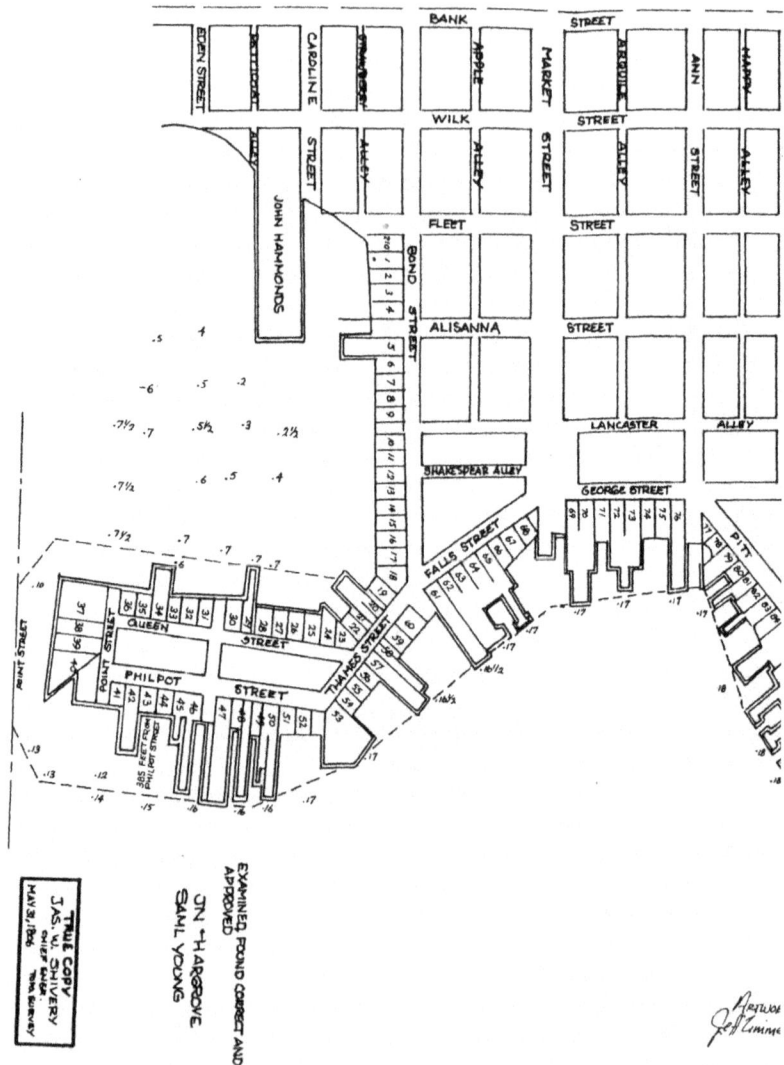

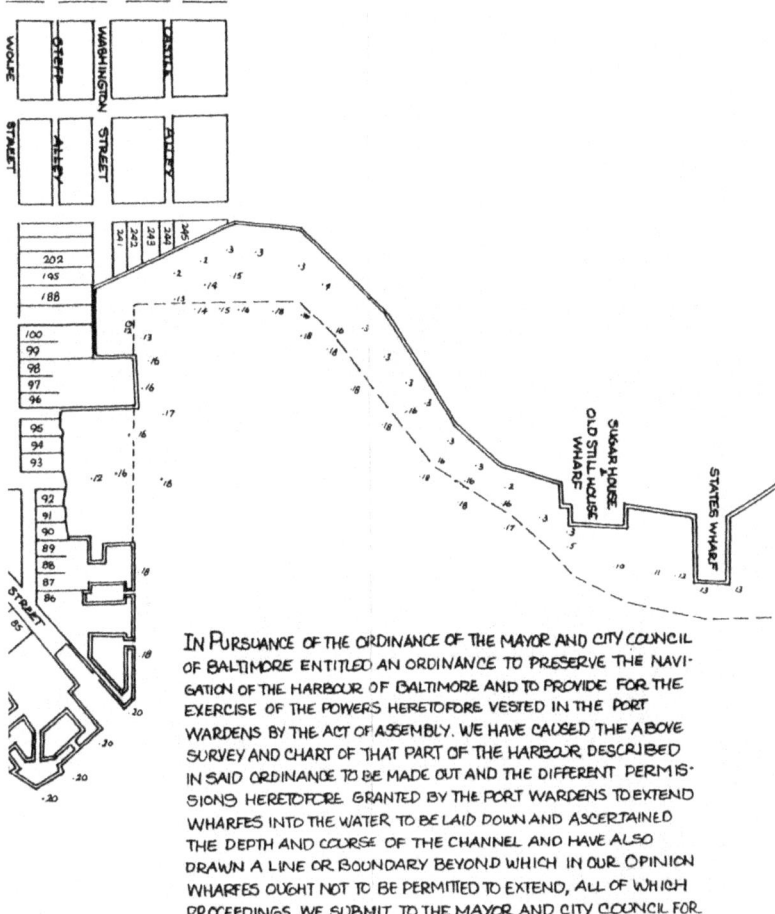

In Pursuance of the Ordinance of the Mayor and City Council of Baltimore entitled an ordinance to preserve the navigation of the harbour of Baltimore and to provide for the exercise of the powers heretofore vested in the Port Wardens by the Act of Assembly. We have caused the above survey and chart of that part of the harbour described in said ordinance to be made out and the different permissions heretofore granted by the Port Wardens to extend wharfes into the water to be laid down and ascertained the depth and course of the channel and have also drawn a line or boundary beyond which in our opinion wharfes ought not to be permitted to extend, all of which proceedings we submit to the Mayor and City Council for their consideration. Given under our hands at the City of Baltimore this 18th July 1799.

WM PATTERSON
SETH BARTON

TRUE COPY
JEHU BOULDIN

SECTION NO. 1

EXPLANATIONS

THE BLACK LINES WITH THE STRONG BLUE SHADE FROM THE SOUTHWEST CORNER OF PATTERSON'S WHARF AT ROUND TO THE EAST END OF GEORGE STREET AT ON THE PLAT SHOWS THE PRESENT WHARVES & PLATFORMS.

THE EXTENT OF WHICH SEVERAL WHARVES & PLATFORMS ARE SHOWN BY BLACK DOTTED LINES WITH THE DISTANCES STATED THEREON AS FOLLOWS THAT IS TO SAY

WILLIAM PATTERSON'S WHARF IN FRONT OF LOT NO. 42 FROM A TO A IS 360 FEET.
JOSEPH DESBOUILLON'S WHARF IN FRONT OF LOT NO. 45 FROM B TO B IS 383 FEET.
WEST'S OLD WHARF IN FRONT OF LOTS NO. 40 & 49 FROM X C TO C IS 378 FEET.
COONEY'S OLD WHARF IN FRONT OF LOT NO. 53 FROM X TO D IS 389 FEET.
CHASE'S WHARF IN FRONT OF LOT NO. 54 FROM E TO E IS 350 FEET.
SAVORY'S BOARDINGS WHARF IN FRONT OF LOTS NO. 55 FROM F TO F IS 350 FEET.
RAMSEY'S & GARDINER'S WHARF IN FRONT OF LOT NO. 56 FROM G TO G IS 397½ FEET.
JAMES BIAS'S OLD WHARF IN FRONT OF LOT NO. 57 FROM G TO B IS 409½ FEET.
JACKSON'S WHARF IN FRONT OF LOT NO. 61 FROM I TO I IS 454 FEET.
CAPT. KERR'S WHARF IN FRONT OF LOT NO. 62 FROM J TO J IS 439 FEET.
DAVID OLIVER'S WHARF IN FRONT OF LOTS NO. 64 & 65 FROM K TO K IS 420 FEET.
ROBERT OLIVER'S WHARF IN FRONT OF LOT NO. 69 FROM L TO L IS 367 FEET.
THOMAS TENANT'S WHARF IN FRONT OF LOT NO. 71 FROM M TO M IS 367 FEET.
THOMAS TENANT'S WHARF IN FRONT OF LOT NO. 72 FROM N TO N IS 367 FEET.
BAPTIST MEZICK'S WHARF IN FRONT OF LOT NO. 83 FROM P TO P IS 343 FEET.
WILLIAM PRICE'S WHARF IN FRONT OF LOT NO. 82 FROM P TO Q IS 343 FEET.
CHASE'S WHARF IN FRONT OF LOTS NO. 83 & 84 FROM Q TO Q IS 344 FEET.
GIBSONS WHARF IN FRONT OF LOT NO. 85 FROM R TO R IS 267 FEET.
JOHN DONNELL'S WHARF IN FRONT OF LOT NO. 86 FROM S TO S IS 371 FEET.
HEZEKIAH WATERS'S WHARF IN FRONT OF LOT NO. 86 FROM T TO T IS 362 FEET.
PRICE'S WHARF IN FRONT OF LOT NO. 87 FROM U TO U IS 424 FEET.

THE HARD BROAD LINES AT THE SOUTH EAST END OF PITT STREET SHOWS A PERMISSION HERETOFORE GRANTED TO SETH BARTON & OTHERS TO PRICE'S WHARF IS SHOWN BY PLAIN RED LINES FROM THE SOUTHWEST END OF PATTERSON'S WHARF AS

C SHOWN A POINT 300 FEET SOUTH FROM PATTERSONS WHARF UPON A DIRECT EXTENSION OF THE WESTLINE OF SAID WHARF AS FIXED BY ORDINANCE, APPROVED APRIL THE 8TH 1807 —

TRUE COPY
JAS. W. SHIVERY
CHIEF ENGR.
TOPO. SURVEY
[DATE]

RESOLVED BY THE MAYOR AND CITY COUNCIL OF BALTIMORE, THAT THE PORT WARDENS BE DIRECTED TO MAKE OUT A SURVEY AND CHARTS AS REPORTED OF THE HARBOUR HERETOFORE LAID DOWN IN 1799 SHOWING THE PORT WARDEN'S LINE AT THAT TIME AS WELL AS THE EXTENSIONS SINCE MADE AND BY WHOM, AND TO CAUSE A LINE DRAWN COMFORMABLY TO SUCH EXTENSIONS, COMMENCING AT THE NORTH EAST CORNER OF PRICE'S WHARF AND RUNNING SOUTH WEST WARDLY TO PATTERSON'S WHARF FELL'S POINT, AND THIS SAID CHART IS RETURNED TO THE CITY COUNCIL AT ITS NEXT ANNUAL SESSION FOR SUCH REGISTER WITH THE APPROBATION OF THE MAYOR FOR THE AMOUNT NECESSARY TO PAY THE EXPENSE THEREOF, TO BE PAID OUT OF THE HARBOUR APPROPRIATIONS.

APPROVED FEB. 18TH 1826
SIGNED JACOB SMALL, MAYOR

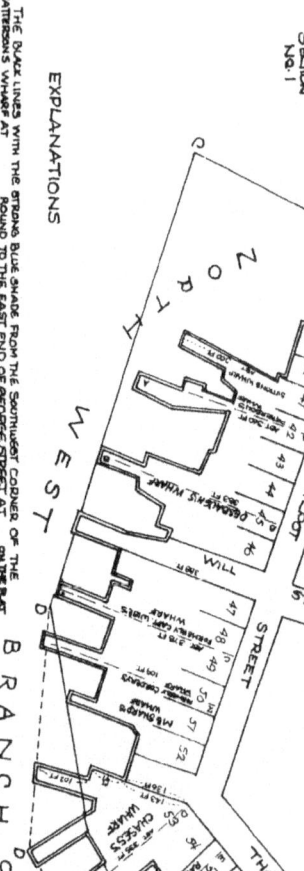

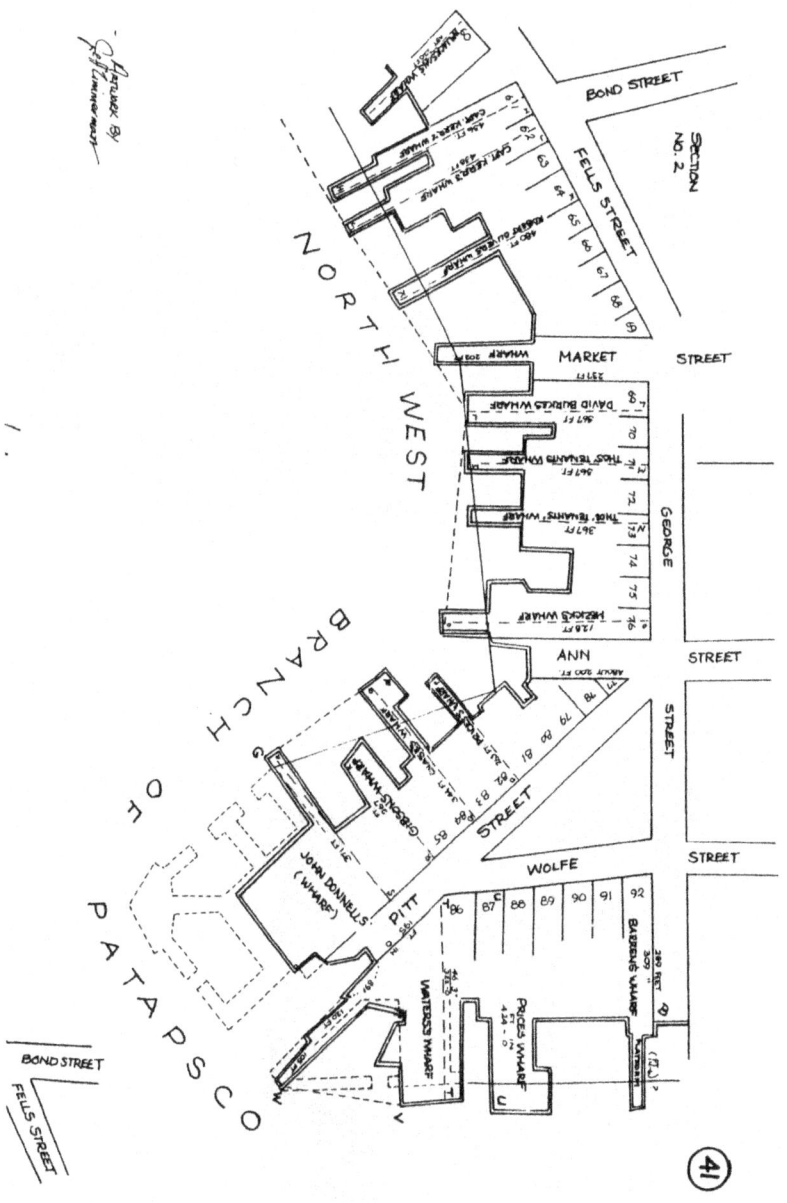

Former Site of Price's Shipyard   William Price's house

Modern day Fells Point (2a, above - Price's shipyard; 2b, left - Price residence)

Photos courtesy of Dan Andberg.

Modern day Fells Point (2c, above - Kemp & Gardner shipyard; 2d, right, rear view of Price residence)

Photos courtesy of Dan Andberg.

Design Makes a Difference

outperformed most European vessels, and the willingness of Maryland investors to maintain the privateer force meant that much of the profit reverted to local coffers. "The port's 122 commissioned vessels took over 500 British vessels and over one thousand six hundred prisoners while doing damage in the millions."[3] However:

> The greatest beneficiary of Baltimore's private armed vessel success during the War of 1812 was the American republic...With Baltimore so active in the prize courts and with its flyers providing the bulk of America's imports at a time when the government had few alternatives, such income was vital to the war effort.[4]

Maritime evolution following 1815 reduced the effectiveness of such a force and there was little call for public participation in later wars. The most thorough work on this subject concluded:

> Unfortunately, Baltimore's extraordinary efforts and performance during the War of 1812 garnered the community few long-term advantages lasting beyond 1819. Profits from the private armed vessel system were more desirable than losses from idleness, and they were helpful in the port's efforts to build railroads and expand manufacturing in the 1820's but they were inadequate for the task of maintaining the city's preeminence as a seaport. *Privateering turned out to be Baltimore's single greatest contribution to maritime history.* During the 1820's Baltimore and other Atlantic ports were unable to stem the gravitation of their trade to the expanding port of New York.[5] (my italics)

Although merchandise was being shipped regularly from the mid eighteenth century, the record of Baltimore-built vessels is inconsistent prior to 1800. It is probable that the early merchants either did not own their own vessels or, if they did, had purchased

Design Makes a Difference

them in another location, Philadelphia, or the Eastern Shore of Maryland, for example. In any event, economic growth expanded the local market for vessels and the number of shipyards, shipbuilders, and the commercial tonnage they produced increased, as shown in Table 2.1 below.[6]

These years reflect the growth experienced by the Baltimore merchant community as it became more and more active in the neutral carrying trade during the wars between Great Britain and France. The increase in vessel size also reflects the expansion of commercial activity beyond the coastal and Island trade as larger ships sailed to Europe and Asia. A major study[7] of eighteenth century shipping in Philadelphia indicates that the mean tonnage for vessels was directly proportional to the destination of the goods: 76.4 tons carried cargo to the West Indies; 56.9 tons carried goods coastwise and north; 48.7 tons coastwise and south; 122 tons shipped to Southern Europe; and 147.9 tons and 124.6 tons respectively to England and Ireland. Although this study covers an earlier period,

Table 2.1

Year	# Ships Built	# Tons Built	# Ship-builders	Average Tonnage/Yr
1797	1	89.75	1	89.75
1798	5	610.40	4	122.08
1799	2	517.00	2	258.50
1801	1	78.60	1	78.60
1802	3	196.74	3	65.58
1803	11	602.25	10	54.75
1804	8	864.56	3	108.07
1805	18	2257.20	8	125.40
1806	18	2260.26	8	125.57
1807	24	3318.72	8	138.28
1808	16	1888.96	7	118.06
1809	13	1798.42	7	138.34
1810	4	858.96	3	214.74

it gives a rough measure of which vessels travelled where. Aside from the increase of vessel capacity from the eighteenth to the nineteenth centuries, the technology used in construction of sailing vessels was fairly stable between the mid 1770's and the early nineteenth century, thus these mean tonnages, after adjustment for capacity changes over time, provide a standard of comparison by which to estimate the varied ports for which the ships built in Baltimore were destined. The importance of ship size in relation to the task to be performed cannot be overlooked:

> Consider, for example, the degree of specialization involved necessarily in the ownership of a specific vessel. A vessel that was too large for a port would glut its market upon arriving. On the other hand, larger vessels were generally preferable because their running costs were proportionally lower, chiefly because of higher ton/crew ratios and lower port charges per ton. Furthermore, there were apparently gains in efficiency from having a vessel especially designed to carry a particular cargo, such as flour or lumber.[8]

Extrapolating the probable use of a vessel by its carrying capacity can indicate the principal trading goals of the merchants who commissioned the ship's construction. For example, in the year 1807, carpenter certificates were recorded with tonnage listed, for twenty-five vessels. Nine of these vessels were between 111 tons and 141 tons; of the remaining sixteen, six were less than 110 tons, four were between 152 and 160 tons, three between 172 and 195 tons, with the remaining three being 211, 244, and 332 tons. The average tonnage was 135.57. Using the Philadelphia vessel sizes as a guide, it is reasonable to estimate that the six vessels under 110 tons each were probably used for local transport, trade, or fishing. The nine vessels between 111 tons and 141 tons appear to be coastal vessels, with perhaps the largest (141 tons) venturing to the West Indies. The seven vessels between 152 and 195 tons were surely Island traders, with the three largest vessels destined for the transatlantic trade. With

Design Makes a Difference

some degree of accuracy, these vessel categories can point to the direction the Baltimore merchants hoped their goods would travel to procure the maximum profit. Appendices 1 and 2 provide a list, by year, of merchant vessels built in Baltimore between 1797 and 1835, with, in many cases, the names of the purchasers.

Had conditions in 1807 remained unchanged, it can be projected that prosperity would have continued unabated for Baltimore's merchants. However, in 1808, records indicate only sixteen ships were built, totaling 1,888.89 tons, an average vessel tonnage of approximately 118.06. There are thirteen Carpenter Certificates recorded for the year 1809, and only five for 1810. Politics, both international and national, had interrupted Baltimore's prosperity and new investment paths were sought.

Political unrest had affected Baltimore shipping prior to this period: the late 1790's was a period of stress between the United States and France and the merchants of Baltimore took an active part in defending their commercial interests. The Quasi-War, which lasted from 1797 until 1801, was primarily an economic and diplomatic war. The only battles were fought at sea, most of them between French and American privateers, merchant vessels and raiders possessing letters of marque and reprisal from their respective governments. These letters legalized the confiscation of vessels and cargoes and the courts in both countries were quick to approve the seizures. Neither nation had sufficient naval power to do much damage to the other: The United States, as mentioned above, preferred to minimize their armed forces, and the French navy was spread quite thin because of its continuing war with Great Britain.

The construction of merchant vessels in Baltimore was negligible in 1797 in comparison to the demand for naval vessels. There are Carpenter Certificates for four shipbuilders in Fells Point in 1798, two of these were engaged in the construction of vessels to be used in defense of the United States. Louis DeRochebrune and William Price, his friend and confidante, were each commissioned by the merchants of the city to construct a vessel that would be loaned to the American government and used to bolster the strength of the very weak U. S. Navy. These two vessels, begun in 1797 were launched in 1799, with considerable fanfare and patriotic fervor.[9]

Design Makes a Difference

Unfortunately, the vessels were shunted from one trivial task to another and never did achieve great distinction. DeRochebrune's vessel, the *Patapsco*, was honored with the duty of transporting to France the diplomats and the treaty that ended the Quasi-War in 1801. Neither of these shipyards recorded construction of merchant vessels until 1803 when Carpenter Certificates indicate a reopening of William Price's shipyard to merchant buyers. During the years 1798 to 1805, there was great demand for Coast Guard and U.S. Navy cutters and there is some record of Price's involvement in construction of these vessels until the early 1800's.[10] Louis DeRochebrune died in 1802 and there is no record of any shipyard activity for him after 1799. As a matter of fact, there was very little shipbuilding activity recorded in Baltimore until 1803 when activity surfaced with renewed energy. In that year, there were eleven men constructing vessels, only two of whom had been building before the turn of the century. It was a new era and the city of Baltimore was about to embark on a fantastic prosperity.

The seclusion provided by the Chesapeake Bay which had favored Baltimore's port activities became less meaningful in view of the peacetime trade patterns which emerged after 1815, however. The vessels that had evolved during the more adventurous periods preceding the Congress of Vienna could no longer provide the margin of profit that had prevailed when the risk factor was preeminent and swift, light traders were more successful than the bulky, heavily laden cargo ships that succeeded them. The economic changes as exemplified in this maritime shift required new financial arrangements. New York's merchants and financiers recreated the shipping industry, maximizing transatlantic monetary alliances and developing the interlocking web which still characterizes the global interdependence of modern nations. The United States' movement from colonial dependence to economic adulthood was propelled through its final phase in the War of 1812 and the sophisticated systems of a mature nation emerged in New York, a city which had focused on finance rather than trade. Baltimore's maritime specialization would give way to a more balanced economy as import and export patterns shifted away from colonial patterns and the Industrial Revolution expanded economic opportunities.

Design Makes a Difference

Baltimore's early merchants, however, bridged the old and the new. From the earliest years of the nineteenth century, they searched for ways to maximize their capital yields as they led themselves and their city to a prominent position in the new nation. Their partners in this endeavor were the shipbuilders of Fells Point and the ancillary industries that equipped, supplied and manned the vessels that enriched the port.[11]

The relationship between international affairs and United States trade is direct and, while demonstrating an overall upward trend, also shows slumps in two periods: the war years 1810-1814, and the postwar years between 1820 and 1824. The 1810-1814 period showed a drastic decline in imports of -50.5% with an export decline of -46.8%. After a gain between 1815 and 1819, the postwar recession recorded a loss of -32.3% of import tonnage and -7.2% of export tonnage. After 1825, import tonnage increased 11.6% by 1829 and 20.6% between 1830-1834. Export increases were 12.9% and 7.9% respectively. (See Table 2.2)

From the first period 1790-1794 which shows that 69.3% of the import tonnage and 66.4% of the export tonnage was carried by American vessels, the number jumps to 91.7% and 87.6% for the period 1795-1799. Import carriage remains consistently high except for the immediate postwar period 1815-1819 when it reaches a low of 77.8% and export tonnage drops to a low of 75.4% in the same years and 78.4% after 1830, another recessionary period.

Analysis of import-export balance shows great inconsistency, particularly between 1810 and 1824. During the war years the import and export drops of -50.5% and -46.8% show up as an overall reduction of -49.9% of the United States' foreign trade and as shown on Table 2.3, a decline of vessels registered for foreign trade of -5.1% (154,500 gross tons). At the same time, there is a small increase in coastal/internal tonnage of 11.5% (247,100 gross tons), as well as an increase of 905.6% (9,100 gross tons) of steam vessels and 5.6% (34,500 gross tons) growth of sailing vessels. These numbers reflect the unsettled international conditions as well as the dawn of the steamboat, the engine of westward expansion within the United States. The 1815-1819 period shows imports up 127.2% and exports up 91.1%, but only 75.4% of this tonnage was carried in

Design Makes a Difference

United States vessels. The U.S. actually had a decrease in registered foreign trade tonnage in this period of -5.7%, with an increase in coastal/internal tonnage of 24.7%, a net gain of 5.9%. This foreign trade imbalance was a major contribution to the depression that occurred in the following period 1820-1824 and resulted in a tonnage loss for U.S. vessels in both external and internal trade of -17.5% and -17.8% respectively, a trade loss of both imports (-32.3%) and exports (-7.2%), and total gross tonnage loss of -17.6%.

In 1762, an Irish immigrant, William Moore, purchased flour milling establishments from Edward Fell, beginning the industry that was to open world markets to Baltimore traders. Other mills were established quickly and, by 1769, flour exports from Baltimore totaled 45,868 tons. Quality control and inspection of exports quickly raised the demand for and the cost of wheat shipped from Maryland to markets such as the West Indies. Although early statistics are inconsistent for the port of Baltimore, continuing efforts of millers such as the Ellicotts, John, Joseph and Andrew, and later their sons, resulted in increased exports. "In 1800 there were within four miles of Baltimore eighteen large merchant flour-mills and in 1822 the manufacture of flour around Baltimore amounted to 300,000 barrels."[12]

In studying the shipbuilding statistics of the city of Baltimore, the most conspicuous relationship is the small number of vessels built in the city as compared to the total built throughout the United States. Once the industry got under way the percentage was consistently between 2.5% and 3.2% with the exception of the war years 1810-1814, when it reached a high of 4.9%. One of the major reasons for this seeming imbalance is that shipyards during this period were local enterprises and were not concentrated in urban industrial blocs. In Maryland, for instance, ships were built in several locations on the Eastern Shore as well as islands such as St. Michaels.

> "Vessels generally remained under one hundred feet in length, so they could be constructed by a master builder and a handful of helpers nearly anywhere the ground could support a shipway and the water could float the finished hull....Until the Civil War,

shipbuilding was a highly competitive industry, essentially a handicraft one, demanding only limited capital to enter. Most yards were small, often operated by a master carpenter who designed the vessels...A hull could be built by as few as three men...Only the largest yards maintained a level of activity high enough to warrant specialization or even a permanent work force....The average annual production was not high; in 1850, it was slightly above one per yard."[13]

Appendix 1 shows that before 1804, the average shipbuilder in Baltimore built about one merchant vessel per year. The heavy demand after 1805 more than doubled that amount so that fewer people built more and larger vessels, but ship construction in the early nineteenth century never came close to mass production levels. Baltimore's total output ranged from eighteen in 1805 and 1806, and four vessels in 1810 to 26 in 1811, and again in 1812, and their all-time high prior to 1815, 39 in 1813. There was an overall total increase of 62.2% in the years from 1810 to1814. This highly productive period was one in which total United States tonnage construction was off by -11.7%, and import and export off as indicated above. Clearly, Baltimore shipbuilders were responding to an unconventional demand.

Although national construction increased in the 1815-19 period by 31.0%, and Baltimore's construction decreased by -22.7%, these numbers must be compared to the previous period 1810-1814, where U. S. construction decreased by -11.7% and Baltimore's increased by 77.3%. There was a nationwide decline as well in the 1820-24 period which was a direct result of the import loss of -32.3% and export reduction of -19.8%. During these periods, Baltimore shippers had lost the edge provided by their early vessels and not yet reached the advantageous position they would resume with their later Baltimore clippers. The shipbuilding industry went into a slump that could not be overcome by the small gains afforded by steam propulsion or inland waterways. It would require a new generation of engineers to create sailing vessels with the capacity to round the

Table 2.2
Carriage of Foreign Trade ($ millions)

Years	Total Imports	% +/-	American Vessels	Total Exports	% +/-	US Merch Exported	US Merch % +/-	US Merch % For Tr	American Vessels
1790-94	150			119		88.0		74.0	66.4
1795-99	374	149.3	69.3	298	150.4	157.5	79.0	52.9	87.6
1800-04	428	14.4	91.7	370	24.2	198.1	25.8	53.5	85.7
1805-09	505	18.0	89.7	380	2.7	173.2	-12.6	45.6	88.7
1810-14	250	-50.5	92.5	202	-46.8	149.5	-13.7	74.0	82.2
1815-19	568	127.2	86.4	386	91.1	303.0	102.7	78.5	75.4
1820-24	379	-32.3	77.8	358	-7.2	243.3	-19.8	68.0	86.6
1825-29	423	11.6	92.1	404	12.9	282.5	16.1	69.9	87.6
1830-34	510	20.6	94.3	436	7.9	330.0	16.8	75.7	78.4

U. S. Bureau of the Census, *Historical Statistics of the United States 1789-1945*. Washington, D. C., pp. 218, 245.

Design Makes a Difference

Table 2.3: United States Merchant Marine Tonnage 1790-1840 (000's)

Year	Total Gr Tons	% +/-	Sail	% +/-	Steam/Motor	% +/-	Foreign Trade	% +/-	Coastal/Internal	% +/-
1790-94	2,694.4		2,694.4				1,927.4		767.0	
1795-99	4,294.5	59.4	4,294.5	59.4			2,964.5	53.8	1,330.0	73.4
1800-04	4,803.8	11.9	4,803.8	11.9			3,101.9	4.6	1,701.9	28.0
1805-09	6,210.5	29.3	6,209.6	29.3	.9		4,055.0	30.7	2,155.5	26.7
1810-14	6,253.2	.7	6,244.1	5.6	9.1	905.6	3,850.6	-5.1	2,402.6	11.5
1815-19	6,626.2	5.9	6,577.5	5.3	48.7	435.2	3,631.1	-5.7	2,995.1	24.7
1820-24	5,459.6	-17.6	5,345.3	-18.7	114.3	134.7	2,997.0	-17.5	2,462.6	-17.8
1825-29	7,580.1	38.8	7,389.3	38.2	190.8	66.9	3,414.0	13.9	4,166.1	69.2
1830-34	7,264.1	-4.2	6,814.7	-7.8	449.4	135.5	3,087.1	-9.6	4,177.0	.3

U. S. Bureau of the Census, *Historical Statistics of the United States 1789-1945*. Washington, D. C., 1949, p. 208.

Design Makes a Difference

Table 2.4 Vessel Construction 1797-1834.
Baltimore Merchant Vessel Tonnage vs. Total U.S. Merchant Vessel Tonnage

Years	# Vessels Total US	Gross Tonnage	% +/-	# Vessels Baltimore	Gross Tonnage	%+/-	% Total US Tons
1797-99	1,452	184,035		8	845		.5
1800-04	995*	423,317	130.0	24	2,882	241.1	.7
1805-09	*	477,535	12.8	94	11,695	305.8	2.5
1810-14	861*	421,748	-11.7	114	20,738	77.3	4.9
1815-19	5646	552,407	31.0	116	13,758	-33.7	2.5
1820-24	3138	354,893	-35.8	73	9,767	-29.9	2.8
1825-29	4666	531,665	49.8	84	15,910	62.9	3.0
1830-34	4,569	568,541	6.9	111	18,114	13.9	3.2

*Incomplete totalss were recorded in some years.
U. S. Bureau of the Census, *Historical Statistics of the United States, 1789-1945*. Washington, D. C., 1975, p. 211; National Archives, Bureau of Marine Inspection & Navigation, RG 41 "Master Carpenter Certificates 1790-1835". Washington, D.C.; MHS: "Brewington Compilation of Carpenter Certificates" File C, Baltimore, Maryland.

Design Makes a Difference

Table 2.5a
Total U. S. Merchant Vessels Built & Documented by Type 1797-1840

Years	# Vessels	Gross Tons	% +/-	Steam Tonnage	% +/-	Sail Tonnage	% +/-
1797-99	1,402*	184,035				184,035	
1800-04	995*	423,317	130.0			423,317	130.0
1805-09	*	477,535	12.8			477,535	12.8
1810-14	861*	421,748	-11.7			421,748	-11.7
1815-19	5,646	552,407	31.0	15,534		536,873	27.3
1820-24	3,138	354,893	-35.7	19,432	25.1	335,461	-37.5
1825-29	4,666	531,665	49.8	49,161	152.9	482,504	43.8
1830-34	4,569	568,541	6.9	63,617	29.4	504,924	4.7

U. S. Bureau of the Census, *Historical Statistics of the United States, Colonial Times to 1970, Bicentennial Edition, Part 1.* Washington, D. C., 1975, p. 751.

Table 2.5b
Baltimore Merchant Vessels Built & Documented by Type 1797-1840

Years	# Vessels	Gross Tons	% +/-	Steam Tonnage	% +/-	Sail Tonnage	% +/-
1797-99	8	845				845	
1800-04	24	2,882	241.1			2,882	241.1
1805-09	94	11,695	305.8			11,695	305.8
1810-14	114	20,738	77.3	205		20,533	75.6
1815-19	116	13,758	-33.7	624	204.4	13,134	-36.0
1820-24	73	9,767	-29.9	359	-42.5	9,408	-28.4
1825-29	84	15,910	62.9	2,219	518.2	13,691	45.5
1830-34	111	18,114	13.9	1,028	-53.7	17,086	24.8

National Archives, Bureau of Marine Inspection & Navigation, RG 41 "Master Carpenter Certificates 1790-1835, Washington, D. C.; MHS: "Brewington Compilation of Carpenter Certificates" File C, Baltimore, Maryland.

Design Makes a Difference

Cape of Good Hope carrying goods and people to the new markets in California.[14] But in 1835, the shipyards of Baltimore were closing as people sought more lucrative ways to earn a living.

If the period between 1790 and 1815 was one of headlong progress for the city of Baltimore, the next fifteen years were a time of instability and stagnation. The change from commerce to manufacturing involved transfers of capital in an era of credit collapse, unsound currency, and little or no banking services. What capital was available, although invested wisely, did not bring about industrial development overnight. Cloth and flour mills, long present in the area surrounding the city, were brought into it following the Embargo, but the export flour market declined substantially with the return of peace to Europe. Cloth milling increased the quantity of output, but quality took longer to achieve; the early product was less than the sophisticated city markets of the northeast were willing to accept.

The answer to these problems was, of course, to ship merchandise to the newly opened west but Baltimore was unable to do so without first developing roads, canals, and railroads to carry the goods to the settlers. Because of the mountains that intervened, this was a complex situation that took money, technology, and time to overcome, and in fact, all three elements would begin to coalesce after 1830, giving new energy to Baltimore's economy. In the meantime, the social and economic life of the city were suspended. The old guard had been swept away in the banking scandals of 1819 and those who remained carried on as best they could. The fabric that had been so carefully woven together by the early Baltimoreans, although optimum for the beginnings of the eighteenth century, was insufficient for the postwar era.[15]

In 1796, however, when Fells Point and Baltimore Town merged into Baltimore City, the future looked uncompromisingly rosy. The two communities were different but aware of their mutual interdependence: financial success in the maritime community of Fells Point often led to acceptance in City society, but this social favor from the "Old City" as it was called, was not important to the Fells Point merchants and shippers of the late 1790's. Only after the turn of the century did successful merchants and craftsmen seek social parity within the City. This divided growth and its accompanying social and political development would have been cumbersome or impossible in a colonial city, but worked well in Baltimore and, in Fells Point resulted in the rapid maturation of a core community devoted to realizing profits through trade.

Baltimore's population increased 96.4% between 1790 and 1800, and 75.6% between 1800 and 1810, providing a huge increase in the manpower needed to produce economic growth. During this same period Philadelphia's population increase was 39.6% in the first decade and 41.8% in the second and New York grew by 82.7% and 66.5%, respectively, both reflecting a healthy growth, but neither being equal to Baltimore's. One of the major reasons suggested for Philadelphia's relatively conservative growth during this period is that it was adversely affected by Baltimore's expansion: "Even more serious was the constricted nature of Philadelphia's agricultural hinterland. By the 1790's the burgeoning city of Baltimore was draining off produce from Maryland's Eastern Shore and from western Pennsylvania, which was connected with the Chesapeake Bay by the Susquehanna River."[16] During this same period, the state was growing at a much more conservative rate (see Table 2.6), indicating the specific focus of the expansion in the new city.

Table 2.6 Population Expansion Comparison:
Baltimore City vs State of Maryland

Year	Maryland Population	# Inc	% Inc	Baltimore Population	# Inc	% Inc
1840	470,019	22,979	4.8	102,213	21,588	21.1
1830	447,040	39,690	8.8	80,625	53,470	66.3
1820	407,350	26,804	6.5	62,738	27,155	43.2
1810	380,546	38,898	10.2	35,583	9,469	26.6
1800	341,648	21,920	6.4	26,114	12,611	48.2
1790	319,729	74,254	23.2	13,503	5,503	40.7

Design Makes a Difference

In this table we see an initial growth spurt in the state in 1790 of 23.2%, a rate that seems best explained by the variation in methods of counting between 1780 and in the first official U. S. Census in 1790. The fact that the city rate increase is consistent with the 1800 increase can be attributed to better demographic records in the city before the first census than existed in the countryside at large. Even considering these limitations, the contrast between population growth in the state and the city are extreme, with the city experiencing a mean growth of 43.7% and an average of 41%, and the state 14% and 8.3% respectively. A significant deviation occurred in 1810, with a major expansion in the state and a drop in growth in the city. It cannot be coincidence that this anomaly happened during the turbulent years following the Embargo and preceding the War of 1812 when trade was at an ebb.

Table 2.7
Population Comparison: United States Total vs Average Urban vs. Baltimore Total (000's)

Years	Total US	% +/-	Urban US	% +/-	Baltimore	% +/-
1790	3,929.2		201.7		13.5	
1800	5,308.5	35.1	322.4	59.8	26.5	48.2
1810	7,239.9	36.4	525.5	63.0	46.6	26.6
1820	9,638.5	33.1	693.3	31.9	62.7	43.2
1830	12,866.0	33.5	1,127.3	62.6	80.6	66.3

Population Abstract of the United States, John L. Andriot, ed. McLean, VA: Andriot Associates, 1980, p. 361; U. S. Bureau of the Census, *Historical Statistics of the United States 1789-1945*. Washington, D. C., p. 25.

A major component of urban growth in America during the early nineteenth century was immigration and Baltimore was surely no exception. It is impossible, however, to be specific about this aspect of Baltimore's development since no data are available. In 1951 a thesis was published which concluded: "One can not examine the newspapers of this period and study the meager statistics available without arriving at the conclusion that Baltimore immigration was small from 1790 to 1830."[17] The "meager statistics" used in Crotty's study were obtained from *House Documents* for the years 1820-1830. The author searched files from the Maryland Historical Society, the Maryland Archives, the Enoch Pratt Free Library, the Baltimore Custom House, the *Records of the Bureau of Customs* and, finally, the *U. S. Congress House Documents*. In this final record, he found "reports not only incomplete but also misleading." Just to be certain that no stone was left unturned, Crotty also searched the *Niles Weekly Register* "from its commencement in 1811 through 1830 and found no usable statistics," as well as the *Baltimore American* and the *Commercial Daily Advertiser* to no avail.[18] For the current study the search was expanded to include computer data bases and still no reliable statistics are available on immigration to Baltimore.

Another component of population growth in Baltimore was the shift of blacks from the category of slave to that of free black. One author concluded: "that the free Black community (of Baltimore) reached a peak of positive growth by 1830." One of the negative influences that he believed influenced the post-1830 decline was "the introduction of hundreds of thousands of German and Irish nationals into the labor market between 1835 and 1865...Baltimore ship lists indicate that in 1852 alone, more than 13,500 German and Irish citizens entered the port of Baltimore."[19]

Table 2.8
Slave vs. Free Black Population: Total US vs. Baltimore (000's)

Years	US/ Slaves	% +/-	US/ Free	% +/-	Balt/ Slaves	% +/-	Balt/ Free	% +/-
1790	697.7		59.5		.4		.3	
1800	893.6	28.1	108.4	82.2	2.8	250.0	2.7	800.0
1810	1,191.4	33.3	186.4	72.0	3.7	32.2	4.0	48.2
1820	1,538.0	29.1	233.7	25.4	4.7	27.0	10.3	157.5
1830	2,009.0	30.6	319.6	36.8	4.1	-12.8	14.8	43.7

U. S. Bureau of the Census, first through fifth census. Washington, D. C.

Design Makes a Difference

The free black population growth before 1830 was fueled by both local emancipation and the influx of slaves freed in other states. This latter group was influenced by the job opportunities that were found in the racially mixed culture of the city, as well as a relative lack of punitive legislation. The free black population grew from 323 in 1790 to 14,800 in 1830, an indication of the huge shift that occurred in the city within the forty-year period. This massive expansion provided a major labor force and a study of the 1831 Baltimore Directory census indicates that blacks contributed considerably to the city's economy.

The 1831 Baltimore Directory listed occupations of free blacks as: laborer 18.9%, washer 10.9%, sawyer 5.5%, drayman 5.1%, porter 3.6%, waiter 3.6%, laundress 2.7%, mariner 1.9%, caulker 1.8%, brickmaker 1.7% and blacksmith 1.6%. Other occupations were counted less than 1% in a total of 2,017 persons. In contrast, a recent survey[20] indicates that in 1850, the occupations of more than half of the slaveholders in the city could be identified, a total of 646 individuals. Of these men, 18.9% were merchants, 6.5% were clerks, 6.0% were grocers, 5.0% were physicians, and 3.4% were carpenters. Other major occupations cited were tavern keepers, hotel keepers, lawyers, shoemakers, and butchers.

Further comparison shows that although 18.9% of the slaveholders were merchants, only four blacks were shopkeepers. The category of carpenter shows 0.64% of the slave population were so skilled, yet 3.4% of slaveholders were carpenters. The question arises: were the blacks not trained, considered untrainable, or simply unable to use their training after they achieved freedom? Unfortunately a statistical answer to this question is outside the scope of this work. The history of labor in early Baltimore, from slave to immigrant is complex and will involve massive correlation of scattered data. However, in one skill, caulking, both slaves and free blacks excelled in Baltimore, monopolizing the trade until late in the 1830's when immigrants began to resent the black presence.[21] This conflict was described in detail by Frederick Douglass and although there is not a great deal of recorded corroboration of his account, there is little reason to consider it atypical.

Design Makes a Difference

Frederick Douglass was born about 1818, son of a white man and black woman. He was never sure which white man was his father and he was separated from his mother as an infant. His childhood was typical for a plantation slave:

> As to my own treatment while I lived on Colonel Lloyd's plantation, it was very similar to that of the other slave children. I was not old enough to work in the field and there being little else than field work to do, I had a great deal of leisure time.[22]

Douglass also relates that this time was spent hungry, unclothed, unshod and with few luxuries such as bedding, while at the same time he was exposed to the violence, cruelty, and murder that were common in the lives of plantation slaves. Between the ages of seven and eight, Douglass was sent to Baltimore to care for the child of Hugh Auld, a relative of his master. To prepare for this move, Douglass spent three days washing himself and was given his first pair of trousers. In looking back on this move, Douglass described it as the most pivotal event in his life: "Going to live at Baltimore laid the foundation, and opened the gateway, to all my subsequent prosperity."[23] His emphasis on this move as critical in his life reflected the vast difference between the world of the plantation slave and the urban slave during the early nineteenth century.

Sophie Auld, Hugh's wife, was a Northerner by birth and a weaver by trade. She rejected the servile attitude of her new slave and began almost immediately to teach him to read and spell. Although this instruction was discovered by her husband and halted immediately, it did not discourage Douglass; rather it inspired him to recognize the power inherent in literacy and he used every opportunity to increase his knowledge. "From that moment, I understood the pathway from slavery to freedom."[24] It did not take Douglass long to understand the difference between city and country:

> A city slave is almost a freeman, compared with a slave on the plantation. He is much better fed and clothed, and enjoys privileges altogether unknown

Design Makes a Difference

to a slave on the plantation. There is a vestige of decency, a sense of shame, that does much to curb and check those outbreaks of atrocious cruelty so commonly enacted upon the plantation...Every city slaveholder is anxious to have it known of him, that he feeds his slaves well; and it is due to them to say, that most of them do give their slaves enough to eat.[25]

It was no great surprise that when Douglass was returned to the countryside, at about age fourteen, he was unable to adapt. He was let out to a disciplinarian whose job it was to break him for field work; he was not a typical plantation slave, however, and this only resulted in his successful challenge to authority and a renewed sense of self-worth and independence. Douglass taught an underground Bible class and, after being caught in an escape plan was finally returned to Baltimore to the Auld household, there to learn a trade. Thus, in 1835, when he was about eighteen years old, he was hired out to William Gardner, a shipbuilder, to learn caulking. Labor problems were just beginning in Baltimore and Douglass was one of the early casualties. After eight months as a common laborer, four white apprentices beat him severely. He describes the event succinctly:

> Until a little while after I went there, white and black ship-carpenters worked side by side, and no one seemed to see any impropriety in it. All hands seemed to be very well satisfied. Many of the black carpenters were freemen. Things seemed to be going on very well. All at once, the white carpenters knocked off, and said they would not work with free colored workmen. Their reason for this, as alleged, was, that if free carpenters were encouraged, they would soon take the trade into their own hands, and poor white men would be thrown out of employment. They therefore felt called upon at once to put a stop to it. And, taking

advantage of Mr. Gardner's necessities, they broke off, swearing they would work no longer, unless he would discharge his black carpenters.[26]

Following this beating and unrest at Gardner's shipyard, Auld apprenticed Douglass at the Price shipyard which he was managing for Walter Price. It is there that Douglass learned to caulk, and from there that he was able to escape to freedom in the North. Baltimore's geographic position at the northernmost boundary of slavery and the southernmost edge of freedom combined with the constant movements of water traffic out of the city in all directions increased the likelihood that slaves could successfully reach freedom and must surely have affected their treatment. The sense of self-worth and individualism that arose out of the circumstance of Douglass' early life combined with his own natural optimism, independence, and the opportunity to escape, resulted in his achieving freedom before age twenty. Although unusual in its outcome, this combination of events was more common than is realized. Urban slavery was an economic factor that affected the bottom line of the ledger sheet. Most industrial urban slaves were skilled workers, men whose abilities and temperaments made them unsuitable for plantations. They carried these skills with them to freedom and passed them on to others until technological gain made them obsolete and competition for jobs stifled opportunity.

The labor shortage in the early Republican years in Fells Point was experienced by the shipbuilders and merchants in the community, and was overcome by whatever means were most efficient. Census records indicate that several of these businessmen owned slaves, a reliable and consistent labor force in the booming economy that existed from the 1790's into the early nineteenth century (see Tables 2.9 and Table 2.10). The growth of Fells Point after 1800 provided a larger free labor pool and slavery began a rapid decline. Part of the new workers were free blacks and, in fact: "From 1810 to the abolition of slavery in the state in November 1864, Maryland contained the largest free Negro population in the country."[27]

Design Makes a Difference

Table 2.9: Slaveholding Shipbuilders, Number of Slaves Owned (as shown in US Census[28])

Name	1790	1800	1810	1820	1830
Richard Bell	2	2		1	
Robert Cooper			1		
James Cordery		3	1		
Peter Davis		12			
Daniel Delozier		4			
Wm (Spry) Denny				2	
L DeRochebrune		12			
Joseph Despaux		8	8		
Wm Flannigain			10		
George Gardner	2?*	0	1	1	
Thos Hall(Harf Co)		(57)	(56)		
Thomas Kemp(Talb)	(2)		7		0
Richard Lawrence					2
Joseph Pearce			7		
Brian Philpot	16				
John Price			14		
William Price			22	25	23
John/Eliz Steel	6	11	11		
Alexander Stephens			3		1
David Stodder	25	17			
Lemuel Taylor				7	
Joseph Turner	11		3		

*Indicates questionable identification on Census Report.
( ) Indicates Baltimore shipbuilder holding slaves in another location.

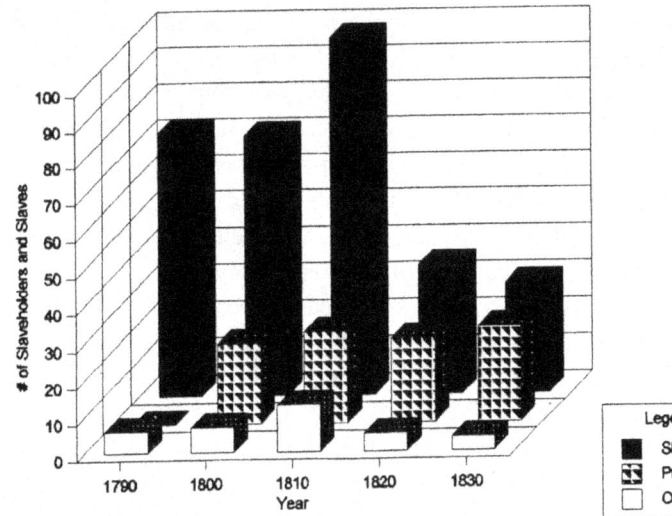

Graph 2.10   Slaveholding Shipbuilders   1790-1830

Design Makes a Difference

Table 2.11: Other Fells Point Slaveholders

Name	1790	1800	1810	1820	1830
Joseph Allender	5	6	7		
James Belt Jr.			2	3	
James Bias		3		20	
Capt Richard Bishop			10	1	
Dr. George Buchanan	3				
David Burke	1	10	8		
Archibald Campbell		6	8		
Samuel Chase	4	6	6		
Nate Childs			4		
Thomas Cole			2		
Jesse Hollingsworth	5		2		
Thomas Hollingsworth	3		6		
Samuel Hollingsworth	4		12		
William Jackson		1	7	5	6?
Capt Baptiste Mezick			2	2	2
Thomas Pamphilion	5		4	1	
Thomas Shepherd			7		
Thomas Tenant		9	5		
Abraham VanBibber	12				
Andrew VanBibber		4			
Isaac VanBibber	7				

Pitt Street, as shown on the Fells Point map (Map 2.2), exemplified a typical neighborhood in the late 1790's, illustrating the extent of economy of agglomeration present in the community. This street began at George and Ann Streets and extended into the harbor, a perfect location for wharves, shipyards, and chandlers. William Price, a shipbuilder, had his residence and business at number thirteen and fourteen, (part of lot #78 and lot #79) and John Steel, another shipbuilder, was across the street at number nineteen (lot #123). The houses of both of these men have survived and attest to their lifestyles. South of Mr. Price's home and office was a ship chandlery shop operated first alone by Ann Belt, and later with a partner, Thomas Cole, and finally by her son, James Belt, Jr.

Edward Collins, an innkeeper, owned a boarding house on the street in 1799, and numbered among his residents the Swedish and Danish Vice Consul, Peter Collins, and Samuel Dodge and Joseph Smith, both customs officials. By 1805, there was a blacksmith shop on the corner of Pitt and Ann Streets, owned by McKenzie & Thomas. James Pilch, a tallow chandler and soap boiler, whose

Design Makes a Difference

business was at 66 Fleet Street, resided on Pitt Street. From 1799 on there was a grocery store at the corner of Ann and George Streets, and as early as 1796, a bakery nearby. Two lots away from Mr. Steel's house was a smaller home which has not survived. It was occupied from 1799 by Louis DeRochebrune, a shipbuilder who had his yard on Fountain Street. And, of course, the street housed traders, ship joiners, sail makers, riggers, sea captains, ship masters and mariners, as well as house carpenters, bottlers, tailors, seamstresses, and laborers. Peter Weary ran a woodyard near Price's shipyard, and Hezekiah Waters owned a large wharf at the end of the street.

George Stiles, who served as mayor of Baltimore from 1816 to 1819, owned property on Pitt Street, and was listed in the 1796 City Directory as a sea captain, residing at 27 George Street, just around the corner. Dr. Joseph Allender was also a nearby resident; he lived at number 17 Thames Street in 1796, and was a prominent physician in the community. His practice in the port had shown him the horrors of yellow fever and the misfortune it posed to those left untreated, mainly indigents, slaves, and seamen. There were several outbreaks of the fever between 1793 and 1825, and his efforts to alleviate the sufferings of the afflicted were resolute and constant.[29]

In 1796, James Biays, a ship joiner, had his shop at 21 Thames Street, along with his residence. He, too, invested in trade and, in 1805, purchased a 328 ton ship, the *United States*, from William Price. Other early merchants also appear in the nineteenth century records as purchasers of vessels. John Hollins acquired a 132 ton schooner, *Ann of Baltimore* in 1798 from John Steel; Thomas Tenant bought the *Paragon*, a sixty-six ton schooner in 1803 and, along with Isaac McKim, the *Maryland*, a 110 ton schooner in 1804, from shipbuilders James Cordery and Thomas Kemp, respectively.

All of the personal interconnections that sustained the commercial and productive activities of this pedestrian city crumbled after the war of 1812. It was a new era for business and most of the old enterprises gave way to new. The company form of business organization more and more replaced the individual as vessels were purchased and operated by the Union Line Steamboats in 1818, and the Pennsylvania, Delaware & Maryland Navigation Company in

Design Makes a Difference

1829, and as technology moved industry from the home into the factory. By 1830, after Charles Crook, Jr. had begun to operate the Baltimore City Cotton Factory with about two hundred employees, industrial manufacturing increasingly changed the direction of Baltimore's social economy.[30]

The period between 1815 and 1835 was one of extreme unrest for the United States as technology and a rapidly expanding population pushed the industrialization of the country. As Baltimore struggled to stay abreast of the technological changes, the capital reserves that had been earned during the 1795-1815 period stood the city in good stead. Merchants who had begun diversification in the first ten years of the century continued to expand their local industrial underpinnings, others moved to New York after 1815, following the commercial establishment which was becoming the primary market in the country. Still others, looking to the West, pushed for the development of new roads, railroads, and canals over which to transport their goods. For those who remained active in commerce in the port of Baltimore, the vessels continued to adapt to their needs. In the following chapter, an analysis of Baltimore's vessels will attempt to clarify the response of the shipbuilders of Fells Point to the changing needs of Baltimore's merchants.

Chapter Three

Baltimore's Vessels

Overwhelmingly, the schooner was the most popular vessel built in Baltimore between 1795 and 1835. It was the main mover of trade goods between Baltimore and the Islands, being specifically designed for the task in terms of style and size. Before discussing Baltimore's schooners and other vessels, however, it is critical to understand how the Carpenter Certificates, mentioned in Chapter One, are used in this study to describe vessel construction in the late-eighteenth, early nineteenth-century.

This information, imperfect as it is, provides the most comprehensive description of the vessels built in Baltimore after 1797, and will be used here to analyze the relationship of the shipbuilding industry in the city to other economic and political influences which affected Baltimore's development. Vessel descriptions varied from time to time and place to place, but have usually been based on a vessel's mast and rigging.[1] For the purpose of this study, the type of vessel, be it barque, sloop, or whatever, is taken directly from the carpenters and Appendix 1 lists these descriptions as fully as space allows. A statistical recap of these certificates follows on page 117 and the vessels are more completely described below.

The 421 schooners built in Baltimore between 1797 and 1835 comprised 68.6% of the total number of vessels and 54.4% of the total tonnage recorded. The total tonnage for these schooners was 48,678.11, or an average of 115.63; the smallest was 19.31 tons, the largest 470.38 tons. Keel lengths ranged from 25' to 114.83', averaged 58.61' and their mean was 69.92'.

These fore and aft rigged vessels with two or more masts and gaffsails[2] were built by eighty-three builders: thirty-nine (47.0%)

constructed only one vessel each (8.8%); ten (12.1%) carpenters built only two vessels each (4.5%). The thirteen (15.7%) most productive carpenters built 268 (60.6%) of these schooners. They were:

William Price	43	James Beacham	17
Kemp & Gardner	11	Thomas Kemp	39
William Flannigain	17	Bailey & Dorgin	11
William Parsons	30	Gardner/Robson	16
Levin H Dunkin	11	George Gardner	22
John Price	15	James Cordery	10
Joseph Turner	13		

These thirteen carpenters illustrate some typical business relationships that existed over time within the shipbuilding community. For example: William and John Price together (father and son), along with William Price & Co., built seventy-seven schooners between 1798 and 1835, an annual average of 2.75. John Price died in 1821 and William in 1831, but the company survived until at least 1835, owned by another son, Walter. Thomas Kemp, alone and together with George Gardner built sixty-one schooners between 1804 and 1816, an annual average of 5.08. Gardner alone and together with Kemp and Joseph Robson, built a total of seventy schooners between 1815 and 1835, an annual average of 3.5; Flannigain & Beacham built eight schooners together between 1817 and 1820. William Parsons alone worked independently, building forty-three vessels between 1801 and 1816, an average of 2.87 per year.

As mentioned above, average annual production for a shipyard as late as 1850 was slightly over one vessel; these numbers far exceeded the average and some did so over long periods of time. Since shipbuilding skills were acquired on the job, it was likely that Joseph Robson apprenticed under George Gardner and George Gardner under Thomas Kemp. William Price most likely trained his son John, but Walter became a merchant and had to hire a manager for the shipyard after his father's and brother's deaths. These builders were the heart of the shipbuilding community between the turn of the century and 1835 because the schooners they built were responsible for the success of the merchant community in Baltimore.

Design Makes a Difference

Graph 3.1

Vessel Type	# Built	% Total #	Average Tons	% Total Tons	Average Keel Length	Decks[1] # / %	Masts[2] # / %	Builders Total/Major[3]
Schooner	421	69.8	115.63	54.4	58.61	1/94.8	2/95.5	83/13
Brig	88	13.8	190.54	18.6	73.9	1/83.5	2/98.7	31/3
Sloop	39	6.5	60.76	2.6	44.27	1/69.2	1/82.1	32/2
Ship	30	4.7	455.52	15.3	93.28	2/73.3	3/83.3	12/6
Steam Power	19	3.2	273.95	5.8	114.22	1/100	N/A	8/4
Barque	6	0.9	263.57	1.8	85.69	2/60.0	3/80.0	6/0
Misc.	12	2	N/A	2.1	N/A	N/A	N/A	12/1

[1] This column lists the number of decks most common for each vessel type and the % of vessels with this number, i.e. 94.8% of the schooners have one deck.

[2] This column lists the number of masts most common for each vessel type and the % of vessels with this number, i.e. 95.5% of the schooners have two masts.

[3] The Builders column shows the total number of shipbuilders for each vessel type and the number who were most active for each type. Again, for schooners, although 83 shipbuilders built schooners, only thirteen were responsible for the production of 60.6% of total schooner construction. Conversely, the six barques were each constructed by a different builder. This category is explained more fully in the following text for each type of vessel.

Graph 3.2

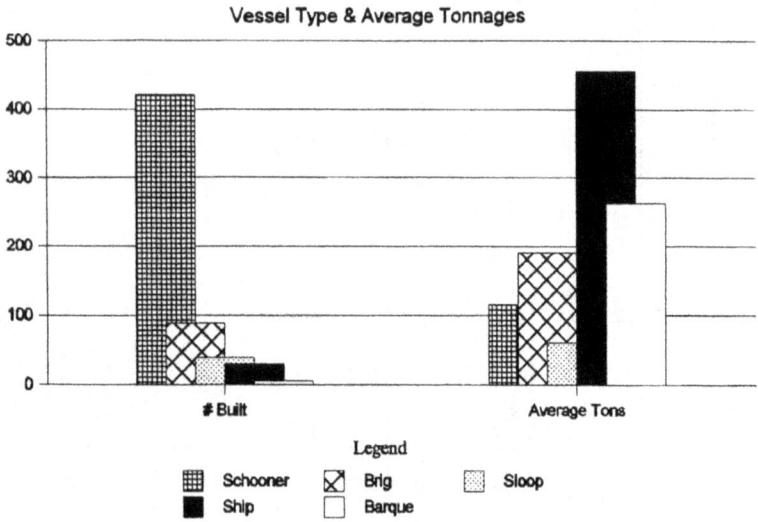

Fells Point Vessels 1795-1835
Vessel Type & Average Tonnages

Legend: Schooner, Brig, Sloop, Ship, Barque

Construction of schooners was more variable than other vessels: nearly all, 308 (93.3%) had one deck and two masts, ten (3.0%) had one deck and three masts, five (1.5%) had two decks and three masts, two (.6%) had a half-deck and two masts, and one had two decks and two masts. The remainder of the schooner deck/mast specifications were incomplete or missing. The most important element of schooners, speed, was determined, among other factors, by the weight of the vessel and the amount of sail that caught the wind to provide propulsion. Baltimore schooners, having only one deck, and that one with a shallow draft, were light but limited in the amount of cargo they could transport. Ships, on the other hand, were heavier and usually had two or more decks to handle larger, bulkier or heavier cargoes. In this study, for example, twenty-three of the thirty ships built in Baltimore had at least two decks, and one of these, the *James Beacham*, built in 1826, had four.

Rigging and rake also determined the speed that a vessel could attain and the number of masts controlled the amount of sail that a

Design Makes a Difference

ship could carry. The design of the sharp-built schooner, with its "fine lines, narrow, fine bow, and long run aft," and its sharply raked masts, allowed the most efficient use of wind for the size and weight of the vessel, while still barely maintaining maneuverability by an experienced captain and crew. During the War of 1812, the preferred material for American sails was cotton, rather than the heavier flaxen duck that had been used previously. "Cotton sails held their shape better, were lighter, and required less wetting down to catch a wind than flaxen sails."[3] These qualities were of paramount importance in the success of the schooner as Baltimore's supreme example of merchant transport. Some builders, such as Thomas Kemp, apparently specialized in rerigging schooners, early in his career, adding masts, sail, rake, and thus speed, to vessels.[4] Later "Baltimore Clippers" sacrificed these qualities in favor of more ample cargo space and larger crew quarters and facilities, thus making feasible the longer, slower journeys from the East to the West coasts in the latter half of the century.

Total tonnage for the schooners was 48,678.11 or, an average of 115.63; the smallest was 19.31 tons, the largest 470.38 tons. Keel lengths ranged from 25' to 114.83', averaged 58.61', and their mean length was 69.92'.

Baltimore schooners were built for speed. Light, sharp, and sitting low in the water, their carpenter-builders described them as "round tuck" or "round tuck pilot boat schooner" (William Price), "round tuck pilot boat schooner" or "round tuck privateer fashion schooner" (Thomas Kemp), "sharp built schooner" or "pilot boat schooner" (William Parsons), "round tuck pilot boat (or built) schooner" (George Gardner). It has been suggested that Kemp, a Quaker whose religion forbade newspaper advertising, was the most specific in his carpenter certificate descriptions. These were not the famous Baltimore "clippers" of the following generation. In fact the word "clipper" was not used in the Baltimore Carpenter Certificates. Twentieth century historians investigating the technological forebears of the later clipper ship, misapplied the name with confusing results.[5] Nevertheless, all agree that the driving force behind the development of the schooner was speed:

> It must be kept in mind that, during the life of the Baltimore type, its whole existence was centered in the necessity for speed...As it happened the

demand for this type, so able to fulfill the privateering and naval needs of a young and struggling nation, became so great that the type became national.[6]

The speed of Baltimore's schooners was so dependable that "...S. Smith and Buchanan told a Philadelphia insurance company 'we seldom insured our West Indian risques'."[7]

To economic value, speed added safety; thus sailors were aggressive in seeking berths on Baltimore vessels. The gathering of a schooner's crew was a competitive business with the private armed vessels usually getting first choice. Highly competent crews were needed because Baltimore's schooners were not particularly easy to sail; good leadership and an experienced crew were an integral part of the schooners' speed. By 1810, Baltimore swarmed with recruiting agents who procured crews for the private armed vessels. "Captains and ship's husbands resorted to recruiting agents whenever they needed more than a handful of men in times of heavy competition."[8] Baltimore's busy port abounded with seamen who filled crews on the privateers, on commercial vessels, and last as well as least, on U.S. naval vessels.

The economic impetus of Baltimore's schooners compelled the captains to capture prizes rather than sink enemy vessels, and the crews shared in the earnings of each voyage. "The navy's efforts to man its Jeffersonian gunboats in Baltimore ran afoul of the private service's attractions. Gunboats would not take many prizes."[9] This was also true for the Royal Navy; victory was their goal and capture of a sound vessel was unimportant:

> The speed of the Baltimore schooners baffled their pursuers and made the vessels objects of nautical curiosity...When captured, Baltimore schooners were sometimes brought into the British navy where sailors and captains inexperienced in the handling of such creations, tried unsuccessfully to sail them...Baltimore seamen had long experience with such vessels, but even they were not anxious to head a schooner around the Horn too often or to

Design Makes a Difference

remain long in northern latitudes with ice-laden sails on light rigging.[10]

The British Navy favored heavy barrages at short ranges, endeavoring to sink their opponent, while the American private armed vessels fired long guns from greater distances, aimed at the rigging, then swooped in to board the floundering vessel and take her as a prize. If this strategy did not work, the schooner would outrun the British vessel and return to fight at a later time. When Great Britain attempted to copy the schooner's construction, they met with failure and Jefferson knew this when he advised continued use of Baltimore's schooners: "The British cannot counter-work us by building similar ones, because the fact is, however accountable, that our builders alone understand the construction."[11] Thus, American schooners were a formidable safeguard by the time of the War of 1812, as well as profitable business ventures in risky seas between the wars.

Though light weight–the average capacity for a Baltimore schooner, over the forty-year period of study was almost 116 tons–the difference between a merchant ship and a privately armed vessel, or privateer was its arms, and such armament required larger vessels. Consequently, it should not be surprising that the ninety-five schooners built during the peak war years from 1811 to 1815 averaged over 158 tons; and then, during the four years following the war, Baltimore's shipyards constructed seventy-seven schooners averaging 107 tons.

Besides arms, the wartime vessels carried larger crews which increased their strength during boarding forays and provided spare mariners to bring the prizes into port. The size of the schooner was most favorable to efficient and economic use of crewmen because the schooners were sailed with less than 150 men. United States law provided for a surety bond which, from time to time, doubled if the vessel size was over one hundred tons or if the crew exceeded one hundred fifty men:[12]

> In practice, the Baltimore owners avoided the $10,000 bond perhaps because of the smallness of their schooners or simply out of a disinclination to waste money. Privateers out of Baltimore carried

Design Makes a Difference

as many as 120, 130, or 140 men on numerous occasions, but the closest they came to exceeding the 150 limit on the $5,000 bond was the case of the famous *Chasseur*. Commander Boyle took out 148 men on one cruise and exactly 150 on another.[13]

Baltimore's experience with privateering and schooner building originated during the American Revolution and was then perfected during the stressful period of almost constant warfare that followed. The British Royal Navy patrolled the Atlantic coastline constantly during the Revolution, blockaded American ports, and halted the importation of arms, clothing, and other wartime necessities. Small vessels that could hide in coves and estuaries had the best chance of getting their cargoes through. With their shallower draft, they did not require deep docking facilities which meant that their cargoes could be off-loaded where needed most.

It did not take these enterprising sailors long to realize the value of taking prizes at sea. This was even more efficient when it worked to the advantage of the nation as well as the vessel owner and crew. In Baltimore, the need to legitimize the system of private armed vessels resulted in the establishment of an Admiralty Court in 1776. Thus, a captured vessel could be brought into port, condemned, and the vessels and goods turned over in short order. This system, perfected early, stood in good stead as the War of 1812 approached, for many in the maritime community had captained vessels during the Revolution and were more than ready to defend their freedom once again.

The period following the Revolution was a wrenching readjustment for American merchants. They had been abruptly ejected from a complex system of worldwide trade. Parliament, in an attempt to injure the United States, and without proper consideration of long-term effects, restricted trade with her American colonies. The result was chaos as mentioned in Chapter One, and the pressure for ultra-legal measures became readily apparent. The British were not ready to supply their American colonies with everyday necessities; they had relied on the North American colonies for too long and did not have substitutes immediately in place. Smuggling was the answer, of course, and

Design Makes a Difference

both sides quietly acquiesced to its necessity. The perfect vessel for this role was the Baltimore schooner.

One of the first tests presented to the young country was the Quasi-War with France. The effectiveness of the Revolutionary privateer system was not forgotten and, when an emergency surfaced at the end of the eighteenth century, Baltimoreans remained steadfast in the appreciation of the value of smaller vessels. The naval strength of the new nation, wholly inadequate to the task it faced, consisted of three frigates not completed until 1798, a few small cutters, and one captured French ship. By 1799, ten Revenue Marine cutters were added to the count (Chapter 1, pp. 3 & 4 above). American merchants realized that their interests could not be protected by this inadequate force and pooled their money and efforts to provide additional vessels for the U.S. Navy. On 23 May 1798, Newburyport, Massachusetts began the movement to provide subscription ships to the federal government. The city would provide a warship within ninety days which would be loaned to the government, compensation being: "an interest of six per cent per annum on the net cost of the ship and equipments, and a final reimbursement, at the convenience of the government, of the said net cost."[14] Philadelphia followed quickly on Newburyport's heels and, by June 16 the citizens of Baltimore held a meeting at the Exchange and agreed to join the other cities in contributing to the war effort. Newburyport had agreed to furnish a 20-gun ship, Philadelphia subscribed $100,000 within one month to construct two 20-gun ships. By the time the Senate bill emerged as law, four frigates mounting thirty-two guns or more each were called for. These ships were comparable to the *Constellation*. Philadelphia, New York and Boston agreed to provide three of the four, and the Navy requested that Baltimore supply the fourth. Instead two twenty-gun vessels were pledged and built.

Although the *Constellation* had just been completed in Baltimore by David Stodder[t], the city's subscribers did not favor construction of another frigate. Under extreme pressure, they built two smaller vessels designated sloops of war. Perhaps this was because the *Constellation*, commissioned 27 March 1794, was not launched until 7 September 1797. This long-term construction project was not what the merchants had in mind when they put up their money to safeguard their vessels and cargoes. They wanted immediate

Design Makes a Difference

protection. Two shipbuilders, William Price and Louis DeRochebrune were chosen to quickly build the smaller vessels that could fulfill the requirements of the legislation which authorized their acceptance by the federal government. The bill allowing smaller vessels was passed on 14 June 1798 and allowed that: "...the President might accept such vessels 'on such terms as he may deem beneficial to the public interest'; but the maximum number of ships accepted could be twelve, none 'of a force less than twenty guns, nine pounders'."[15]

In addition to the subscription ships, Price's yard was a major constructor of naval vessels for both the Revenue Marine and the U.S. Navy but the Carpenter Certificates used as the basis for this thesis recorded merchant vessels only; consequently the extensive information they provide is not available for the Baltimore-built warships and, particularly, for the subscription ships built in 1799. Naval records must suffice and these describe the two subscription ships as follows: (a) the *Maryland*, built at the Price shipyard and launched 3 June 1799, with Captain John Rodgers in command, was 380 tons and carried thirty nine-pounders and six six-pounders; (b) the *Patapsco*, 380 tons, 87' keel, 20 guns, first named *Chesapeake* but later renamed because of another vessel in the navy with the same name, was launched 20 June 1799 by Louis DeRochebrune, and commanded by Captain Henry Geddes.

Questions may arise as to the motivation of the merchants who subscribed the funds to construct these vessels, but there was little question as to the general public response. The launch of the *Maryland* was noted in the Baltimore *American* of 4 June 1799, which proclaimed the majesty of the occasion:

> Yesterday the United States sloop of War *Maryland* was launched from her ways, at Price's ship yard Fells Point...The steady and majestic movement of the ship, the immence [sic] crowd of spectators which occupied the surrounding wharves and eminencies [sic] the continued roar of cannon, and repeated huzzas, which seemed to rend the circumambiant air, formed a *tout ensemble*, which we have not witnessed since the launching of the *Constellation*.[16]

Design Makes a Difference

The *Patapsco/Chesapeake* was launched as extravagantly: "On no occasion was there ever a launch conducted in a more masterly manner, or one that terminated more to the honor or satisfactory to the feelings of the builder."[17]

What we know of these early American war vessels is minimal, but a debate emerged at this time, and continued throughout the period of Baltimore's shipbuilding ascendancy because non-sailors criticized their naval capability. This provoked Baltimoreans to defend their unusual ship design. *Maryland* sat low in the water:

> She is Sir a Charming Little Ship, Exceedingly well fitted w^h The best Materials I ever Saw- looks most Beautiful[l], & has only Two Faults in my opinion- Tho' The first is certainly not esteem'd So, by The Builder or Designer- a *whole* Deck laid over Her Guns, in place of Gang Boards, & a Partial Deck only- all British & French Ships (not 2 Deckers) having The Deck *open*, From The Quarter Deck. to the Foremast- But The other is irremediable- Viz: Swimming too low in The Water. & Her Gun-Ports being too near The Waters Edge- a Fault The *Constellation* had, *in a great degree*, & indeed every American Man of War, I have yet Seen which I am sorry For, as it makes Them allways [sic] *Crank*, or *Tender*, & even Dangerous Ships, either in a Gale of Wind- or in Battle if any Sea is Going, or an observing Enemy Compells [sic] Them, to Fight their Lee Guns-[18]

The author of this description, James Buchanan, Baltimore merchant, knew more about Baltimore vessels than his addressee, Secretary of State Timothy Pickering ever did; and in fact, both the *Maryland* and the *Patapsco* survived the war intact. The *Patapsco* was stationed in the West Indies under Commodore Silas Talbot and "She aided *Merrimack* and a British frigate in capturing Curaçao after the French had taken it from the Netherlands."[19] The *Patapsco* was sold in 1801. The *Maryland* served in the Surinam station

Design Makes a Difference

moving between French Guiana and Curaçao from 1 October 1799 to 9 August 1800. After repairs in Baltimore, *Maryland* "departed Baltimore 22 March 1801 with Congressman John Dawson of Virginia, President Adams' designated bearer of the amended and ratified Pinckney Treaty with France and arrived in Havre De Grace, France in early May."[20] She was sold in October 1801 for $20,000. As can be seen, there is ample data available about these two vessels, but much less information can be found regarding other naval vessels built at Baltimore. Although these two warships were called sloops by their builders, they hint at what made Baltimore's schooners so formidable in the nineteenth century. The builder of the *Patapsco*, Louis DeRochebrune, only survived the Quasi-War by one year, dying in 1802; William Price, carpenter of the *Maryland* continued building vessels until 1831 when his business was inherited by his son.

Buchanan's comparison of the faults of these two vessels with the problems he saw in the *Constellation*, a warship which certainly had little else in common with them is interesting for another reason. The great deadrise, or relative angle of the vessel's hull between keel and waterline became a hallmark of Baltimore's later schooner construction.[21] This feature, along with the extreme rake, or angle of the masts to the keel that Baltimore builders favored, certainly contributed to the speed that the vessels were able to achieve, although one expert, Howard Chapelle, contends that no particular feature was exclusively responsible:

> Generally speaking, it seems safe to state that no one feature of the design of a fast sailing vessel is the sole reason for her speed. The fairness of her form, the balance of her centers of buoyancy, sail, gravity and lateral area, the position and shape of her mid-section or section of greatest beam are all important, but like deadrise and hollow floors, no one of them can alone make a fast sailer.[22]

While the success of a vessel was less dependent on one particular feature, than on the aggregate of many, the features that were inherited by the clippers and yachts of later years can be clearly identified in their predecessors:

Design Makes a Difference

> ...a vessel of austere simplicity, unburdened by complicated rigging or anything that would decrease its speed...The Virginia pilot boat was characterized by its sharp deadrise, narrow body, fine long run, flush deck, low freeboard [height of vessel's sides from deck to surface of water],[23] fairly shallow draft, and deep drag aft.[24]

But it must be remembered that these schooners were the workhorses of the city's overseas trade. The merchants that settled the city at the end of the eighteenth century established trade routes and contacts that stood Baltimore in good stead until 1815. As trade expanded, the shipyards grew, and the vessels were adapted to meet the needs of the merchants, allowing them to expand their markets as their capital base grew. When the need became severe after 1812, the carpenters adapted the vessels further, allowing for the installation of guns. When the war was over, and guns were superfluous, the vessels were again updated, but, for the first time, local merchants and shipbuilders began to go their separate ways. In times of waning trade, the shipbuilders sought a larger market and, for the most part, were successful. Chapelle, again, has been cited as an authority on the question of Baltimore shipbuilders' contribution to construction of slave transports following the War of 1812; he stated that the end of the war caused some shipbuilders to relocate to other areas to take advantage of the slave trade which made use of fast, light transports for their human cargoes:

> When the American government began to take an active interest in the trade, they kept watch of the Baltimore ship-builders and inquired into the uses to which the vessels were to be put...This interfered with the Baltimore builders somewhat and many migrated to Havana, Cuba, Brazil, and Central America, and for a short time built vessels for the slave trade in these places...This building, of course, died out with the trade.[25]

Design Makes a Difference

The records of Baltimore's shipyards disagree with this contention. Most major shipbuilders continued their work uninterrupted; a break in production occurred with only a very small number of the larger shipyards. James Cordery, who lived at 7 Philpot Street in Fells Point while building fifteen vessels between 1803 and 1815, was listed in the city directory in 1816 and 1817 as a ship carpenter. He disappeared after that year, and his widow, Maria, appeared in the directory for the 1822-23 issue. No other public record mentioning Cordery can be found. He sold his vessels exclusively to local merchants such as Thomas Tenant, Henry Wilson, and Peter Karthaus, all investors in privately armed vessels as well as merchant vessels. Andrew Descande built ten vessels between 1813 and 1816 and seemingly entered into the business in response to heavy demand by investors. Four of his nine vessels were built for G. A. Guestier, a ship broker, a possible indication that he did not deal with a regular local clientele. There is neither record of Descande in the city directories of the period, nor public data available.

Cordery, it turns out, was one exception for most shipyards continued in business after the war. William Flannigain, for example, built twenty-seven vessels between 1804 and 1818; from 1817 through 1819, he collaborated with James Beacham on his construction, and there is record of his death at his seat in Anne Arundel County on 8 August 1821 at age 54. Andrew Flannigain, probably his son, began his shipbuilding career in 1824 and there are two vessels built by William Flannigain in 1827, again the possibility is strong that he is William's son and Andrew's brother, the last record of construction by Andrew is 1825. Thomas Hall resided at 93 East Allisanna Street in Fells Point; his business also continued beyond the war. He built eleven vessels between 1813 and 1817, all schooners but one "sharp sloop", with eight of these schooners being described as "sharp built." No other record of Hall exists.

Thomas Kemp was a second but "semi" exception. He built his last vessel in Fells Point in 1815; but in 1816 he built the *Montazume* at St. Michaels, from which location he continued to supply Baltimore merchants with vessels. William Parsons' career ended similarly to Cordery's. Parsons began constructing vessels in Fells Point in 1801 and ended his career with six vessels built in

Design Makes a Difference

1816; his death on 30 May 1824 is recorded in Cincinnati, Ohio and describes him as "steam boat builder." As mentioned above, William Price and his son, John, continued building vessels in Fells Point until their deaths in 1831 and 1821, respectively.

Actually an extraordinary number of vessels and tonnage were constructed during the War of 1812. They were built almost exclusively through the increased productivity of the larger shipbuilders. In fact, of the number of vessels constructed in the smaller yards–those that produced less than four vessels–only five of fifty-one- or less than ten percent–were constructed during the war. In addition to a burgeoning market for their products, these major shipbuilders invested in the privateers that they built, sometimes taking a share in the prizes as part of their fees. This vast influx of wealth may explain the retirement or semi-retirement of some shipbuilders like Kemp. "Absorbed with orchards and farming, Kemp built no more than two or three more schooners before his death in 1824."[26]

Of the two major shipbuilders during the war whose absence is unexplained after 1816 or 1817, neither had been a Baltimore shipbuilder before the war. This evidence indicates that most Baltimore shipbuilders did not leave the Chesapeake area to migrate to foreign shores and build slavers. Rather, most either died or remained in the Baltimore area, making adjustment to the new conditions in various ways. Some reduced their capital investment, William Price, for example, eventually deeded his second shipyard to his daughter. He had acquired lot number ninety Wolfe Street in 1806 and numbers eighty-seven, eighty-eight, and eighty-nine in 1815. For the 1815 purchase he became obligated on a mortgage to Francis J. Mitchell, his son-in-law's father; this note was satisfied on 23 June 1824. On the same day, Price deeded three Wolfe Street lots (eighty-seven, eighty-eight, and eighty-nine) to his daughter, Ann Maria Mitchell, in exchange for $20,000, and Francis J. Mitchell loaned James and Ann Maria $21,080. For whatever reason, perhaps the death of the elder Mitchell, these three lots went to public auction 3 August 1825 under a decree issued by Baltimore County Court of Equity; they were described as: "A valuable wharf property, situated on Fells Point at the Southeast intersection of George & Wolfe Streets and known by the name of Price's Wharf."[27] This type of private mortgaging was common for the period. It should be remembered that Price's son John, the primary tenant of the Wolfe Street property died in 1821, so it is safe to assume that William Price was using the property to provide financial security for his daughter.

Other schooner shipbuilders, however, continued to construct privateer-style vessels that were surely sold to owners who used them as transports for slaves.[28] This would support the need for the modifications that changed Baltimore's schooners after 1816 as they again adapted to new conditions. One of these was Thomas Kemp, who removed himself from the more public Baltimore community to Talbot County but continued to build the same type of vessel. "For some reason the phrase 'privateer-built' remained on his carpenter certificates."[29] It is important to remember that the post-war slump in shipbuilding was more likely related to the deflation that followed the end of the Napoleonic Wars than to design flaws that restricted the Baltimore schooners to either privateering or slaving. As indicated on Table 2.4 above, although there was an immediate national postwar instability in the shipbuilding industry, Baltimore did not follow the same path as the rest of the nation. While Baltimoreans were actively building vessels during the war, shipbuilders in blockaded and vulnerable locations were not, so it is understandable that Baltimore would have surplus tonnage at the end of the war. Many of these vessels were probably sold outside the city where demand was great, since Baltimore's fleet was more than sufficient for peacetime needs, however, tracing the sale of used vessels is beyond the scope of this study.

As mentioned above, schooner size increased somewhat during the War of 1812, but overall they ranged between 100 and 120 tons. The smaller size of the peacetime vessels both before and after the 1810-1815 period is important because ship tonnage was, and still is, the basis of many maritime regulations which affect the economy of the transport. Mandatory crew size, complement of officers, port dues, taxes, and other factors influenced ship tonnage, hence design. Master carpenters balanced the need for cargo space, supply storage, and crew size and comfort against the demands for speed and economy to reach the optimal vessel proportions.

The advance in the efficiency of the design of American schooners was caused by two major economic factors: one was that the costs of transport were lower in American vessels than in any of

Design Makes a Difference

the European vessels, and the other was that the maritime industry was profitable enough to retain a considerable proportion of investment capitol. Thus, American shipbuilders had both a comparitive and competitive advantage over Europeans. Although American wages became higher than European standards, both in shipyards and on vessels, the advantage of plentiful, inexpensive raw materials offset the wage differential. The supplies of oak timber, oak and hard pine planking, and pine masts were not inexhaustible, but they did affect the cost of wooden vessels into the twentieth century, to the advantage of American shipbuilders:

> ...the cost of operating American vessels was generally considerably above that of the nations of western Europe throughout the period from 1789 to 1914, if the differences in the prices of new ships are not taken into account. Since the advantage in ship operation was based on that in shipbuilding, the depletion of the timber supply was certain to cause a serious contraction in the American shipping industry sooner or later. Until the middle of the nineteenth century, however, the American owners were able to maintain a substantial advantage, and to dominate a large part of the world's carrying trade...The competitive advantage of the American shipping industry appears to have been greatest during the early years of the Republic...This early period was one of extraordinarily vigorous maritime enterprise in which the operation of small-sized private trading ships on speculative voyages to Europe, the West Indies, and the Orient was the characteristic type of activity. The ships employed were small sailing vessels, which rarely exceed 400 gross tons in size and one hundred feet in length.[30]

Vessel construction-materials and workmanship-was haphazardly local. Each vessel, with very rare exceptions, was a unique creation, having its own idiosyncrasies and, while these may have been treasured by the owner or captain, could not interfere with effective performance. The Baltimoreans who designed these schooners were constantly adapting them to changing circumstances, as evidenced by the alterations both during and after the 1811-1815 period. The schooner, ranging from 100 to 120 tons performed most efficiently and economically in the transport of trade with the West Indies, and later South and Central America, since Baltimore's commercial interests centered in those areas. The smaller of these vessels were also used for trade with the North American ports to the south of Baltimore, more likely than they were used to the north, for, as observed by James Buchanan, they did have problems in rough seas, and their captains and owners preferred the more lucrative and less stormy southern routes.

Brigs were the second largest class of vessels built by Baltimore's shipbuilders. Eighty-seven two-masted, square-rigged vessels,[31] or about 14.2% of the total number of all vessels recorded between 1797 and 1835 were brigs. Their average keel was 73.90' with a tonnage of over 191. Their higher-than-average tonnage is reflected in their proportion of 18.6% of the total tonnage constructed in Baltimore. Most brigs (83.5%) had one deck and almost always (98.7%) had two masts; only one brig had three masts. These vessels were built by thirty-one different builders, fifteen (48.4%) of whom built only one each. Of the remaining sixteen builders, five carpenters constructed only two apiece and three built three each. Thomas Kemp, Isaac H. Miles, Bailey & Dorgin, and Levin Dunkin each built four brigs. Three builders constructed the remaining thirty-seven brigs: George Gardner built sixteen, the Price shipyards fourteen, and James Beacham, seven. No brigs were built between 1811 and 1816, an indication that the speed and maneuverability which typified the schooner and enhanced its wartime demand was not characteristic of the brig. In fact, only seventeen brigs were constructed before 1816; that the remaining 80.5% were built between that year and 1835 indicates brigs were best suited for the peacetime carrying trade.

The third largest class of vessels built were sloops. Thirty-nine of them, single-masted fore and aft rigged vessels,[32] (6.4%) were built between 1799 and 1834 by 23 shipbuilders, ten (41.0%) of whom built only one apiece, and five (25.5%) of whom built two each. The other builders were William Flannigain who built nine (23.1%) and Thomas Kemp who built four (10.3%). Seven of the

Design Makes a Difference

sloops were built for the builders' own use and six of these were the smallest in tonnage. All of the sloops were under 50' in length and 76 tons except two: one, the *Patapsco*, the subscription ship built by Louis DeRochebrune, and called by him a war sloop. She was 380 tons and built in 1799. The other, *Splendid*, 458 tons, built by Robb & Donaldson in 1832, listed as "full built sloop." This may mean that it was what was referred to at the time as a ship-sloop since, in addition to its size, it also had the two-deck, three-mast design of a ship. This was in sharp contrast to the almost exclusive one deck, one mast configuration for other sloops. Sloops were built continuously throughout the forty-year period, nineteen by 1815, twenty built between 1815 and 1834. Eliminating the two atypical vessels from the statistics, average tonnage of the sloops was 60.76, average keel length 44.27'; it was the smallest recorded vessel built in Baltimore (commercial vessels under five tons did not have to be recorded). The sloop accounted for 6.5% of the number of vessels built, but only 2.6% of the tonnage. Probable uses for sloops, aside from pleasure craft, would include local transport, dock to ship, for example, or from point to point within the bay or along local rivers.

The fourth largest class of vessels built in Baltimore, ships, were large, square-rigged trans-oceanic vessels, designed to carry bulky cargoes[33]. There were thirty (4.9% of total vessels) built in Baltimore between 1804 and 1835 with a record five built in 1811. These thirty comprised 15.3% of total tonnage. The average ship had a keel length of 93.28' and a capacity of 455.52 tons. They usually had two decks (73.3%) and three masts (83.3%). Only twelve yards built ships, six of whom built one each. The remaining twenty-four were constructed by: the Prices, eight (26.7%), Beacham, seven (23.3%), Parsons, three (10.0%), and, finally, Kemp, Gardner, and Flannigain, who built two each totaling 19.8%. The average tonnage of the first fifteen ships built was lower (336.53) than that of the later half.

Two exceptionally large ships were the *Hannibal*, finished in 1811 by William Price, 790.18 tons (see pp. 85, 87 and Appendix 3), and the *Baltimore*, 2,028.71 tons built in 1826 by James Beacham. Between 1809 and 1810, the Price shipyard was commissioned to build a corvette for Henry Christophe, ruler of the new Haitian Republic. Through his agents, VonKapff and Brune, Christophe sent goods and bills of exchange worth $136,000 to cover the cost of construction. All was not well, however, with Christophe's financial standing in Baltimore. During the island's revolution, guns and munitions had been shipped to Haiti and not paid for, so Christophe's ship was ordered to auction to settle the debts. When the auction was published by VonKapff & Brune, legal action was brought to stop the sale. The claimants, John and James Thompson and Henry Davis felt that, because of the imminence of war with Great Britain, prices would be depressed and they would not recover all of what was owed to them. They sued to delay the sale but were unsuccessful and on July 6, 1811, an auction was held. Newspaper advertisements describe the vessel:

> She is allowed by the best of judges to be a very handsome and well finished ship, and from her model, it is supposed she will be a very fast sailor. She is corvette built, pierced for 26 guns, burthen 850 tons, is 136' 6" on upper deck and 37' 8" in breadth; is copper fastened to the bends, and coppered [...] deep line mark.[34]

She is further described as having a gun deck of 129'6", a keel of 110', and square rigging. Her main mast was 76' 9", topmast 60' 6" and her foremast 72'.[35] Messrs. Thompson and Davis estimated the cost of construction of this ship at "upwards of $90,000" but felt that the auction "would not bring more than the sum of $30,000."[36] No record of the sale price remains, but the ship, originally named the *Hope* was purchased by Robert and John Oliver, Abraham Von Kapff, Courtney D'Arcy, Henry Didier and others, renamed the *Hannibal*, and the ownership was recorded on November 25.

While the *Hannibal* was being fitted, the owners were busy putting together a shipment for her maiden voyage. Henry Didier, Jr. wrote a letter to Messrs. D'Arcy Dodge & Co. from Baltimore on October 11 offering an interest in this voyage:

> Mr. D'Arcy made you an offer in his last letters of an interest in our coffee on board of the ship *Hannibal* and if you thought proper an interest in the ship. I am in hopes she will more than clear herself this voyage by her Freight, him and myself

Design Makes a Difference

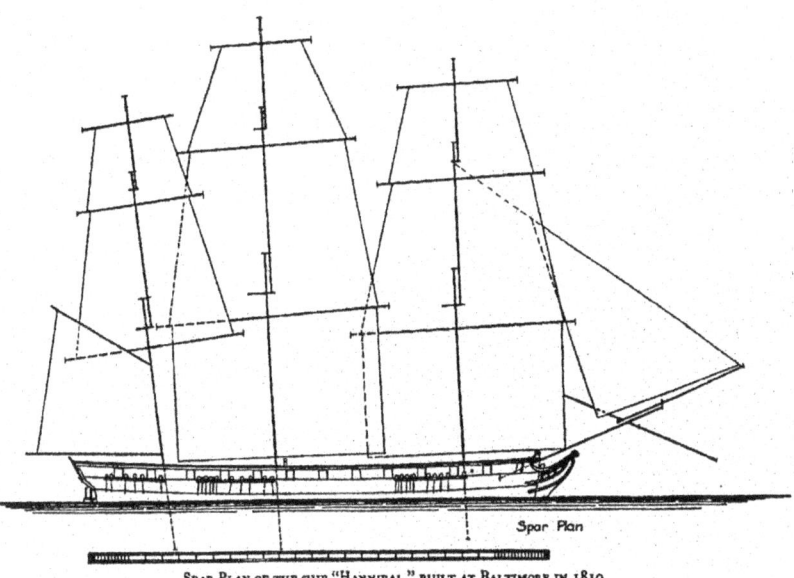

Spar Plan of the ship "Hannibal," built at Baltimore in 1810

3.3 HANNIBAL[37]

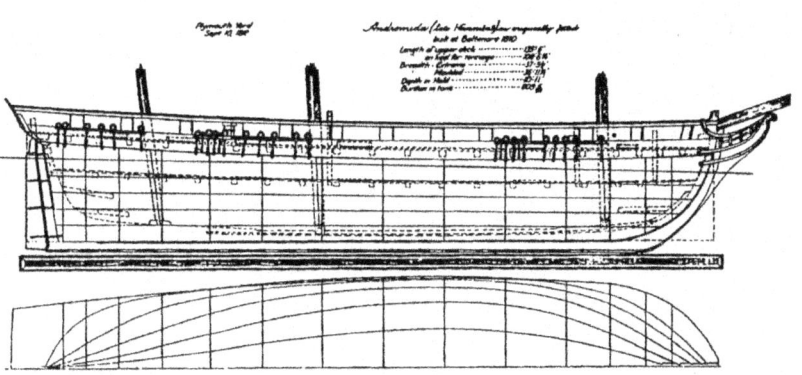

Design Makes a Difference

> own one third of the ship which we purchased of Mr. Oliver. I repeat Mr.D'Arcy's's offer and if Mr. Marple and Dodge think proper will allow them to take one third or one half of our interest. We have on board three hundred thousand pounds of coffee, they may either take one hundred or one hundred fifty thousand pounds. In that case they will send the same quantity to Mr. D'Arcy here and cash to pay for their interest in the vessel and charges on the coffee. We shall try to get into Bordeaux or if chased into the first port in France. Coffee by the last accounts was seventy five to eighty cents and there has not been one return cargo that has sold for upwards of one hundred percent in this country. We have the only licinse [sic] now in this country for colonial produce, so that I have no fear of the markets being glutted. [38]

On December 3, 1811, the *American & Commercial Daily Advertiser* reports, the *Hannibal* cleared Baltimore, bound for Bordeaux. Although war was not declared until the following June, the *Hannibal* was an early victim, being taken by the British Royal Navy on 31 January 1812; she was studied, refitted and renamed *Andromeda*. She was sold 18 April 1816 and disappears from history. The architects at Plymouth [England] Yard, however, recorded the refitting and Chapelle describes what he found:

> The plan is of a very rare type, an American merchantman of the period of 1812. There are very few draughts in existence of American vessels of this date. Above the water she has the appearance of a French sloop of war of this period, but her underbody is an enlargement of the Baltimore clipper schooner, without as much rake to her sternport. The amount of deadrise is very great for a vessel of this size and rig. A comparison of this draught with that of the *Ann McKim*, another Baltimore ship of a later date,

3.4 HANNIBAL

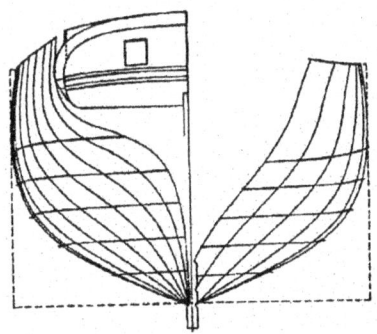

shows some similarity in ideas, though the last named is far more extreme in type. The *Hannibal* or *Andromeda*, has less drag to her keel, but the builder, like the builder of the *Ann McKim*, had the same general idea for a design of a fast ship. The *Hannibal*, we may therefore assume, is an example of a very early clipper ship. She is mentioned in James' 'History of the Royal Navy' abstract 21, as being an extraordinarily fine ship and that her model should have been used for the class of ship-sloops to be built to oppose the American ship-sloops of the *Frolic* class.[39]

At 2,208.71 tons, three times the capacity of the *Hannibal*, Beacham's *Baltimore*, was built in 1826 for Henry Eckford. *Baltimore* was a very large ship, the largest recorded in Baltimore before 1835, excepting the *Constellation* which was a ship of war, not a merchant ship. *Baltimore* had four decks and three masts; her keel measured 166.42'. Because there seems to be no trace of the vessel in Maryland records, it is highly likely that she was turned over immediately to Eckford. Henry Eckford was a well known and well connected shipbuilder in New York City after the War of 1812. During that war, he had supervised construction of the fleet on Lake

Design Makes a Difference

Ontario. He was constructor at the Brooklyn Navy Yard for three years during the Monroe Administration. After resigning this post, he returned to his yard in Brooklyn where he built the *Robert Fulton*, a steamboat which made the first successful trip from New York to New Orleans and Cuba in 1822. In his later years he built a corvette for the Sultan of Turkey and died there while organizing a navy yard[40]. Why this man would have requested James Beacham to construct a ship for him is open to conjecture since they do not seem to have more than the *Baltimore* in common. The most likely guess is that he wished to study Baltimore-style construction, but this vessel, large as it was, was not typical of Baltimore, so this remains a mystery.

The *Ann McKim*, mentioned above, was 420 tons and built in 1833 by Kinard [Kennard] & Williamson. She is described as a ship with two decks, three masts, a keel length of 109' 7" and was built for Isaac McKim, a Baltimore merchant who named her for his wife.

Although many merchant houses failed in the Panic of 1819, others held on: "The McKims, Pattersons, and others continued as shipping operatives and business leaders right into the period of clipper ships. They carried on trade with the Orient, South America, and the West Indies in flour, tobacco, coffee, hides, and other products."[41] The *Ann McKim* undoubtedly represents the best of the type of ship engaged in transoceanic trade in the 1830's. She is still touted today as the premier forerunner of the clippers that would arise in the antebellum period.

The use of steam to power vessels began in Baltimore in 1813 and they constituted the fifth largest class of vessel. William Flannigain and James Beacham, together and singly constructed ten (52.6%) of the nineteen built before 1836. Four steamships were constructed, one each by William Parsons, Levi and Israel Riggin, George Gardner, and Culley & Rogers. William Skinner built two (10.5%), John Robb and Robb & Donaldson built three (15.8%). Purchasers were usually (63.2%) steamboat companies; these vessels were large and required substantial investment. Two smaller steamboats were bought by local notables, one, *Experiment*, of 46.45 tons by Charles Ridgley, the other, *Antelope* (registered as *Surprise*), 85.23 tons by George Stiles in 1816 while he was mayor of Baltimore. Hugh McElderry and James Corner, local merchants, bought *Patuxent*, 214.68 tons, in 1827. Lamar, Long, Glaghorn,

Design Makes a Difference

Wood, Gaudroy, Segriel, and Mills of Savannah, Georgia bought John Robb's *Bazil Lamar* in 1832.

Tonnage ranged from 39.07 t. to 461.56 t., with an average of 273.95 tons and keel length 58' to 169', an average of 114.22'. They comprised 3.1% of the total number of vessels built and 5.8% of total tonnage. All of the steamboats had one deck; four (34.6%) of the eleven with complete records had one mast, three (27.3%) had two masts, and four (36.4%) had none.

All six of the sixth largest class of vessels built, barques, which appeared before 1835 were built after 1832. A barque is defined as a three-masted vessel with fore and main-masts square-rigged and mizzen mast fore-and-aft rigged.[42] According to the Baltimore shipbuilders, the barque had two decks in three of five records and three masts in four of five other cases. The earliest-built barque had only one mast and two decks, representing perhaps a prototype or crossover from the brig, which usually had one mast and two decks, or the smallest ships, only two of which were this configuration. The barque seems to have been a tentative move in a new direction, perhaps an early step toward the Baltimore Clipper of later fame. The average keel length of 85.69' and tonnage of 263.57 indicate that the barque may well have substituted for a vessel larger than a brig but smaller than a ship, probably filling both needs as the situation demanded. The six were each built by a different builder, and it is interesting that a third of the buyers were from out of state: the *Ann Louisa* was built by and purchased from the estate of James Beacham in 1834 by Horatio G. Ward of New York and John Land of Ipswich, Massachusetts, and the *Louisa* by Messrs Bevin, Humphreys, and Frazier of Philadelphia from John Robb in 1833.

Baltimore shipbuilders were in business for profit. Through good times and bad, their vessels kept Baltimore's freight moving. The economics of industry were most complex at that time; a man's ability to raise capital in tight periods depended on his good name and community regard. When capital was plentiful, Baltimore shipbuilders tended to invest in land and the Fells Point system of ground rents made this venture easy and profitable. Interest in real property became divided between the owners of the ground and the owners of the improvements such as houses, workshops, offices, and outbuildings. Landowners had title to the lot and were included in deciding major alterations that affected the ground; this was not

Design Makes a Difference

uncommon in Fells Point since the waterline was constantly being extended (see maps, pp. 40a, 40b).[43] Property lines were moved out into the water when the port was dredged and harbor sludge moved onto land. This procedure became increasingly popular after 1791 with the construction of a dredging machine by Baltimorean Peter Zacharie.[44] Existent wharves were extended and new ones built by the merchants and shipbuilders in business along the waterfront. Thus, as can be seen on the Port Warden's map of 1828 (p. 40a), wharves occupied as much of the waterfront as possible along the point. Businesses and residences were located adjacent to the wharves.

In many instances the complex financial climate of Baltimore encouraged businessmen to diversify their investments. Fells Point was a community of entrepreneurs; most fortunes were made by a lucky combination of skill, hard work, thrift, and good investment; they could be readily lost by a deficiency of any of these ingredients, especially luck. Although the merchant class was important to the early development of Baltimore, it is well to give the shipbuilders their due credit. Their social involvement in the community will be discussed in the following chapter and the importance of their overall contributions to the growth of the city will be evaluated. Their financial interactions with family and friends will be discussed as well because these aspects of commerce were much more vital during that period when banking was more personal than societal.

Chapter Four

The Shipbuilders

Although early nineteenth century Baltimore did not leave many public business records, and the 1790's even fewer, by looking at conditions that flourished in the shipyards of Fells Point we can begin to understand how this maritime community prospered. One instance of this process, the shop system, helped train new artisans as the master shipbuilders passed on their skills as well as their capital. Baltimore's labor system was in flux, however, and between 1795 and 1835 underwent significant changes: sole ownership and management by masters to partnerships and companies run by managers rather than owners, slave to free black, native labor to immigrant workers. Banking was primitive or nonexistent in 1795, but by 1835 had evolved into the intricate structure necessary to maintain more consistency in the local business community. Insurance companies were formed locally to respond to Baltimore's specific needs. Local government and municipal services moved from voluntary organizations of citizens to government employees. A small maritime community became part of a thriving, successful city. Baltimore's shipyards are excellent examples of this evolution.

Pre-capitalist urban American labor practices were in great flux in the late seventeenth and early eighteenth centuries. The transition from the traditional shop methods to the more modern wage laborer had just begun. In a border city like Baltimore, the old and the new lived in close proximity, with slavery a viable part of the entrepreneurial system. Artisan slaves were hired out to work next to European immigrants whose skills were nominal; racial biases determined the almost inevitable ascendancy of the white over the black worker and where economics was not the determinative, violence was. To understand the resentment of the white workers, it is instructive to examine the general labor conditions of the time. No inquiry has yet been done in Baltimore, but a major study of early nineteenth century artisans of New York has. This work examines both the masters and the journeymen in the traditional system. Citing an analysis of wealth relative to occupation in 1815, an author concludes: "Overall these masters [artisans], ranking on an average but one economic class below that of the merchant community, possessed sufficient means for a comfortable if not wealthy existence." Further, he explained, "The 1819 Jury List for the Sixth Ward reveals that of the ninety-eight masters listed in traditional crafts, twenty-five, or just over one-fourth (25.5 percent) owned real property. The wills of the more prosperous artisans testify to the popularity of such investment."[1]

Under the shop system, a father, William Price for example, trained his son John and provided a shipyard for him to begin his business. Had John Price outlived his father, his future would have been secure. William Flannigain built vessels from 1804 to 1821; James Beacham worked for Flannigain between 1817 and 1819, and continued to build ships on his own until 1835 or longer. George Gardner worked with Thomas Kemp between 1815 and 1818, with Joseph Robson between 1817 and 1820, and on his own until his death in 1833. Chart 4.1 illustrates the interactions among Baltimore's shipyards.

Of course, these were not the only shipbuilders in the city, but they were among the most productive, especially in terms of privateering vessels. Garitee's accounting of the private armed vessels shows that of the 111 Maryland vessels for which certificates have been found, sixty were built in Baltimore, and of that sixty, the Prices' built twelve and Thomas Kemp seventeen, almost 50% of the total. These men were the industry leaders, then, and it is interesting to consider the economic atmosphere of the era and how it might have affected shipyard finances.

The scarcity of public banking facilities in the early period of Baltimore's growth was serious in a city of merchants. Attempts were made from 1784 to begin the Bank of Maryland; incorporation of the bank was finally approved by the Maryland legislature in 1790

Design Makes a Difference

Chart 4.1 SHIPBUILDERS CAREER LONGEVITY

Name/ # Built	1795	1800	1805	1810	1815	1820	1825	1830	1835
William Price			1797-1831 --- d.1831						
John Price				1811-1821 ------------------d. 1821					
William Price & Son (Walter)								1831-1835 ------d.1840	
William Flannigain		1804-1818 --d. 1821							
Flannigain & Beacham					1817-1819 ----------				
James Beacham					1817-1835 ---------------------------d.1842				
Thomas Kemp		1804-1816 -------------------d.1824 (ret'd St. Michaels 1816)							
Gardner & Kemp					1815-1818 ----------				
Gardner & Robson					1817-1820 ----------				
George Gardner					1815-1835 --------------------------------d. 1833				

and two hundred thousand dollars were raised within fourteen days. The first directors were merchants and lawyers, elected in March 1791 when the bank finally opened. A Baltimore branch of the Bank of the United States opened in February 1792, and in December 1792, the National Bank of Baltimore was chartered, and called the Bank of Baltimore. The directors of all of these banks overlapped: Samuel Smith, Isaac Vanbibber, Samuel Hollingsworth, and Archibald Campbell, among others, served as officers of more than one financial institution. This particular group of bankers favored risky methods, particularly following the War of 1812, and the overall poor economic climate of those years pushed them over the brink into fraud. "More than any other single factor, the financial collapse on May 20, 21, and 22, of the 'Club' of speculators who were officers of the branch [Bank of the United States] triggered the depression of 1819 in Baltimore."[2] The bank failures in the Panic years took many merchants along with them.

Design Makes a Difference

There was a need in Baltimore for more than merchant finance, however, and this was addressed with the establishment of the Mechanics' Bank of Baltimore, located at the corner of Calvert and Fayette Streets in 1806, capitalized at one million dollars. The commissioners included shipbuilder William Price and George Jessop, one of the founders of Calverton Mills. Also commissioners were George Decker and James Mosher, members of the Athenian Society which promoted domestic manufactures, and William Gwynn, who would later become secretary of The American Society for the Promotion of Domestic Manufactures and National Industry, organized in 1817. The second article of the constitution "...required that nine of the directors should be practical mechanics or manufacturers..."[3]

The Franklin Bank was founded in March 1810 and the list of commissioners and directors consisted of many names familiar to the shipbuilding community: Lemuel Taylor, William Flannigain, and William Price, for example. In 1810, other waterfront businessmen cooperated to found the National Marine Bank: Hezekiah Waters, Joseph Biays, Archibald Kerr, John Lee, John Coulter, Thorndike Chase, and Baptiste Mezick incorporated the bank, the first one in Fells Point, and capitalized it at six hundred thousand dollars. Hezekiah Waters, a wharf owner on Pitt Street, became the first President, remaining in that office until 1835, and the bank opened its doors on Broadway, then relocated in 1832 to Gay and Second Streets.[4] This type of enterprise was common during the Federalist period. "The first banks were conservative enterprises funded and directed by members of the mercantile community, who sought both new investment opportunities and a means of supplying greater outside financing for their own trading ventures."[5] The Mechanics Bank and the National Marine Bank were later converted into national banks, in 1865, and 1880, respectively.

These banks helped the shipyard community cross the bridge from the personal economic climate of the late eighteenth and early nineteenth century into the more modern banking system that grew out of the Panic of 1819. The "first pervasive monetization of credit in American society" arose during the 1820's under the leadership of the second Bank of the United States, and "[T]he operations of the

Design Makes a Difference

Bank of the United States thus changed the nature of the seaport markets...The new system democratized the seaport markets by effecting a shift to a buyers' market and money system."[6]

The period between 1800 and 1835 was not an easy one for those who depended on the sea for a livelihood; the Embargo years preceding the War of 1812, the depressed years following the war, and the many slump periods that came and went periodically threw much of the maritime industry on very hard times. Neither was it an easy period for marginal trades, and cities such as Boston, New York, and Philadelphia were faced with major increases in expenditures for poor relief. For example, "The formation of the Assistance Society in December 1808 provides further evidence of increased economic dependency in New York City during the Embargo years...The Assistance Society remained active until after 1825, occasionally reinstituting general relief during periods of extreme distress."[7] Although comparable records were not kept in Baltimore, the maritime focus of America's economy brought about equal distress in all of the Atlantic seaports and had disastrous consequences for maritime laborers and their dependents.

In the late eighteenth century, artisans throughout the young nation faced considerable economic difficulties, credit being primary. There was no banking system which would deal with local businessmen; they relied on personal contacts or cash reserves to protect their cash flow irregularities, but this was often inadequate. Legal problems arose for some tradesmen, and for others, federal legislation created difficulties. Foreign competition was a constant problem to early American merchants and manufacturers, and attempts were made from the 1790's on to encourage local manufacturers. There was little response until the Embargo period when capital was moved from international trade to new investments in industry. Part of this problem was the merchants dependence on the importation of finished goods to maintain their returns; conversely, native producers were negatively affected by the increased cost of imported raw materials.

An early attempt to stabilize the peril inherent in the early merchant system was the establishment of insurance companies to offset high-risk investment. The insurance industry, important as it

Design Makes a Difference

was to a seaport such as Baltimore, was begun by Maryland's General Assembly in 1787. This legislation approved the establishment of The Baltimore Insurance Company to insure local residents in case of fire, but by 1796, additional authorization was extended to allow the company to insure "freight on ships or vessels, and goods or merchandise on board of ships or vessels."[8] This company was followed by two more before 1810.

Seamen were especially conscious of the dangers of fire and the large amount of lumber present in a shipbuilding community encouraged not only insurance, but the formation of fire companies to control the dangers to business as well as personal property. Several shipbuilders were active in forming volunteer fire companies. There were two early fire companies reported in Fells Point, the Deptford Fire Company instituted in 1792, and the Columbian Fire Company begun in 1809. Until 1833, the Deptford Fire Company was located at the corner of Market (Broadway, today) and Fleet Streets. Hezekiah Waters, wharf owner and banker, was a director in 1806, as were Thomas Cole, ship chandler located on Pitt Street close to the Waters wharf, and James Biays, initially a ship joiner, later a merchant. Two other traders, Thomas Tenant, and William Wilson were a Lane-man, and Property-man, respectively. It was the duty of the Lane-man to clear a path through the crowd for those who fought the fire. "Armed with eight-foot staffs, they cleared a path from the closest water source to the fire. Others, wearing white-topped hats, acted as 'property-men' whose job was to protect the household goods firemen took out of a burning house."[9]

The Columbian Fire Company appears to have succeeded the Deptford, or perhaps coexisted with it because it reportedly was located on the same corner of Fleet and Market Streets in Fells Point. It elected officers in 1809: the President was Joseph Allender, local physician. There were several directors such as Thorndike Chase, a prominent merchant in the community. William Price, shipbuilder, was a Lane-man, as was Baptiste Mezick, ship owner, captain, and merchant.[10] These businessmen, carried their management and leadership skills into the general community, benefitting their fellow citizens as well as themselves. Civic responsibility in this era moved easily from fire fighting to security as illustrated by the courageous community spirit and involvement that emerged in the defense of Baltimore and Fort McHenry in the War of 1812.

Along with the difficulties of the changing economy, the independence of the working class also created problems. Up to the late eighteenth century, journeymen were domiciled with their masters and did not marry until they had become proficient enough to open their own shops. This became almost impossible in the mushrooming cities of America: rapid population growth reduced the housing availability drastically, with a concurrent increase in cost. If only one-quarter of the masters could purchase their own homes, the rest must rent quarters as an expense of business. The cost of providing lodging as well as shop space drove the margin of profit down, so more and more journeymen were forced to provide their own lodgings, thus restricting the income available to support a family or open an independent shop.

The hours worked were long and hard, and most labor was seasonal, constrained outdoors by the weather and indoors by light or lack of it. The construction trade in New York is an example: "In all, a journeyman's workday, inside or out, consisted of ten or more hours of labor for six days a week, including, for indoor tradesmen, the strain of working for hours by the glimmering light of candles."[11] Incomes for journeymen were minimal; a study of journeymen carpenters and masons in the 1810's concluded "the journeymen were barely making a subsistence living, with less than ten percent owning more than $150 of personal property."[12] In addition to low wages, work was seasonal, with the winter being particularly bleak for maritime workers: work was less available and living expenses increased.

If journeymen were barely making a living, what was the case for common laborers: draymen, dockmen, and other menial jobs provided less reliable income than the trades. If merchants and masters could fail in business, plunging into poverty, how uncertain then was life for those lower down the economic ladder. Some cities had welfare agencies and these communities experienced huge increases in petitions for relief. Baltimore had no public provision for the indigent until after 1818,[13] but the situation in New York was well recorded: "Vagrants multiply on our Hands to an amazing

Degree...Immigration swelled the almshouse and the poor lists during the 1790's...The crisis of the city deepened decade by decade. Natural disaster and man-made catastrophe contributed to this disturbing dimension of urban life."[14] Although discussing New York, the author may well have been describing the problems that assailed Baltimore: yellow fever epidemics, extremely cold winters, the Embargo, post-war depression following the War of 1812. These problems were so common that New York's liberals "accepted poverty as the normal condition of the laboring classes," whereas they decried pauperism, defined as "dependence on public relief or private charity, an intolerable and unnecessary evil."[15] One of the causes of poverty is described as: "[T]he vicissitudes of maritime employment [which] affected the families of seamen." A large category of urban poor were the working poor and, in New York:

> The city was full of able-bodied men and women with low-paying jobs or without regular employment-urban workers...'whose servile employments are necessary in furnishing the opulent with the conveniences and luxuries of life.' Such laborers included indentured servants, free blacks, apprentices, seamstresses, washwomen, and domestic workers. Similarly, seamen worked only sporadically. The largest group consisted of unskilled common laborers-cartmen, scavengers, chimney sweeps, wood cutters, stevedores, and dock workers-men and boys who sought new jobs each day...The irregular nature of employment available to unskilled workers dictated that they would rarely move above subsistence levels...The virtual suspension of commerce and shipping in winter also brought seasonal unemployment to laborers and craftsmen, whose livelihood depended on a bustling harbor-dock workers, bargemen, river boatmen, ship carpenters, caulkers, and riggers.[16]

Design Makes a Difference

Although Baltimore was a vibrant, growing city between 1795 and 1835, there were hard times for many, particularly those of the lower class.

The master carpenters, most prosperous in the shipbuilding economy, left little record of their business activities. Some, like Thomas Kemp and William Flannigain tend to be remembered for their most famous vessels, and in searching for more information, there is a risk of incorrect details being passed along. William Flannigain, for example, recorded his first Carpenter Certificate in 1804. This vessel, the *Dart*, was a seventy-one ton "pilot boat" schooner and was sold to a Mr. L. M. Dunan; it was much smaller than Flannigain's average vessel but about average for the three vessels he built that first year. He continued building his schooners-seventeen of the twenty-seven vessels he built independently were schooners-until 1818. George Stiles was reputed to have paid $40,000 for the *Siro*, built by William Flannigain, but the Carpenter Certificate for this vessel has not been found, perhaps because she was not considered a commercial vessel, but rather exclusively a privateer. Engineering skills were evidenced in Flannigain's vessels:

> Shipbuilder William Flannigain demonstrated flexibility of rig when he advertised a 226-ton pilot-boat built vessel for sale that could be 'fitted [as] a brig or schooner. With British merchant captains fleeing at the first sight of a schooner-rigged vessel, a brig profile had advantages at sea when one was willing to sacrifice some speed.[17]

William Flannigain, as most Fells Point businessmen, was active in the real estate market. He owned property on Wolfe Street, a corner lot at Albemarle and Duke Streets, another corner at Aliceanna and Burke Streets. The Wolfe Street lot, acquired in 1802 was transferred to Elizabeth Herring in 1820, a lot on the east side of "Centre market Space," deeded to him in 1810 was in turn deeded by him to Charles Crook in 1817. He also satisfied a mortgage on the Duke and Albemarle corner property in 1812 to James Taylor. His brother Andrew succeeded him in his shipyard, constructing his first vessel in 1824. William died, at age 54, on 8 August 1821 at his seat in Ann Arundel County. Andrew married Catherine Eliza Taylor on 30 January 1831 and lived a long life until his passing on 21 June 1870.

Catherine Taylor was the eldest daughter of Captain Lemuel Taylor who had also been a Fells Point shipbuilder during the years 1817 to 1821. There was little information on Lemuel Taylor, other than his several attempts to escape bachelorhood. Taylor wed Mary Merryman at Clover Hill in Baltimore County 20 April 1815. He married again 6 June 1816, a Miss Margaret Fowler. She died 4 April 1817. Taylor was married again 11 November 1817 to Miss Ann Rawlings in Annapolis, his final recorded marriage. In 1812 Lemuel Taylor, along with other Fells Point citizens Hezekiah Waters, Thomas Tenant, and James Biays, was active in establishing a "'Home of Industry' for the care of deserving females and needy children and young street vagrants.:" That same year, Taylor joined James Buchanan, Luke Tiernan, Levi Hollingsworth, George Stiles, James Biays, and Thorndike Chase, among others, in signing resolutions calling "for war against England, and against France also, if the latter should not afford redress for the wrongs inflicted."[18]

Taylor built two vessels with Joseph Turner, whose Fells Point shipyard began operating in 1812. The Turner yard was small, building not more than two vessels in any but one year, a total of seventeen in the period 1812 to 1827, including two that Turner built with Taylor. Turner married Rebecca Sinclair at the Friends Meeting House 21 October 1812. He died at his residence in Harford County 16 October 1832 at age 54 leaving his wife with "a large family of children." In 1865, when Turner's son died in New Orleans at age 33, Rebecca was still alive.

William Parsons was listed as a shipbuilder in Baltimore's first directory in 1796, but the first record of a vessel built by him was in 1801, a 78 ton schooner sold to R. C. Boislandry. His shipyard was located at that time on Hanover Street in Federal Hill. He later moved to Fells Point where he continued to build until 1816. In his sixteen years in business he built 42 ships, almost three per year, a higher than average output. He died near Cincinnatti, Ohio on 30 May 1824 and was described in his obituary as a steamboat builder.

Design Makes a Difference

Since he built only one steamboat in Baltimore, it is possible that he was involved in steamboat construction in Ohio prior to his death there. The one steamboat that he built in Baltimore was launched in 1816. It was built for George Stiles, Baltimore's then mayor, and was named the *Antelope* "in honor of the famous Revolutionary privateer of that name. It was only 76 feet in length...Its rotary engine was acclaimed as a great forward step in the improvement of steam propulsion."[19]

James Beacham was a latecomer to the Fells Point shipbuilding community, beginning his independent career in 1820 and continuing until 1834. In 1828, he bought property adjacent to the water on Wolfe Street, two lots that he may have used for his shipyard. He also purchased a lot on the west side of Strawberry Street [Alley], one street away from Wolfe street. He mortgaged a property to the Maryland Savings Institution in 1829, an innovative transaction because most mortgages prior to this period were on private residences. Beacham built 36 vessels, an average of two and a half vessels per year. His vessels were larger, on the average, than any other major shipbuilder, reflecting his preference for ships (6), steamboats (5), and full built brigs (6). James Beacham worked from 1817 to 1820 with William Flannigain, most likely as an apprentice.

George Gardner's career spanned more than two decades. During this twenty-two year career he collaborated with Thomas Kemp (1815-1816), and later (1817-1822), with Joseph Robson. He built a total of seventy vessels, an average annual output of over three vessels. His last vessel, built in 1835, was constructed with or by his son William. He died about 1835, but an obituary was not found; his will was filed in 1833. George Gardner built schooners, for the most part, his total independent output averaged 134.26 tons, as opposed to 145 for Thomas Kemp or 197.61 for William Price. His schooners were described by him as "round tuck pilot built schooners" Some of his vessels were sold to buyers in New York, but for the most part Baltimore merchants such as Thomas Tenant, Edmond Didier, Isaac McKim, C. W. Karthaus, James Corner, William Wilson & Sons to name just a few, were regular customers over the years. Gardner also invested in Fells Point real estate, but not to any great degree.

Thomas Kemp is probably the most famous of Baltimore's early shipbuilders; his vessels sailed to glory during the War of 1812. Considerable research has been done on Kemp's life, probably because there is ample material to draw from. His Quaker background did not deter his construction of privateers, in fact he took great pains to let the public know that he built "round tuck privateer fashion schooners." He worked for the most part alone, constructing fifty-two vessels in Baltimore between 1804 and 1816, in addition to the twelve he built with George Gardner, a total of sixty-four in thirteen years or an average annual output of almost five vessels. This is the highest production rate of any Baltimore shipbuilder and, in spite of the speed of construction, the quality was so high that his vessels were renowned for their durability and speed, as well as their lack of cargo space. By 1815 Kemp had made his fortune; a one hundred seventy acre parcel of land that he had mortgaged in 1815 was free and clear before the year was out. Kemp's shipbuilding enterprise was at odds with his religious background; the Quaker community "absolutely rejected military activities of any kind" and Kemp's privateer fashion schooners were specifically designed to attack other vessels. Kemp's interest in the success of his vessels was personal as well as commercial; he invested, along with other shipbuilders, in the privateering enterprises of the *Chasseur*, for example, as Joseph Despaux invested in the *Caroline* and William Price in the *Revenge*.[20] Kemp's genius for constructing fast, light schooners was unmatched by any other shipbuilder of the time. His vessels were captained by heroes like Thomas Boyle who so trusted his privateer fashion schooner, the *Chasseur*, that he sailed directly into British waters, on their side of the Atlantic, and announced that he was placing the English coast under blockade. While such brash actions create legends, they also illustrate the tremendous confidence that the captain felt in his vessel, certainly a tribute to its maker. At the end of the war, Thomas Kemp retired to his Eastern Shore home, Wade's Point Farm. Here he continued to build ships but with less intensity, turning the work over to his brother, Joseph. He instructed his agent to dispose of the home

Design Makes a Difference

that he owned in Fells Point at the corner of Fountain and Fleet streets. The property was then occupied by George Gardner and was described as "a Very Comfortable and Roomy two story frame Dwelling house, a good brick Kitchen and Smoke house, A large work shop and very good counting house."[21] Kemp died 3 March 1824, aged 45.

Much has already been said about the Price family shipyards which built a total of seventy-seven vessels over four decades; of these, fifty-nine were schooners. The average size of a vessel built by William Price was 197.61 tons, John's average vessel was somewhat lighter, 166.56 tons. William Price & Son, the company owned by William's son Walter and managed by Hugh Auld and probably others had an average vessel size of 191.86, close to William's own. The superior quality of a Price vessel was attested to by the demand for his vessels in Baltimore and in foreign ports over a forty-year span. These vessels were built by slaves, those at the very bottom of the social and economic scale. This paper makes no attempt to apologize for slave owners, but rather seeks to explain the information that has unfolded as research into shipbuilding has progressed. It is a fact that the Price shipyard on Fell Street was operated with slave labor from the first tax records in 1798 until its disappearance in 1840. It is certain as well that the yard was productive and successful throughout this period, a tribute to the management skills of the owner. It is also true that the vessels that were built in Price's yards were consistently in demand over a forty-year period, evidence of the skills and professionalism of the workers. If slaves on plantations and farms were protesting their condition by subversion, those at the Price shipyards were not. Not only was the work skillfully performed, but the crafts were passed on to others such as Frederick Douglass who became a caulker during his employment at the Price yard. It is ironic that this proficiency could never be put to use after Douglass left Baltimore; he reports that skilled black men were not hired in the shipyards of the free North. The competition for jobs affected the hiring of slaves in southern cities as well and legal steps were taken to curtail the hiring out of black slaves as skilled laborers.[22]

Design Makes a Difference

The occupations of free black laborers in Baltimore, as listed for the first time in the 1831 City Directory, shows that 25.88% did not have occupations indicated and 29.75% are listed as laborers (male) and washers (male and female), a total of 55.63% of the labor force with minimal skills. The balance of 44.37% of free black workers possessed numerous skills: 111 (5.5%) were sawyers, 102 (5.06%) were draymen, 73 (3.62%) were porters, 72 (3.57%) were carters, 55 (2.73%) were waiters. Among the other occupations listed for free blacks were laundress, mariner, caulker, brickmaker, blacksmith, stevedore, carpenter, hair dresser, gardener, teacher, waterman, shopkeeper, physician, midwife, cook shop owners, tanners, a wide range of skills which reflected those that existed among the working class white occupations.[23]

There was a total of 4.36% of the free black labor force employed in maritime occupations, 3 rope makers, 10 ship carpenters, 37 caulkers, and 38 seamen. It is highly likely that these skills were acquired during slavery and records show that several shipbuilders manumitted their slaves in their wills. David Stodder, builder of the *Constellation* in the late 1790's provided for the freedom of all his young slaves at age twenty-five and "all my old negroes to be free immediately, and also I desire that my negroe Lewis have all the iron and tools in my blacksmith shop..." This stipulation of Stodder's will dated 14 September 1806 covered the slave Lewis Dixson along with Anna West, Henry Morris and others, as well as the youngsters mentioned in Stodder's estate inventory: 1 Negro Darcus, 1 Negro Girl & Boy, 1 Negro Boy.[24]

The *Constellation* was built by slaves; in 1790 David Stodder owned twenty-five slaves but only seventeen in 1800. This 32% decrease in the number of slaves may indicate a deliberate shrinkage of his work force because of retirement or illness. There is no record of Stodder building commercial vessels in Baltimore after he completed the *Constellation*.

Louis DeRochebrune, another Fells Point shipbuilder, provided for both his heirs and his slaves by stipulating that his slaves were to labor for a time to benefit his estate, and then be freed: "I will and bequeath unto my executors hereinafter named in trust for the benefit of my estate my Negro Law to serve three years from my death and

Design Makes a Difference

then to be manumitted and set free. Also my negro Charles 3 years, negro Harry 3 years, negro Will 3 years, negro Leon 6 years, Stephen 15 years and negro Jack 7 years."[25] DeRochebrune died in 1802 and at this time, this method of manumission was not uncommon in the maritime community of Fells Point. Also common practice was the indenture of youths to masters to learn a trade and Louis DeRochebrune illustrates this custom. His father, Thomas DeRochebrune had directed in his will that his son Louis, who was twelve at the time of the probate, be "bound" to such a trade "as appeared to be to advantage."[26] The early years of his shipbuilding career have not been documented but he built vessels in Fells Point from 1797 to the end of the century.

In comparing the list of shipbuilders with that of slave owners, it is only infrequently that one name appears on both lists, especially when the number of slaves indicates that their use was commercial rather than domestic. Census records indicate that in 1790 a Peter Davis in Queen Anne's County owned twelve slaves, Thomas Hall in Harford County owned fifty-seven, Hugh Auld in Talbot County, five, William Gardner in Charles County, fourteen, John Steel in Baltimore owned six and David Stodder owned twenty-five. Joseph Turner, a Quaker, owned eleven in Charles County and James Ball in Baltimore owned five slaves. In addition to these major holdings, eight shipbuilders owned 14 slaves, less than two each, an indication that they were house slaves rather than skilled laborers. Chapter 2 (p. 62) lists several shipbuilders that have been cross-checked for the period 1795-1835 and indicates the rare occurrences of slave labor forces in the shipyards of Fells Point. In 1800, only four shipyards owned more than five slaves, in 1810 that number increased to twelve, one of which may be in an error because shipbuilder John Steel died in 1809 and it is unknown whether or not his wife kept the shipyard running with the slaves she inherited. By 1820, only one shipyard, that of William Price, still employed more than five slaves and this remained true until 1830. William Price died in 1831, and his son and heir Walter, in 1840. Walter died intestate and records do not show whether these slaves were manumitted or sold. In fact, there is no record of these people, either as slave or free, after the

Design Makes a Difference

1830 census showing them to be Price's property, not even in the records of the black Baltimoreans who migrated to Liberia.

There are many such gaps in manumission documents in Maryland because the records have been lost or destroyed. The few that remain do not tell the whole story, but the available evidence suggests that the independent-minded shipbuilders in Fells Point, and the men they did business with did not rely to any great extent on slave labor. In the manumission records that did survive, early Fells Point residents are strongly in evidence. Hezekiah Waters not only freed his own slaves but testified as to the claims of freedom of other blacks. The merchant Abraham VonBibber freed at least two of his twelve slaves upon his death in 1805; Dr. Joseph Allender freed Philip Buchanan and Francis Buchanan in 1837, the year of his death. Baptiste Mezick, sea captain and merchant freed Tom Green in 1832, and Jeremiah Yellott freed several slaves in 1805. It was the rule, rather than the exception, to manumit slaves through will, and for the most part, care was taken to protect the very young or very old from being cast out without provision being made for sustenance.

The presence of a considerable number of maritime skills among the free blacks of Baltimore attests to the fact that, once trained and manumitted, these workers tended to remain in Baltimore where they were most likely to find jobs that would utilize their skills. Frederick Douglass was scathing in his condemnation of the northern cities which pretended to acknowledge the humanity of the free black, but would not employ a skilled black man in the trade in which he was proficient, preferring to keep him subservient and poor with only the meanest jobs open to him. The Southern seaports were openly hostile to free black artisans, the Northern cities covertly prejudiced, but Baltimore was a fairly open city in the early nineteenth century. The situation deteriorated as the antebellum period approached, but from 1790 to the early 1830's skilled labor was appreciated and employed without much bother about the color of the laborer's skin.

Dr. Joseph Allender's eldest daughter, Eliza Ann, married Walter Price on 16 March 1824. Dr. Allender was a prominent physician in Fells Point; he treated William Price's oldest son, William, who was either retarded or epileptic. He treated, as well, the many poor and

Design Makes a Difference

slave folk who labored in Fells Point. Following the influx of the refugees who fled the San Domingo revolution in 1793, most Atlantic seaboard communities experienced an upsurge of yellow fever. While the epidemic of that year was less severe in Baltimore than it was in Philadelphia where the dead were uncountable, many people died and the death continued each autumn for the next generation. Many of the fatalities were caused by improper treatment, or no treatment at all. Physicians did not understand the etiology of the disease, consequently fear caused people to flee the cities in the hopes of avoiding contagion.

Quarantine was the official weapon, but it was, of course, ineffective. It is now recognized that the damage had occurred in 1793 when the St. Domingan refugees brought yellow fever in their blood streams and transmitted it to the local mosquito population.[27]

During the yellow fever epidemic of 1797, Dr. Allender warned the Board of Health "That a malignant epidemic prevails and urges the members to inspect the Point themselves (September 2)"[28]. In late August 1800 Dr. Allender pleaded for a "better accommodation for the poor" and by September the fever was spreading like wildfire. A temporary hospital was set up but "[T]here was no room in it for colored persons."[29] Although there was little comfort for Baltimore's poorest sick, until his death in 1834, Dr. Allender did not waver in his quest for adequate treatment for all.

Because of the rapid expansion of the city, home construction became a priority. There are no building permits to tell us the patterns of development, and deeds rarely mention improvements on lots, so it is difficult to track just when or by whom buildings were constructed. An example, however, of how the profits from Baltimore's shipbuilding industry enhanced this growth will illustrate how one man's investments created lasting wealth in the city. William Price owned the following property in 1798: an improved water lot assessed at £700, an unimproved water lot at £75, a house and lot at £100, a house and lot, rented at £125, and ten slaves. At his death in 1832, he left homes in Fells Point to each of his eight grandchildren, and in addition, owned a lot with a brick stable as well as seven income properties which provided support for his widow and handicapped son.

Design Makes a Difference

Price's home is still standing in Fells Point and the archaeologist who worked on its excavation commented on the fact that the master bedroom closely resembled a ship captain's cabin.[30] It is probable that the same carpenters who built Mr. Price's ships worked, when they were not building vessels, on the many homes he left to his heirs as well as others in the city.

Baltimore's early city directories list the profession of house carpenter for a very few men around 1800; it would appear that this craft is comparable to what we today might call a general contractor. Where would this man get his workers? There are few bricklayers, carpenters, or laborers listed in the directory. The most logical answer is that unskilled labor was used, most probably the many laborers both black and white listed in the directories of that period. Slaves were also hired out by their owners when they were not needed in the city's homes. No records were kept in early Baltimore; there are no statistical sources to support the type of workers that might have been hired, the amount or kind of work they did, or how well or poorly they were treated. There are newspaper advertisements that attempt to place slave laborers, most of whom are skilled. They were hired by contract for a term of months or years. It was common for owners to require the employer to keep the slave within the state. Maryland law forbade abuses to the liberty of blacks; unscrupulous persons sometimes sold hired slaves and even free blacks to plantations in the deep South.

The ten slaves that William Price owned in 1798 increased and their number fluctuated from a total of twenty-two in 1800, to twenty-five in 1810, twenty-three in 1820 and twenty-six in July of 1828 when his will was drafted. This was a large labor force to maintain in a city and it was necessary to generate income to support so large a group when there was little or no demand for vessels. Rather than risk hiring out his skilled slaves, he might well have turned to home building as a second trade, but no record remains to support this. Further study of the original carpentry in his own home, compared to others in the area that survive from the 1790's might clarify this. The relative stability of the number of slaves, between twenty-two and twenty-five, over a thirty-year period indicates the labor force and skills necessary to produce Price's annual output which was also stable.

His estate inventory, done in 1832, lists ten male adults, ranging in age from fourteen to fifty-eight. This number is somewhat smaller than the crew he listed in the 1820 census, fourteen slaves, ranging in age from three males under age fourteen to four males over the age of forty-five. A reduction in Price's labor force is no surprise since his age in 1830 was over seventy. His older son John who had followed him in the shipbuilding business had died in 1821. His youngest son Walter, although he continued the shipyard after his father's death, had become a successful merchant who did not personally supervise the yard; rather he hired a manager. Throughout most of the period under study, Price was probably not procuring new skilled workers, but rather training the young that were born to the families that he owned.

Price's inventory provides other information about urban slaves, for example, in 1831, he owned ten women over the age of fourteen, the average age of these women was 32.0, about the same as the average for the males fourteen and over which was 32.4 years. The ratio of men to women (both groups fourteen years of age and over) was 1:1 in the estate inventory of 1831 and the presence of small children as well seems to reinforce the probability of family groups within the slave population.

Walter Price operated the shipyard after his father's death with slave labor, according to Frederick Douglass who described in detail his employment at Price's yard. When Walter died in 1840, however, his estate inventory lists only seven slaves, one of whom, Major, was sixty years of age, and infirm. Two other men, Harris and Frank were caulkers, perhaps the same men who instructed Frederick Douglass. Two more were boys, thirteen and fourteen, and two were female house servants, aged twenty-five and twelve. This major reduction in staff is probably due to economic constriction as well as the death of William and the gradual reduction of the shipyard production. The manager in the period discussed by Frederick Douglass (roughly 1835) was his owner, Hugh Auld, and his employment may have been influenced by Auld's proficiency in handling slaves as much as any shipbuilding knowledge he had.

Design Makes a Difference

Auld was born on the Eastern Shore and had experience in shipyards there. Whether or not slaves were used in these yards is beyond the scope of this study, but it is certainly a probability.

Douglass's descriptions of Price's yard with its slave labor, and Gardner's yard, which hired slaves, but did not own them, points out important differences in relations between whites and blacks in Baltimore in the early nineteenth century. Disregarding personal relationships, which we do not know in this instance, slaves were economic units and, especially in the cities, possessed skills that gave them value. A prudent owner cared for such capital investments, especially in a border city such as Baltimore, where freedom was only a few steps away. One factor that must be taken into account when comparing the free black and slave quality of life was the constant threat that the free black faced, in Baltimore as well as most Northern cities. Free blacks were frequently kidnapped to be sold further south, or convicted of crimes whereby they were punished by being sold as slaves. A skilled and valued worker in a positive family environment had security that no free black could find. Whether or not such people were more or less happy than their free brethren must remain a mystery.

We do have the abundant writings of Frederick Douglass, a man who fled slavery, and dedicated the balance of his life to the abolitionist cause. However, although many slaves fled, many did not and those who remained have not told us why they did. It is almost inconceivable that men who lived and worked on the waterfront for decades could not flee if they chose to do so. Therefore, it seems safe to presume that they preferred the security of the shipyards in Fells Point, where they exercised their skills when the work was plentiful, and were fed when it was not.

Slaves were owned by blacks as well as whites in Baltimore and ownership by blacks is described as "largely humanitarian in nature" by one historian. "Relatives or friends could be purchased (when economically and politically feasible) in order to keep them out of the hands of a white slaveholder until manumission could be successfully obtained."[31] Keeping in mind that people's attitudes are not totally determined by racial characteristics, it is surely possible that white

Design Makes a Difference

men could treat their slaves humanely and, conversely, black men might be unkind to those whose destinies they controlled.

Social mobility was an important part of the Baltimore atmosphere. High-risk, wartime investment brought both exorbitant earnings and heavy losses. Maritime trade, even in peacetime was not without substantial hazard: pirates, weather, bad luck, or market fluctuations could reduce a successful businessman to poverty in almost no time at all. Many, however, thrived and, in doing so, moved up the social ladder. George Stiles, mayor of Baltimore immediately following the War of 1812, who began his career as a seaman, became a ship's captain in the 1790's. When he retired from the sea in 1810, he became a merchant and established a dwelling and "counting house" on King George Street in Baltimore where he lived until his election as Baltimore's mayor.[32]

In 1809, Stiles bought a piece of land on Pitt Street in Fells Point; the home on that lot was William Price's. Over the years, Price improved the lot, expanding the wharf behind his home, but he never seemed interested in purchasing the lot himself even though he and his wife lived there until both died. When Mayor Stiles died, his son and heir, John S. Stiles and another seaman, Christopher Deshon, and Julie Claire Ganteaume signed over the ground lease to Francis Gallega, also a sea captain. Deshon, ship's husband before the War of 1812, prize master during it, shared other interests with Stiles: both were directors of the Chesapeake Insurance Company, members of the City Marine Committee, letter-of-marque bond surety agents, and Republicans. Ms. Ganteaume was the daughter of a merchant, James Ganteaume, whose shop was located on the corner of Ann and George Streets, very close to the Pitt Street property. The complexities of this type of private financial arrangements were commonplace in a business community with little access to an established banking system. Personal relationships were intricately woven into the fabric of the economy.

The growth of Baltimore, and even more so, of Fells Point, was a maritime phenomenon, unique at that time among the seaboard cities. Philadelphia, Annapolis, Boston, New York, all were begun as colonial ports and derived their social systems from their origin as British satellites. Baltimore, however, evolved from the merchant

Design Makes a Difference

community that settled there at the end of the eighteenth century and the cooperative ethic shared by the maritime folk was an integral part of the city's growth pattern. This maritime spirit, shared by the merchants and shipbuilders as well as the seamen, encouraged patriotism and civic responsibility, which, along with hard work, thrift, and good luck forged the base for a community that is still strong two hundred years later.

Conclusion

It has been said that the times create the person and this can certainly be applied to America in the last quarter of the eighteenth century. Thomas Jefferson, John Adams, and George Washington rose to roles of leadership on the national level and have left indelible marks in American history. Others, less known in their own time and less remembered in ours, also rose to the demands of their times and circumstances. It is the responsibility of the local historian to help bring these people recognition and the late eighteenth-century city of Baltimore produced many who deserve to be remembered. This study has focused on the little-known artisans who supplied the means for the early merchants of Baltimore to prosper.

The United States was in a severe economic depression following the Revolution. Cut off from the mercantile system that had sustained it as a colonial dependent, it had to scurry to find another way to survive. There was no industry to speak of. There was little capital and much debt. The government had no power to tax and no way to raise an army or navy. The only asset the new nation possessed was its merchant community, the people who moved goods around the world for a profit. The first matter that the new government attended to was the establishment of a port system, which included of course, tax revenues to keep the government solvent.

This tenuous position existed for almost two decades, until the profits which had been earned through trade were redeployed into native industry and manufactures in greater measure. The industrial base of our nation, begun in earnest after the Embargo of 1809, was fueled by the profits earned by the previous generation. These profits were possible because the shipbuilding industry in the United States could provide a commodity that was in demand throughout the world, transport, and provide it at a price that was more than competitive

Design Makes a Difference

until the middle of the nineteenth century. The raw material wealth of the American continent was certainly a help, the forests that provided the lumber for the ships, the tar from the northern pine forests, and, last but not least, the skills of the labor force that turned the raw material into a finished product.

In the beginning, the United States had virtually nothing to export and a severe dependency on Europe for finished goods. Resistance to this dependence began in the Revolutionary spirit of 1776, but could not be sustained without innovative alternatives. Becoming an entrepôt, trans-shipping Europe's goods to the West Indies, returning their coffee and sugar to the eager European markets, along with the Mid-Atlantic tobacco, provided the key to unlock the economic stagnation that immediately followed the Revolution.

This opportunity would not have been as lucrative without Baltimore's speedy little schooners. These vessels and the men who built them were a response to their constantly shifting opportunities. As demand changed, so did the vessels, and this flexibility was what kept them on the leading edge of technology until they were usurped by major land improvements. Roads and trucks, bridges and railroads, canals and barges overcame the economic advantages that the schooners provided; but still they survived, evolving into the beautiful yachts and clippers that were so popular in the latter half of the nineteenth century. They survive today in the "Pride II," the vessel designed in the manner of Thomas Kemp's *Chasseur*.

Throughout Baltimore's history, her vessels have been a measure of the city's spirit. The men of the shipyards, black and white, rich and poor, cooperated to produce a competitive product which enriched the economic base of the city. As cities age and decay, their underlying spirit diminishes. Two hundred years later, recollection of this founding vigor can breathe new life and energy and, along with it, a rediscovery of civic pride that can provide a catalyst to enhance the success of urban renewal.

APPENDIX 1:
COMMERCIAL VESSELS BUILT IN BALTIMORE 1795-1835
Recap by Year

Year	# Vessels Built	Average Tonnage
1797	1	89.75
1798	5	122.08
1799	2	258.50
1801	1	78.60
1802	3	65.58
1803	11	54.75
1804	8	108.07
1805	18	125.40
1806	18	125.57
1807	24	138.28
1808	16	118.06
1809	13	138.34
1810	4	214.74
1811	25	219.28
1812	26	199.67
1813	35	152.05
1814	15	115.72
1815	26	131.70
1816	36	108.25
1817	17	113.42
1818	13	170.41
1819	16	96.96
1820	13	143.75
1821	9	97.66
1822	12	154.93
1823	15	118.49
1824	18	141.02
1825	15	138.04
1826	10	328.65
1827	16	140.28
1828	21	145.64
1829	20	199.90
1830	21	137.68
1831	20	111.62
1832	33	184.22
1833	20	181.87
1834	16	161.75
1835	22	162.24

APPENDIX 1

COMMERCIAL VESSELS BUILT IN BALTIMORE 1795-1835*

Builder/#Built	Vessel Name	Date	Style	Decks	Masts	KeelLng (ft)	BrdthBeam (ft)	HoldDpth (ft)	Tonnage	Built For:
DeRochebrune, L	Argo	1797	Schooner	1	2	52.50	19.50	8.25	89.75	
1			Averages			52.50	19.50	8.25	89.75	
DeRochebrune, L	Nancy	1798	Sq Stern Schoon/fhd	1	2	65.25	22.92	10.13	159.25	Luis Noailles, witnessed by Thomas Cole
DeRochebrune, L	Swallow	1798	Brigantine	1	2	68.31	23.29	9.17	160.00	Mark Pringle with Indian Head
Pearce, Charles	Elizabeth	1798	Sq Stern Schooner	1	2	30.00		5.50	25.00	William Halfpenny/Richard Johns
Price, William	Buckskin	1798	Schooner	1	2	61.29	22.46	9.5	134.16	
Steel, John	Ann of Baltimore	1798	Schooner	1	2	60.00	21.42	9.75	132.00	John Hollins
5			Averages			56.97	22.50	8.80	122.08	
DeRochebrune, L	Patapsco*	1799	Twenty-gun Sloop	1		87.00	29.00	12.50	380.00	*Dictionary of Amer Naval Fighting Ships
Turnbull, Andrew	Activer	1799	Brig	1	2	62.75	22.75	9.83	137.00	William Dunham
2			Averages			74.88	25.86	21.83	258.50	
Parsons, William	S(c)ample	1801	Schooner	1	?	50.00	20.00	7.42	78.60	R C Boislandry
1			Averages			50.00	20.00	7.42	78.60	
Delozier, Daniel	Betsy	1802	Sq Stern Sloop	1	1	30.00	10.83	3.92	10.48	Himself
Spencer, Richard	Munroe	1802	Schooner			54.00	21.83	10.33	126.27	M McBlair

*Master Carpenter Certificates (see endnote.)

APPENDIX 1 COMMERCIAL VESSELS BUILT IN BALTIMORE 1795-1835*

Builder/#Built	Vessel Name	Date	Style	Decks	Masts	KeelLng	BrdthBeam	HoldDpth	Tonnage	Built For:
Sutton, Isaac	Coquette	1802	Sharp Schooner	1	2	36.00	17.00	8.33	60.00	Isaac Sutton
3			Averages			40.00	16.6	7.53	65.58	
Ball, James	Susan	1803	Schooner			25.00	12.25	4.83	45.57	William Shield
Cordery, James	Paragon	1803	Schooner			41.83	18.0	8.33	66.00	Thomas Tenant
Dawson	Racer	1803	Schooner			49.00	19.25	8.00	78.00	Thomas Charley Howe
Parsons, William	Experiment	1803	Sharp Blt Sloop	1	1	19.66	8.75	4.17	7.60	Himself
Parsons, William	Cornelia	1803	Sharp Blt Schooner	1	2	33.92	16.25	5.75	33.53	Richard Lawrence/Daniel Nye
Pearce, Charles	Favourite	1803	Full Blt Schooner	1	2	40.00	18.5	6.66	53.03	Himself
Price, William	Amphion	1803	Schooner			58.58	22.00	9.30	126.37	Capt R Wilburn/S Taylor
Robins, John	Berry	1803			2	36.33	16.42	6.50	40.82	Captain James Curtis
Skinner, John	Antilope	1803				39.25	18.33	7.17	54.28	Wingate Rotten
Smith, Daniel	Mary	1803	Full Built Sloop	1	1	42.00	15.00	5.25	30.00	Himself @ Beaver Creek
Watson, David	Hannah Maria	1803	ShBlt SqStern Schnr	1	2	46.00	18.50	7.50	67.00	William Pitt/James Taylor
11			Averages			39.23	16.66	6.68	54.75	
Flannigain, Wm	Dart	1804	Pilot Boat Schooner	1	2	50.75	19.67	6.75	70.96	L M Dunan
Flannigain, Wm	Twin Brothers	1804	Pilot Boat Schooner	1	2	50.75	19.66	6.75	70.96	L M Dunan
Flannigain, Wm	Harriet	1804	Pilot Boat Sch Rig	1	2	50.75	19.66	6.75	70.96	L M Dunan
Kemp, Thomas	Maryland	1804	Sharp Blt Schooner	1	2	55.00	21.75	8.75	110.00	Isaac McKim, Thomas Tenant

*Master Carpenter Certificates (see endnote.)

APPENDIX 1 COMMERCIAL VESSELS BUILT IN BALTIMORE 1795-1835*

Builder/#Built	Vessel Name	Date	Style	Decks	Masts	KeelLng	BrdthBeam	HoldDpth	Tonnage	Built For:
Parsons, William	Dash	1804	Sharp Blt Schooner	1	2	50.67	19.42	7.50	77.70	Lemuel Tayrlor
Parsons, William	Fells Point	1804	Sharp Blt Schooner	1	2	51.00	20.00	8.58	92.16	Jonathan Barney
Parsons, William	Erin	1804	Full Built	1	3	62.08	27.66	16.00	200.59	Falls/Brown/Daniel Howland
Parsons, William	Nancy	1804	Sharp Built Bng	2	2	62.83	22.75	14.17	171.20	William Patterson
8			Averages			54.23	21.32	9.41	108.07	
Auld, Hugh	Dart	1805	Schooner			55.5	21.25	8.04	105.46	John Sherlock
Flannigain, Wm	Orestes	1805	Round Tk Schooner	1	3	62.58	23.00	8.00	121.00	Bernard Salenaves
Flannigain, Wm	Luna	1805	Square Tuck Schoon	1	3	67.00	22.17	8.08	126.37	Bernard Salenaves
Flannigain, Wm	Mary Ann	1805	Sq Stern Schooner	1	2	59.50	21.25	7.57	100.93	Lewis M Dunan
Flannigain, Wm	Revenge	1805	Sq Stern Schooner	1	3	59.50	21.25	8.00	106.47	B Salenaves (BOS 5June1808,$7,000)
Geoghyan, Moses	Enterprise	1805	Sharp Blt Schooner	1	2	47.00	22.00	8.75	95.00	Himself
Kemp, Thomas	Arrow	1805	Rnd Tk Schooner	1		60.50	21.25	8.13	150.00	Jack/Ottesen BOS:McNeal/Anderson $8,000
Kemp, Thomas	Spy	1805	Round Tuck	1		54.00	19.50	7.33	81.25	Lemuel Taylor
Kemp, Thomas	Fanny	1805	Rnd Tk Schooner	1		58.00	21.00	8.25	105.77	Alexander Modier
Kemp, Thomas	Meteor	1805				67.00	19.00	7.75	87.50	Henry Wilson/Thomas Frazier, merchants
McHuerin, James	Restitution	1805	SqTk PilBt Schnr	1	2	35.00	16.33	6.00	36.13	Anthony Harrow/William Harrow
Parsons, William	Fair American	1805	Full Built	2	3	73.25	27.66	13.83	295.00	William Taylor, merchant
Parsons, William	Nimble	1805	Pil Bt Rnd Tk Schnr	1	2	60.00	20.75	7.50	98.28	Marche/Salenaves/Harf Co/BOS:$5,500 '07
Parsons, William	Matchless	1805	Sharp Blt Schooner	1	2	55.33	19.5	8.17	92.77	Thomas Tenant

*Master Carpenter Certificates (see endnote.)

APPENDIX 1 COMMERCIAL VESSELS BUILT IN BALTIMORE 1795-1835*

Builder/#Built	Vessel Name	Date	Style	Decks	Masts	KeelLng	BrdthBeam	HoldDpth	Tonnage	Built For:
Price, William	United States	1805	Schooner			76.44	28.58	14.29	328.05	James Byas
Price, William	Ranger	1805	Sq Tuck Schooner	1		63.58	21.83	9.21	132.21	Capt W (Harrison)
Wills, Joshua	Mohawk	1805	Sq Tuck Schooner	1		59.00	21.00	8.17	110.71	Jonathan Hudson
Wills, Joshua	Imperial	1805	Sq Stern Schooner	1	2	53.17	19.63	7.71	84.21	Mc?saints & Bazzon
18			Averages			59.24	21.49	8.60	125.40	
Flannigain, Wm	Restitution	1806	Sharp Blt Schooner	1	2	41.58	16.81	5.92	43.35	William Harrow & Co
Flannigain, Wm	Pinckney	1806	Sharp Blt Sloop	Q	1	35.17	18.50	6.25	35.00	Joshua Ward/George Ward/Thomas Taylor
Flannigain, Wm	Superb	1806	Sharp Blt Sloop	Q	1	45.17	18.50	6.25	35.00	Joshua Ward/George Ward/Edward Tripple
Gayle, Joseph	Harriet	1806	Schooner	1 Fl	2	38.00	16.04	6.50	41.70	Wm Halfpenny, George & Thomas Powell
Hutton, John	Parope	1806	Schooner	1	3	72.00	23.00	9.00	156.88	Bernard Salenaves/BOS 16 Oct 1806 $7,000
Hutton, John	Rebecca	1806	Pilot Boat Schooner	1	2	64.50	22.33	8.58	130.11	Bernard Salenaves
Kemp, Thomas	President	1806	Sloop			43.58	18.33	6.25	52.00	Benjamin Ferguson/Jonas Owens
Kemp, Thomas	George Washington	1806	Sloop			44.00	18.33	6.25	53.00	Benjamin Ferguson/Jonas Owens
Kemp, Thomas	Ida	1806	Prv Waist Brig	1	2	70.58	24.08	6.66	190.00	Hollins&McBlaire/JnoPurviance/Buchanan
Kemp, Thomas	Lynx	1806	Rnd Tk Schooner			57.00	21.08	8.25	99.00	Henry Craig
Kemp, Thomas	Cora	1806	Rnd Tk Pil Bt Schnr			62.00	20.00	8.25	107.50	Christopher Deshon/Henry Craig
Nash, Charles	First Attempt	1806	Sharp Schooner	1	2	45.00	18.50	6.50	63.00	Himself
Parsons, William	Margaret	1806	Pilot Boat Schooner	1	2	60.75	20.50	7.50	96.35	John Marche/Bernard Salenaves
Parsons, William	Sainte Ann	1806	Pilot Boat Schooner	1	2	68.67	22.25	8.00	128.67	Marche/Salenaves BOS: S Sanger 26 May

*Master Carpenter Certificates (see endnote.)

APPENDIX 1 COMMERCIAL VESSELS BUILT IN BALTIMORE 1795-1835*

Builder/#Built	Vessel Name	Date	Style	Decks	Masts	KeelLng	BrdthBeam	HoldDpth	Tonnage	Built For:
Parsons, William	Maria	1806	Full Blt Pilot Boat	1	2	39.00	17.25	5.00	35.00	Himself
Parsons, William	Chesapeake	1806	Sharp Built	2	3	93.00	31.00	15.50	470.38	John Darnell
Price, William	Philip	1806	Schooner			74.33	28.54	7.66	318.27	
Wills, Joshua	Advice	1806	RndTk PilBt Schnr	1	2	63.00	21.50	8.50	119.22	Henry Wilson
18			Averages			56.52	20.86	7.60	125.57	
Adams, Zachariah	Neotah	1807	Schooner			52.00	22.00	8.00	102.92	Peter Gold
Cordery, James	Policy	1807	Schooner			67.67	21.58	9.04	139.03	Henry Wilson/Samuel Harris
Cordery, James	Model	1807	Schooner			64.17	21.18	8.58	122.74	Henry Wilson/Samuel Harris
Flannigain, Wm	Mary	1807	Sharp Blt Schooner	1	2	68.58	22.38	9.46	152.78	Jonathan Hodson
Flannigain, Wm	Williams	1807	Ship	2	3	78.25	28.42	18.00	332.69	William Patterson & Sons
Hutton, John	Telegraphe	1807	Pil Bt Rnd Tk Schnr	1	2	60.00	19.50	8.00	98.53	Bernard Salenaves/BOS 12 Nov 1807 $5,600
Hutton, John	Blossom	1807	Pilot Boat Schooner	1	2	56.00	18.75	7.00	77.37	Bernard Salenaves/BOS $5,800 undated
Hutton, John	Betsy	1807	Rnd Tuck Brig	1	2	78.00	24.58	10.50	211.94	Bernard Salenaves
Hutton, John	Jason	1807	Round Tuck Schnr	1	3	76.00	22.83	9.50	173.00	Bernard Salenaves
Kemp, Thomas	Amiable	1807	RndTkPilotBtSchnr			65.00	20.25	8.25	114.27	Henry Craig
Kemp, Thomas	Annacostia	1807	Rnd Tk Pil Bt Schnr	1	2	60.00	20.50	8.50	111.39	James David Barry
Kemp, Thomas	Superior	1807	Pilot Boat Schooner			42.00	17.75	6.75	52.97	William Harrow & Company
Kemp, Thomas	Rossie	1807	Rnd Tk Prtv Fin Sch			70.00	23.00	10.18	172.00	Isaac McKim/Robert Davis, Master
Kemp, Thomas	Breeze	1807	Rnd Tk Pilot Boat			63.00	21.00	9.00	126.50	Wilson/SamlHarris/Reeves Spaulding, mstr

*Master Carpenter Certificates (see endnote.)

APPENDIX 1 COMMERCIAL VESSELS BUILT IN BALTIMORE 1795-1835*

Builder/#Built	Vessel Name	Date	Style	Decks	Masts	KeelLng	BrdthBeam	HoldDpth	Tonnage	Built For:
Kemp, Thomas	Leo	1807	RndTk PrivFsh Brig			76.50	25.75	11.83	244.26	Henry Wilson
Kemp, Thomas	Hebe	1807	Rnd Tk Pil Bt Schnr			62.00	21.00	9.18	125.63	John McKee, I Hudson
Parsons, William	Wasp	1807	Sharp Schooner	1	2	67.00	21.25	9.25	141.12	George Stiles
Parsons, William	Sarah	1807	Sharp Built Sloop	1	1	47.00	18.00	6.25	45.65	Levi Hollingsworth
Price, William	Nonpariell	1807				64.00	23.50	9.83	155.67	
Price, William	Experiment	1807	Full Built Schooner	1	2	40.33	16.25	5.04	34.79	Edward Harris
Price, William	Amphion	1807	Pilot Boat Schooner	1	2	65.08	23.50	9.83	158.45	Lemuel Taylor
Price, William	Inca	1807	Brig	1	2	71.27	23.92	10.75	192.86	James Williams, Charles E Kallman
Price, William	Herald	1807	Pilot Built Schooner	1 Fl	2	66.42	21.79	9.18	106.04	Joseph Conkling
Wills, Joshua	Bee	1807	Round Tk Schooner		2	61.50	21.13	8.92	126.17	Captain ? Deshaune
24			Averages			63.41	22.08	9.2	138.28	
Cordery, James	Whim	1808	Schooner			66.08	21.92	9.17	138.61	Christian Deshon
Cordery, James	Fly	1808	Sloop			32.00	14.75	3.83	19.04	Dennis Nowland
Flannigain, Wm	Rosamond	1808	Full Built Schooner	1	2	67.58	22.25	9.17	145.08	John & George Barber
Flannigain, Wm	Superior	1808	Sharp Blt Sloop	1	1	45.75	18.50	6.50	57.91	? Henderson
Flannigain, Wm	Eclipse	1808	Sharp Sloop	1	1	46.46	18.54	6.42	58.08	Benjamin Ferguson/Jonas Owings
Hutton, John	Emma	1808	Rnd Tuck Schooner	1 Fl	2	72.00	21.25	9.00	144.90	L M Duncan
Hutton, John	LePregoire	1808	Brig	1	2	78.75	24.00	11.25	221.68	Bernard Salenaves
Hutton, John	Fiznacier	1808	Round Tuck Schnr	1	2	68.00	21.46	9.13	140.24	William Taylor & Sloat

*Master Carpenter Certificates (see endnote.)

123

APPENDIX 1   COMMERCIAL VESSELS BUILT IN BALTIMORE 1795-1835*

Builder/#Built	Vessel Name	Date	Style	Decks	Masts	KeelLng	BrdthBeam	HoldDpth	Tonnage	Built For:
Hutton, John	Robust or Robert	1808	Round Tuck Schnr	1	2	36.00	18.00	6.00	40.42	Bernard Salenaves
Kemp, Thomas	Alexander	1808	Prıv Waist Brig			73.00	23.25	10.00	178.61	Henry Wilson
Kemp, Thomas	Experiment	1808	RndTkPılBtSchoonr			62.00	20.25	8.33	108.00	Capt C Desbon
Montgomery, Jas	Courier	1808	PılBSq(TkSchooner	1	2	36.00	17.00	7.00	45.19	James Curtis
Parsons, William	Hazard	1808	Sharp Schooner	1	2	68.83	21.33	9.58	148.08	George Stiles
Parsons, William	Trim	1808	Sharp Blt Schooner	1	2	69.25	22.42	9.00	147.03	George Stiles
Parsons, William	Brothers	1808	Sharp Schooner	1 Fl	2	46.00	17.58	7.00	59.59	William Harrow @ Harford County
Price, William	Eutaw	1808	Sharp Built Brig			75.17	25.17	11.88	236.43	Messrs Blair & Hollins
16			Averages			58.92	20.48	7.26	118.06	
Cordery, James	Bona	1809	Schooner?	1	1-2	67.00	19.66	8.42	94.88	James Williams
Cordery, James	Cornelia	1809	Sharp Built Schooner	1	2	55.83	19.04	8.33	95.47	Thomas C Howe
Cordery, James	Georgianna	1809	Sharp Built Brig	1	2	70.33	25.17	11.50	238.69	Samuel Shull
Harrison, William	William	1809	Sharp Built Schooner	1	2	54.00	19.00	4.58	47.02	William Bolster
Kemp, Thomas	Louisa	1809	Sharp Built Brig	1	2	66.04	23.17	10.00	162.00	Jonathan Hudson, John McKee
Kemp, Thomas	Savage	1809	Round Tuck Sloop			46.00	18.75	7.08	64.50	James Taylor, James Curtis
Kemp, Thomas	Rolla	1809	RndTkPrıvFashSch			57.00	20.00	8.33	100.00	James Curtis, James Taylor
Kemp, Thomas	Ant	1809	RndTkSharpBltSch	1	2	62.00	20.25	8.58	113.01	Charles F Kalkman
Price, John	Eleanor	1809	RndTkPılBtSchoonr	1 Fl	2	82.54	23.16	9.83	197.80	Capt Wm Robinson/Sold to John Donnell
Price, William	Dolphin	1809	RndTkPılBtSchoonr	1	2	67.96	21.63	9.42	145.58	Capt William Robertson

*Master Carpenter Certificates (see endnote.)

124

APPENDIX 1 COMMERCIAL VESSELS BUILT IN BALTIMORE 1795-1835*

Builder/#Built	Vessel Name	Date	Style	Decks	Masts	KeelLng	BrdthBeam	HoldDpth	Tonnage	Built For:
Price, William	Luna	1809	RndTkPilBtSchoonr	1 Fl	2	70.00	23.83	10.29	182.92	James Williams
Price, William	Congress	1809	RndTkSqSternShip		2	80.17	28.08	14.00	322.64	James Biays
Willis, Joshua	Hornet	1809	SharpBltRndTkSch	1	2	37.00	15.04	5.63	33.90	J Reeves, Jacob Loroy
13			Averages			62.76	21.29	8.92	138.34	
Despaux, Joseph	Alexander	1810	Rnd Tuck Shrp Sch	1	3	87.50	28.00	12.66	301.74	Joseph Despaux for himself
Kemp, Thomas	Charles	1810	RndTkPilBtSchoonr			46.00	17.75	6.50	54.27	William Pitt
Kemp, Thomas	Comet	1810	PrivFashRndTkSch			68.00	23.00	10.00	164.60	Capt Thorndike Chase
Price, William	Melantho	1810		2	3	83.00	28.00	10.00	338.36	
4			Averages			71.13	24.19	9.79	214.74	
Benilant, Stephen	Industry	1811	Full Built Brig	2	2	71.00	22.33	13.25	191.00	Finished for Capt Robinson, deceased
Benilant, Stephen	Proteria	1811	RndTkSch w/Fgrhd	1 Fl	2	70.00	24.00	10.92	193.05	Himself
Elliot, John	Good Hope	1811	Schooner			45.00	22.00	8.50	86.75	Levin Jones, Roger Wallford
Flannigan, Wm	Edward	1811	Full Built (Ship?)	2	3	74.00	27.38		291.00	William Patterson & Sons
Grumby, Stephen	Ann	1811	Full Built Schooner	1	2	59.25	19.83	4.33	64.00	James Holmes/Thomas Holmes
Kemp, Thomas	Wabash	1811	Round Tuck Ship	1 Fl	2	69.75	26.75		262.52	S Smith & Buchanan
Kemp, Thomas	Thomas Kemp	1811	Round Tuck			44.00	17.00	6.50	51.00	Capt William Pitt
Kemp, Thomas	Betsy Kemp	1811	Sharp Blt Schooner	1	2	33.00	14.66	6.00	30.50	Joseph Butler
Kemp, Thomas	Dart	1811	RndTkPilBtSchoonr			44.00	17.00	6.50	51.00	William Pitt

*Master Carpenter Certificates (see endnote.)

APPENDIX 1

COMMERCIAL VESSELS BUILT IN BALTIMORE 1795-1835*

Builder/#Built	Vessel Name	Date	Style	Decks	Masts	KeelLng	BrdthBeam	HoldDpth	Tonnage	Built For:
Kemp, Thomas	Rolla	1811	Rnd Tk Priv Fas Sch			67.00	20.00	8.33	100.00	JasTaylor/JasCurtis(rpt of nonpmt by Kemp)
Kemp, Thomas	Emperor	1811	Round Tuck Ship		3	68.50	30.42		430.75	Charles F Kellman
Kemp, Thomas	Charles	1811	Rnd Tuck Pilot Boat			46.00	17.25	6.50	54.28	William Pitt
Kemp, Thomas	Eclipse	1811	Rnd Tk Pil Bt Brig	1	2	80.58	24.38	12.00	284.06	Capt William Robinson
Kemp, Thomas	Marmion	1811	Schooner w/buckfhd			70.00	25.75		224.21	Smith&Buchan/Brown/Hollingsworth/Mezick
Kemp, Thomas	Comet	1811	Rnd Tk Priv Fin Sch			68.00	23.00	10.00	164.63	Chap Thorndike Chase
Kemp, Thomas	Wabash	1811	Round Tuck			69.75	26.75		262.57	S Smith & Buchanan
Kemp, Thomas	Arrow	1811	Round Tuck Schnr			71.25	23.33	10.33	180.78	Hollins & McBlaire
Kemp, Thomas	Wolfe	1811	Full Built Schooner		2	40.00	16.00	5.42	36.48	Jacob Grafflenn/Benjamin Hardeston
Parsons, William	Aid	1811	Brig	2	2	71.00	23.50	11.75	203.36	George Stiles
Parsons, William	Galathea	1811	Sharp Schooner	1	2	62.33	21.58	9.17	129.83	Built @ Harford County
Parsons, William	Stag	1811	Ship	1	3	83.67	28.00		368.27	Captain C Deshon
Price, John	United States	1811	Round Tuck	1	3	87.00	31.08		443.24	James Biays
Price, William	William & Ann	1811	Round Tuck	1	3	81.00	33.08		386.00	Himself
Price, William	Hannibal	1811	Square	2	3	103.00	37.00	18.00	790.18	R & J Oliver/VonKapf/D'Arcy/Didier etal
Price, William	Henrietta	1811	Pilot Boat Brig	1	2	74.5	24.58	10.50	202.45	Charles & Frederick Knittman, merchants
Salenaves, Bernard			Averages			66.15	23.88	9.29	219.28	
25										
Cordery, James	Lynx	1812	Pilot Boat Schooner	1	2	72.5	24.00	10.66	125.37	James Williams
Cordery, James	Courier	1812	Sharp Schooner	1	2	74.00	24.02	11.66	222.00	John Gooding/William Kricham

*Master Carpenter Certificates (see endnote.)

APPENDIX 1 COMMERCIAL VESSELS BUILT IN BALTIMORE 1795-1835*

Builder/#Built	Vessel Name	Date	Style	Decks	Masts	KeelLng	BrdthBeam	HoldDpth	Tonnage	Built For:
Cordery, James	Bordeaux	1812	Schooner			77.33	25.29	12.25	252.21	Peter Arnold Karthaus, merchant
Descomde, Andrew	Bellona	1812	Pilot Blt Schooner	1 Fl	2	76.00	24.50	11.75	230.28	Francis Brevil
Hunley, James R I	Port of Baltimore	1812	Schooner			52.00	20.33	8.50	94.59	Capt Paul Gold
Kemp, Thomas	Commerce	1812	Full Built Schooner	1	2	52.25	22.25	10.00	122.00	Robert Hamilton
Kemp, Thomas	Cora	1812	Rnd Tuck Prvtr Blt		2	74.33	24.00	11.42	214.33	John (athan) Morton
Kemp, Thomas	Viper	1812	Rnd Tuck Schooner			76.17	24.66	11.50	227.32	John McFadon
Kemp, Thomas	Flight	1812	Rnd Tk Priv Fas Sch			75.00	24.25	11.75	223.25	GeoWilliams/HHolder/MatKelly/ThosKemp
Kemp, Thomas	Patapsco	1812	Rnd Tk Priv Blt Sch			74.25	24.25	11.42	215.59	HFulford/ACloppen/SHollingsworth/?Wms
Parsons, William	Climax	1812	Sharp Built Schooner	1	2	62.00	20.50	9.38	125.4	Capt G Stiles
Parsons, William	Cleaner	1812	Schooner	1	2	45.00	16.25	5.46	42.91	Aquila & George Beaver
Parsons, William	Lee	1812	Sharp Built Schooner	1	2	77.67	25.38	11.71	242.87	Thomas Lewis
Price, John	Elizabeth	1812	RndTkPilBtSchoonr	1 Fl	2	48.33	17.75	7.50	67.69	Johns & Carroll
Price, John	Cashier	1812	RndTkPilBtSchoonr	1	2	79.08	25.50	12.13	247.40	Girard Wilson
Price, John	Active	1812	RndTk PilBt Schnr	1	2	56.25	19.58	8.43	101.06	Anthony Faular
Price, John	Fair American	1812	Ship	1 Fl	3	89.00	30.58		437.67	
Price, John	Phaeton	1812	Rnd Tk Pil Bt Schnr	1	2	72.5	24.66	12.18	228.91	P J Guistier
Price, John	Tom	1812	Rnd Tk Pil Bt Schnr	1	2	79.08	25.50	11.83	251.18	Garrard Wilson
Price, William	The Price	1812	Round Tuck	1	3	70.65	24.96	11.00	204.17	Hollins & McBlair
Price, William	Sabine	1812	Round Tk Schooner	1	2	82.83	26.83	12.50	292.55	Himself/Sold to:Jn Gooden/Jamy Williams
Price, William	Revenge	1812	Round Tuck	1	2	76.25	24.38	12.00	234.78	Charles F Kalkman

*Master Carpenter Certificates (see endnote.)

APPENDIX 1 COMMERCIAL VESSELS BUILT IN BALTIMORE 1795-1835*

Builder/#Built	Vessel Name	Date	Style	Decks	Masts	KeelLng	BrdthBeam	HoldDpth	Tonnage	Built For:
Price, William	Vorhollen	1812	Round Tk Schooner	1	2	65.83	29.58	10.58	172.84	Charles S Kalkner
Salenaves, Bernard	Expedition	1812	Pilot Boat Schooner	1	2	81.67	27.00	12.63	293.02	John Carrere
Salenaves, Bernard	Ossian	1812	Pilot Boat Schooner	1	2	79.00	24.25	10.50	211.04	F A Fuestier
Turner, Joseph	Providence	1812	Schooner	1	2	53.00	21.33	8.33	111.02	Wm Dawson/Agent for Geo B Claston/Phil
26			Averages			61.48	23.91	10.72	199.67	
Cordery, James	Pike/Tunes	1813	Full Built Schooner			77.67	24.50	11.58	232.81	Merchs'Vickers/Karthaus/Waesche/Hurythal
Cordery, James	Planter	1813	Full Blt Sloop/deckd	1	1	40.50	15.33	5.00	25.27	
Cork, Matthew J	Commndr Decatur	1813	RndTk PilBt Schnr	1	2	46.75	18.18	6.50	56.25	James Greggs
Descande, Andrew	Ultor	1813	Schebeck			70.00	19.50	7.50	107.50	Guestier
Descande, Andrew	Adeline	1813	Schooner	1	2	85.00	23.50	9.00	199.70	G A Guestier, Merchant
Descande, Andrew	Cora	1813	Sharp Lugger		3	71.00	23.83	11.33	201.32	Amelaine, Agent for Meyers
Despaux, Joseph	Fathers & Sons	1813	Sharp	2	3	84.5	25.17	15.66	242.00	Joseph Despaux for himself
Flannigan, Wm	Erie	1813	Full Built Sloop	1	1	45.00		5.00	43.00	Himself
Flannigan, Wm	Chesapeake	1813	Full Blt Steamboat	1		130.00	20.00	7.50	205.26	William McDonald/Samuel Lothers
Gardner, George	Torpedo	1813	Pilot Blt Schooner	1	2	69.75	22.83	10.25	171.85	William Patterson
Hall, Thomas	Coquette	1813	Schooner			56.42	19.50	8.33	96.52	H&W for John Gavet, James McLanahan
Hall, Thomas	Unnamed	1813	Sharp Blt Schooner	1	2	50.66	18.25	7.33	71.39	Hall & White/Jonathan Barron, Jr
Kemp, Thomas	Barron	1813	Rnd Tk Priv Blt Sch			undeciph	undeciph	undeciph	119.03	Levin Hall/Baptiste Mezick
Kemp, Thomas	Midas	1813	Rnd Tk Priv Blt Sch			76.00	24.25	11.17	216.63	Baptiste Mezick

*Master Carpenter Certificates (see endnote.)

APPENDIX 1   COMMERCIAL VESSELS BUILT IN BALTIMORE 1795-1835*

Builder/#Built	Vessel Name	Date	Style	Decks	Masts	KeelLng	BrdthBeam	HoldDpth	Tonnage	Built For:
Kemp, Thomas	Perry	1813	Rnd Tk Privateer			61.00	20.25	9.25	120.24	Capt Baptiste Mezick
Kemp, Thomas	Burrows	1813	RndTkPilBtSchoonr			60.00			119.03	Levin Hall, Baptiste Mezick
Kemp, Thomas	Grampus	1813	Rnd Tk Priv Fas Sch			79.00	24.83	11.66	240.97	Cmdr Wms/Clopper/Holngswrh/Wms/Fulford
Kemp, Thomas	Chausseur	1813	Round Tk Schooner			85.66	26.00	12.63	295.95	William Hollins
Parsons, William	Tuckahoe	1813	Sharp Schooner	1	2	69.42	23.83	10.33	180.36	John Cragi/R ? Kilburn
Parsons, William	Transit	1813	Sharp Schooner	1	2	77.00	25.00	11.79	238.84	Amos A Williams/And Clopper/Hnry Fulford
Parsons, William	Hound	1813	Sharp Schooner		2	53.42	19.00	7.33	78.35	Jonathan Barras, Jr.
Parsons, William	Moro	1813	Sharp Schooner	1	2	55.5	17.33	7.25	73.41	George Stiles
Parsons, William	Diamond	1813	Sharp Schooner	1	2	83.42	25.58	12.54	281.76	Andrew Clopper/Henry Fulford
Price, John	Chance	1813	Round Tuck	1	2	61.00	17.79	7.66	71.84	George P Stevenson
Price, John	Premium	1813				61.00	17.83	7.66	72.45	George Wilmot
Price, William	Daedalus	1813	Round Tk Schooner	1	2	55.67	20.66	9.17	111.00	Himself
Price, William	Model	1813				56.5	20.75	9.17	114.00	Hollins/McBlair/Williams
Price, William	Hollins	1813	Round Tk Schooner	1	2	69.33	24.08	11.00	199.00	Hollins & McBlair
Price, William	Maria/Harpy	1813	Round Tk Schooner	1	2	83.67	27.08	12.66	303.13	Msrs D'Arcy & Didier
Salenaves, Bernard	Lawrence	1813	Pilot Boat Schooner	1	2	85.42	27.66	13.33	331.72	John Marche
Saunders, Saml	Dispatch	1813	Rnd Tk Pil Bt Schnr			35.00	16.00	6.33	37.82	Built for Kemp for James Biays
Turner, Joseph	Chippewa	1813	Sharp Schooner	1	2	76.00	22.25	12.00	252.00	Himself
Turner, Joseph	Orb	1813	Sharp Schooner	1	2	70.00	23.25	9.00	154.18	Himself
Walker, Samuel	Robust	1813	Sloop	1	1	39.00	17.25	5.08	35.77	Charles Ridgely

*Master Carpenter Certificates (see endnote.)

129

APPENDIX 1 — COMMERCIAL VESSELS BUILT IN BALTIMORE 1795-1835*

Builder/#Built	Vessel Name	Date	Style	Decks	Masts	KeelLng	BrdthBeam	HoldDpth	Tonnage	Built For:
White, B & Hall, T	Swallow	1813	Sharp Blt Schooner	1	2	50.67	18.25	7.33	21.37	John Barron
35			Averages			66.79	21.55	9.37	152.05	
Cordery, James	Amelia	1814	Schooner			63.5	21.58	9.33	134.31	A Karthaus/Ferdinand Humthal
Cork, Matthew J	Tickler	1814	Schooner	1	2	40.00	15.92	5.83	39.10	Edward Fitzgerald
Denny & Robson	Amphion	1814	Sharp Blt Schooner	1	2	63.17	21.50	10.00	142.96	
Descande, Andrew	Saturn	1814	Schooner	1	2	63.00	21.00	10.50	146.00	N T Bosley
Descande, Andrew	Nereide	1814	Schooner	1	2	75.00	25.50	10.50	260.00	G A Guestler, Merchant
Flannigain, Wm	Swift	1814	Schooner	1	2	80.83	25.33	12.18	268.78	Himself
Hall, Thomas	Black Bird	1814	Sharp Sloop	1	1	30.00	11.33	4.00	14.00	Himself/James Rouse/Thomas Nicoll
Thomas Hall	Flight	1814	Schooner			63.00	19.58	7.83	79.90	James Greggs
Kemp, Thomas	Romp	1814	Rnd Tk Prlv Schnr			62.00	20.83	9.18	124.66	Capt Pearl Durkee BOS-AlexBrown& Sons
Kemp, Thomas	David Porter	1814	Round Tuck			39.00	14.50	3.83	19.31	
Kemp, Thomas	Surprise	1814	Rnd Tk Prlv Blt Sch			79.50	24.75	11.83	245.00	Taylor & Buchanan at St. Michaels
Parsons, William	Cygnet	1814	Sharp Blt Schooner	1	2	57.92	18.50	7.75	87.44	John McFadden/John Barron Jr.
Parsons, William	Clara	1814	Sharp Blt Schooner	1	2	59.66	19.25	8.33	100.76	John Paulac
Parsons, William	Stafford	1814	Schooner	1	2	64.50	19.50	9.50	100.79	John Barron
Salenaves, Bernard	Flash	1814	Pilot Boat Schooner	1	2	79.75	24.83	11.58	241.55	Frederick C Graf, merchant
15			Averages			61.39	20.26	8.78	115.72	

*Master Carpenter Certificates (see endnote.)

APPENDIX 1   COMMERCIAL VESSELS BUILT IN BALTIMORE 1795-1835*

Builder/#Built	Vessel Name	Date	Style	Decks	Masts	KeelLng	BrdthBeam	HoldDpth	Tonnage	Built For:
Cordery, James	Ghent	1815				80.42	29.66	14.83	372.54	A Karthaus, merchant
Denny & Robson	Sisters	1815	Sharp Blt Schooner	1	2	35.67	15.50	6.00	34.87	John McCullough
Descande, Andrew	Laura	1815	Schooner	1	2	62.5	22.50	10.08	148.00	Peter Riverie of New Orleans
Flannigan, Wm	Sarah	1815	Full Built Sloop	1	1	46.33	18.25	6.00	53.40	William Meeten
Gardner, George	Torpedo	1815	Schooner	1	2	69.75	22.83	10.25	171.90	William Patterson
Hall, Thomas	Cuba	1815	Sharp Blt Schooner	1	2	60.00	18.25	7.25	65.53	James Frazier/J Prour/Thomas Wilson
Hall, Thomas	Young Constitution	1815	Sharp Blt Schooner	1	2	64.00	18.42	7.21	74.10	Thomas C Robinson
Hall, Thomas	Commodore Rogers	1815	Sharp Blt Schooner	1	2	51.00	16.75	6.08	43.93	James Griggs
Kemp & Gardner	Rossie	1815	RndTk PrivBlt Schnr		2	74.25	23.00	10.17	182.78	Isaac McKim
Kemp & Gardner	Platsburg	1815	Priv Blt Rnd Tk Schr			74.25	23.00	10.33	185.71	Isaac McKim
Kemp & Gardner	Coquette	1815	Rnd Tk Privateer Blt		2	54.00	19.50	7.83	86.82	In Barron/Assnd to Boyle/Stafford/Craig
Kemp, Thomas	Tangent	1815	Priv Fin Schooner			62.00	20.66	9.08	122.50	Andrew Clopper
Kemp, Thomas	Fox	1815	Rnd Tk Priv Blt Sch			65.00	22.83	9.75	151.00	John Craig
Kennard, Samuel	Dolphin	1815	Full Built Sloop	1	1	50.75	21.42	4.33	38.01	William Patterson & Sons
Kennard, Samuel	Edward	1815	Full Built Sloop	1	1	48.67	16.42	4.33	36.47	William,Joseph, Edward Patterson/Timmons
Parsons, William	Belvidera	1815	Full Built	2	3	83.00	29.00	14.50	367.38	William Lauman/A Brown (sig.verso)
Parsons, William	Stafford	1815	Sharp Blt Schooner	1	2	64.5	19.50	9.13	120.83	John Barron Jr (Assd to Graham/Stump)
Parsons, William	Eugenie	1815	Sharp Blt Schooner	1	2	65.75	20.50	9.00	127.73	D Daniels
Pearce, C & J	Pearce	1815	Full Built Sloop	1	1	40.00	17.00	4.92	32.80	Fin by son Jos J for dec father @ Middle Riv
Price, John	The Franklin	1815	Full Built	2	3	85.00	27.75	13.88	344.64	Matt McLaughlin/John Craig/Luke Lieman

*Master Carpenter Certificates (see endnote.)

131

APPENDIX 1 COMMERCIAL VESSELS BUILT IN BALTIMORE 1795-1835*

Builder/#Built	Vessel Name	Date	Style	Decks	Masts	KeelLng	BrdthBeam	HoldDpth	Tonnage	Built For:
Price, John	Eutaw	1815	Rnd Tk Pil Bt Schnr	1	2	80.17	26.66	12.66	285.17	Himself
Price, John	Elizabeth	1815	RndTk PilBt Schnr	1	2	44.75	18.50	6.33	55.51	
Price, John	Hound	1815	Rnd Tk Pil Bt Schnr	1	2	71.00	20.50	9.50	112.00	Pearl Danker
Stewart, Joseph	Sally	1815	Schooner			39.00	16.00	5'2'	35.25	James Nicker
Turner, Joseph	Opera	1815	Sharp Blt Schooner	1	2	52.00	20.50	8.33	93.61	Brown & Wilson
White, Benjamn	Trimmer/Flight	1815				73.00	19.00	7.83	79.95	James Griggs
26			Averages			61.42	20.92	8.65	131.70	
Cork, Matthew J	Dove	1816	Sharp Blt Schooner	1	2	40.50	17.00	6.33	45.88	Leon & Leoni
Davis, Peter	Fly	1816	Sloop	1	1	23.5	8.33	3.83	6.16	Himself
Denny & Robson	Gilpin	1816	Sharp Blt Schooner	1	2	62.42	23.50	9.83	151.84	Themselves/Transferred to William Hollins
Descande, Andrew	Ea	1816	Brig	2	3	75.00	25.00	17.00	246.71	G A Guestier
Descande, Andrew	Moran	1816	Sharp Blt Schooner	1	2	58.00	21.00	7.50	96.16	Andrew Candalle
Descande, Andrew	G P Stevenson	1816	Brick Rigged Brig	2	2	64.00	25.00	14.50	210.32	Wm Baartschrn/John Jillard/Renne Lemetor
Flannigain, Wm	Philadelphia	1816	Full Blt Steamboat	1		116.67	23.33	8.18	236.06	William McDonald/Tom Lother/Sam Lother
Flannigain, Wm	Comm Patterson	1816	Full Built Sloop	1	1	47.92	18.92	7.75	74.00	George Stole/vrs Shields/Bennett
Flannigain, Wm	Slater	1816	Full Built Sloop	1	1	48.00	19.25	4.50	63.22	William Corman
Hall, Thomas	Fox	1816	Sharp Blt Schooner	1	2	60.00	19.25	7.75	74.32	Capt Pearl Durkee
Hall, Thomas	Curtis	1816	Sharp Blt Schooner	1	2	83.25	23.50	10.00	170.95	CpfThmSheppard/JasCurtis/NichStansbury
Hall, Thomas	Castor	1816	Sharp Blt Schooner	1	2	36.00	17.79	5.33	35.96	Samuel Hall/Levin Hall

*Master Carpenter Certificates (see endnote.)

APPENDIX 1   COMMERCIAL VESSELS BUILT IN BALTIMORE 1795-1835*

Builder/#Built	Vessel Name	Date	Style	Decks	Masts	KeelLng	BrdthBeam	HoldDpth	Tonnage	Built For:
Harrison, William	Trinidad	1816	RndTk PilBt Schnr	1	2	44.00	18.00	6.50	54.19	Isaac McKim
Inloes, William	Davey	1816	Sharp Blt Schooner	1	2	83.83	24.46	11.54	203.80	MajThosSheppard/NichStanbury/HDidier.Ir
Kemp & Gardner	Kemp	1816	Rnd Tk Pil Bt Schnr		2	42.00	16.75	6.00	44.43	Mark
Kemp & Gardner	Mary Ann	1816	Rnd Tuck Pilot Boat		2	41.00	16.33	6.00	42.26	Barton Thomas
Kemp & Gardner	Seagull	1816	Round Tuck Sloop	1	1	36.00	13.50	4.33	18.42	Thomas Kemp
Kemp & Gardner	Vesta	1816	Rnd Tuck Pilot Boat		2	39.00	16.00	6.00	39.41	Richard Johns
Kemp & Gardner	Tyro	1816	Round Tk Schooner		2	46.17	18.75	7.08	64.50	James Corner
Kemp & Gardner	Patriot	1816	RndTk PrivFsh Schn		2	58.67	20.33	9.03	113.18	Capt Joshua Meziok
Kemp & Gardner	Tyro	1816	RndTk PrivBlt Schnr		2	55.50	20.00	9.00	105.16	James Corner
Kemp & Gardner	General Smith	1816	Rnd Tuck w/fhd		3	76.00	26.66		284.33	George Stevenson/Edward Cleazy
Kemp & Gardner	Hero	1816	Rnd Tk Sharp Blt Sch		2	40.00	19.00	6.00	42.52	Capt Plummer Southcomb/A Allen
Parsons, William	Opera	1816	Sharp Blt Schooner			52.00	20.50	8.33	93.61	John Barron
Parsons, William	Surprise/Antelope	1816	Full Blt Steamboat	1		76.00	16.25	6.92	85.21	George Stiles (registered as Surprise)
Parsons, William	Amalthea	1816	Sharp Blt Schooner	1	2	48.25	18.83	6.50	62.18	John Barron Jr./Capt Thomas Basher
Parsons, William	Maria	1816	Sharp Blt Schooner	1	2	67.00	20.33	8.96	128.46	John Barron
Parsons, William	Jane	1816	Sharp Blt Schooner	1	2	47.50	19.38	7.50	72.78	Luke Kiistand
Parsons, William	Alert	1816	Schooner	1	2	44.00	18.42	6.00	51.18	Acquila Deavers/Samuel Wilson
Price, John	Cuba	1816	Rnd Tk Pil Bt Schnr	1	2	49.17	18.58	7.17	69.66	James Curtis/Joseph Clockmer
Price, William	North Point	1816	Sharp Schooner	2	3	84.67	30.75		419.00	John McDonnell
Price, William	Emily	1816	Full Built	2	3	90.75	25.93		266.26	Geo&JnHoffman/HenThompson/PDawson

*Master Carpenter Certificates (see endnote.)

APPENDIX 1 COMMERCIAL VESSELS BUILT IN BALTIMORE 1795-1835*

Builder/#Built	Vessel Name	Date	Style	Decks	Masts	KeelLng	BrdthBeam	HoldDpth	Tonnage	Built For:
Robertson, Robert	Young Halcyon	1816	Full Built Schooner	1	2	50.00	19.75	7.00	72.76	George Weems
Turner, Joseph	Joseph	1816	Sharp Blt Schooner	1	2	43.00	18.75	7.50	63.72	Himself
White, Abe	Vane	1816	Rnd Tuck Schooner			47.5	19.38	7.50	48.80	Joseph Severn
Winch. & Marshall*	Superior	1816	Sloop	1	1	28.00	13.00	4.17	39.55	*ThomasC Winchester/W Marshall/Themslvs
36			Averages			55.70	19.76	7.62	108.25	
Ashcroft&Sherwd	Edward & Margaret	1817	Schooner	1	2	41.25	17.83	6.17	69.73	Themselves
Despaux, Joseph	Mary Ann	1817	Sharp Blt Brig	1	2	63.00	24.00	12.00	194.00	Himself (registration date, not carp cert)
Flannign&Beachm	Vicunia	1817	Sharp Blt Brig	1	2	76.33	25.08	12.00	241.82	Themselves
Gardner & Robson	Lapwing	1817	Sharp Blt Schooner	1	2	53.04	20.36	8.25	94.86	Alexander Grigg
Gardner & Robson	Active	1817	Full Blt Schnr/Sloop	Q	1	48.00	17.00	4.50	38.65	C & J Patterson
Gardner & Robson	Alexander	1817	Sharp Blt Schooner	1	2	72.83	24.21	11.66	216.55	Elihu D Brown
Hall, Thomas	Croghan	1817	Sharp Blt Schooner	1	2	73.87	21.00	9.75	128.50	Thomas Sheppard/James Curtis
Price, John	Brothers	1817	Sharp Pilot Boat	1	2	40.12	14.08	5.00	75.00	Richard Johns
Price, William	Josephina	1817	Sharp Schooner		2	62.00	20.56	10.50	143.07	
Price, William	Lady Monroe	1817	Brig			70.33	24.17	8.58	275.17	Jacob Adams
Riggn, Jamey	Sam	1817	Sharp Blt Schooner	1	2	48.00	19.46	6.50	84.38	Michael Tiernan
Robertson, Robert	Ann & Adeline	1817	Round TK Schooner	1	2	53.00	20.75	7.17	75.19	Capt Thomas Holmes
Taylor, Lemuel G	Margaret	1817	Sharp Blt Schooner	1	2	45.00	19.25		74.54	Built 1806, 1807 for himself
Taylor, Lemuel G	Mary	1817	Sloop	1	2	43.00	14.00	4.25	26.93	Hollingsworth & Worthington

*Master Carpenter Certificates (see endnote.)

APPENDIX 1 COMMERCIAL VESSELS BUILT IN BALTIMORE 1795-1835*

Builder/#Built	Vessel Name	Date	Style	Decks	Masts	KeelLng	BrdthBeam	HoldDpth	Tonnage	Built For:
Taylor, Lemuel G	Margaret Ann	1817	Sharp Blt Schooner	1	2	54.00	17.00	6.50	54.34	Himself
Turner, Joseph	Serpent	1817	Sharp Blt Schooner	1	2	56.00	20.75	8.33	101.93	Himself
Turner, Joseph	Ellen	1817	Full Built Schooner	1	2	37.00	16.25	4.00	35.54	Leaven Kilman/Paca Smith
17			Averages			55.17	19.84	7.82	113.42	
Cooper, Robert	Corinthian	1818	Ship	1	3	108.67	30.58	14.83	423.48	James Inloes (later rebuilt)
Flannigan, Wm	Beacham	1818	Sharp Blt Schooner	1	2	42.00	16.75	6.50	48.13	Wm Halfpenny/Samuel Peal/Samuel Haney
Flannign&Beachm	United States	1818	Full Blt Steamboat	1		124.00	26.42	8.00	304.31	William McDonald/Agent/Union Line Stmbts
Gardner & Robson	Cecilia	1818	Sharp Blt Schooner	1	2	65.5	20.92	8.75	126.45	Archibald Kerr
Gardner & Robson	Amanda	1818	Schooner			60.00	22.50	8.50	151.56	Archibald Kerr
Gardner & Robson	Enterprise	1818	Sh Blt Rnd Tk PBt	1	2	41.00	16.75	5.75	41.52	TWilliams/JasMahon/HHParker/of ChrisSC
Gardner & Robson	Cora	1818	Sharp Blt Schooner	1	2	51.83	17.92	7.08	69.24	A Faulae/Thomas Janvier/J Patrick
Gardner & Robson	Star	1818	Sharp Blt Schooner	1	2	42.00	16.75	5.83	43.16	James Berry/vers: N Stansbury
Gardner & Robson	Jamy H McCulloch	1818	Sharp Blt Schooner	1	2	62.58	21.25	9.46	132.42	James Corner
Gardner & Robson	Montpelier	1818	Sharp Blt Schooner	1	2	63.33	20.79	6.66	120.13	Archibald Kerr
Kennard, Samuel	Cervantes	1818	Full Built Brig	1	2	68.5	25.38	12.66	231.73	William Patterson (finished only by Kinard)
Murry, William	Nancy	1818	Sharp Blt Schooner	1	2	36.00	15.83	5.58	30.00	Himself
Riggin, Levi&Israel	Superb	1818	Full Built	2	3	91.5	32.00	8.30	493.14	William Corner
13			Averages			65.90	21.83	8.30	170.41	

*Master Carpenter Certificates (see endnote.)

135

APPENDIX 1 — COMMERCIAL VESSELS BUILT IN BALTIMORE 1795-1835*

Builder/#Built	Vessel Name	Date	Style	Decks	Masts	KeelLng	BrdthBeam	HoldDpth	Tonnage	Built For:
Despaux, Joseph	Frances Ursula	1819	Sharp Blt Schooner	1	2	62.00	22.83	10.25	152.21	Himself
Flannign&Beachm	Tom	1819	Sharp Blt Schooner	1	2	56.00	21.21	9.66	140.45	Baptiste Mezick/Jas Johnson/Matthew Kelly
Flannign&Beachm	Richard	1819	Sharp Blt Schooner	1	2	59.08	20.83	9.08	117.70	Adam Gantz
Flannign&Beachm	Rocket	1819	Sharp Blt Schooner	1	2	57.50	21.00	9.00	114.39	Charles & Peter Wingenan
Flannign&Beachm	Alexander	1819	Sharp Blt Schooner	1	2	57.50	20.71	9.08	113.91	Alexander Thompson
Gardner & Robson	Yellott	1819	Sharp Blt Schooner	1	2	57.00	21.00	8.83	133.00	Archibald Kerr
Gardner/Robson	Experiment	1819	Flat Bottom Schoon	1	2	53.25	21.25	4.50	52.55	William Patterson & Company
Pearce, Joseph J	Active	1819	Sloop	1	1	27.00	13.00	4.50	17.00	For himself @ Middle River Neck
Price, William	Maria	1819	Sharp Rnd Tk Schnr	1	2	61.47	22.54	9.25	134.93	"on my account"
Price, William	Dart	1819	Sharp Rnd Tk Schnr	1	2	54.00	19.50	9.00	99.76	Mssrs Mezick and Corner
Price, William	Iris	1819	Sharp Rnd Tk Schnr	1	2	61.50	22.00	10.00	142.42	Himself
Riggin, Levi&Israel	Two Brothers	1819	Schooner	1	2	43.00	18.50	6.42	53.73	Themselves
Robinson, Robert	Adonis	1819	Sharp Blt Schooner	1	2	50.33	20.33	7.50	80.79	Capt Charles Baker/Rubin Ross
Robinson, Robert	Aeolus	1819	Full Built Sloop	Q	1	45.00	18.25	6.00	52.00	Stephen H Ford
Turner & Taylor	Speedwell	1819	Full Blt Schooner	1	2	30.50	17.50	5.17	35.00	Themselves
Turner & Taylor	Doe	1819	Sharp Blt Schooner	1	2	59.00	20.75	8.66	111.55	Hollins & McBlair
16			Averages			48.54	20.14	7.93	96.96	
Beacham, James	Clio	1820	Sharp Blt Schooner	1	2	65.00	21.92	9.66	144.95	Matthew Kelly/Charles Malloy
Beacham, James	Lightning	1820	Sharp Blt Schooner	1	2	65.00	21.83	9.66	147.81	Frederick C. Graf

*Master Carpenter Certificates (see endnote.)

APPENDIX 1   COMMERCIAL VESSELS BUILT IN BALTIMORE 1795-1835*

Builder/#Built	Vessel Name	Date	Style	Decks	Masts	KeelLng	BrdthBeam	HoldDpth	Tonnage	Built For:
Bell, Richard	W B	1820	Sharp Blt Schooner			82.00	21.00	8.50	110.00	William Baartcheer/Isaac Thomas Heardie
Cooper, Robert	Corinthian	1820	Rebuild	1	3	108.67	30.04	14.83	423.51	James Inloes (see Gardner 1817/1818)
Despaux, John	Despaux	1820	Sharp Blt Schooner	1	2	56.86	21.37	9.04	115.68	David Parrot
Gardner & Robson	Idas or Ida S	1820	Sh Blt Rnd Tk Schnr	1	2	52.92	18.33	7.63	77.90	Capt Herman Perry
Gardner & Robson	Nephele	1820	RndTk ShBlt Schnr	1	2	61.17	21.54	9.08	125.98	Joel Vickers/James Corner
Gardner & Robson	Hyperion	1820	Rnd Tk Billet Head	2	2	78.33	28.92		344.74	Thomas Tenant
Price, John	Fells Point	1820	ShpRndTk PllBt Sch		2	56.50	16.75	6.33	44.93	Richard Johns
Price, John	Dick	1820	Sharp RndTk Schnr	1	2	62.50	18.50	7.50	75.07	Richard Johns
Price, William	Theban or Trojan	1820	Round Tk Schooner	1		76.00	22.42	10.08	148.91	Himself/Sold to Capt Archibald Kerr
Price, William	Beauty	1820	Rebuild			46.00	12.58	4.00	29.32	
Robinson, Robert	Virginia Ross	1820	Schooner	1	2	47.00	20.25	7.82	80.00	Reuben Ross
13			Averages			65.54	21.19	8.68	143.75	
Gardner, George	Dido	1821	Sharp Blt Schooner	1	2	56.92	19.83	8.83	103.09	James Corner
Price, John	Abarilla	1821	Sharp Rnd Tk Schnr	1	2	66.75	20.17	7.79	90.42	Jacob Gasseff
Price, William	Walter	1821	Rnd Tuck Schooner	1		60.67	22.25	9.08	129.07	Himself
Richardson, Tristm	Hector	1821	Schooner	1	2	38.00	19.00	6.00	46.23	George Nister
Riggin, Levi&Israel	Martha	1821	Round Tk Schooner			52.00	21.50	9.00	105.92	Isiah Mankin
Taylor, Lemuel G	Caduceus	1821	Sharp Blt Schooner	1	2	52.00	19.25	8.17	85.52	J T Heartter & others

*Master Carpenter Certificates (see endnote.)

APPENDIX 1   COMMERCIAL VESSELS BUILT IN BALTIMORE 1795-1835*

Builder/#Built	Vessel Name	Date	Style	Decks	Masts	KeelLng	BrdthBeam	HoldDpth	Tonnage	Built For:
Turner & Taylor	General Stricker	1821	Sharp Blt Schooner	1	2	55.00	21.00	8.00	97.15	Harrison & Thompson
Turner & Taylor	Maryland	1821	Sharp Blt Schooner	1	2	69.00	24.42	10.17	180.91	John Megarity
Turner, Joseph	Pilot	1821	Pilot Built			58.25	17.25	5.83	40.64	James Griggs
9			Averages			56.51	20.52	8.10	97.66	
Beacham, James	Peter	1822	Sharp Blt Brig	1	2	75.75	25.38	12.38	220.62	Robert Barry
Beacham, James	Constitution	1822	Full Blt Steamboat	1	0	122.00	26.75	9.50	320.35	Wm McDonald & Sons & others
Gardner & Robson	Corinthian	1822	Rnd Tk Sh Blt/bfhd	2	3	90.83	29.66	14.83	423.25	Mezick & Johnson
Gardner, George	La Fille Sauvage	1822	Rnd Tk Pil Blt Sch	1	2	50.00	16.04	6.08	47.47	Mayer & Brantz
Gardner, George	Thessalian	1822	Rnd Tk Pil Blt Brig	1	2	74.83	23.50	10.58	196.51	Archibald Kerr
Price, William	Maria	1822	Rnd Tk Schooner	1	2	58.33	20.17	8.83	109.38	Daniel Gardner
Price, William	Recompense	1822	Rnd Tk Schooner	1	2	53.75	19.50	8.50	94.11	Mr. R. Barry (of Havana)
Price, William	Liberal	1822	Rnd Tk Schooner	1	2	63.33	22.33	9.38	139.90	Mr. Walter Price
Price, William	Fawn	1822	Rnd Tk Schooner	1	2	48.75	20.00	8.29	85.09	Richard H. Johns
Riggin, Levi&Israel	Port Deposit of Bal	1822	Sq Tuck Steamboat	1	0	58.00	16.00	4.00	39.07	John McCourland for George Rogers
Turner, Joseph	Damsel	1822	Schooner	1	2	42.50	17.50	7.17	55.44	Henry Payson/Agent for Stephen Trowbridge
Turner, Joseph	Greek	1822	Hermaphrodite Brig	1	2	52.00	22.00	18.92	128.00	Thomas Sprigg/William League
12			Averages			65.84	21.57	9.87	154.93	

*Master Carpenter Certificates (see endnote.)

APPENDIX 1 — COMMERCIAL VESSELS BUILT IN BALTIMORE 1795-1835*

Builder/#Built	Vessel Name	Date	Style	Decks	Masts	KeelLng	BrdthBeam	HoldDpth	Tonnage	Built For:
Beacham, James	George Stiles	1823	Sharp Blt Schooner	1	2	67.00	22.66	10.17	162.31	Buck/Hendrick/Himself
Beacham, James	Catherine	1823	Sharp Blt Brig	1	2	67.50	22.50	10.50	167.91	Benjamin Buck/Thomas Hendrick/Himself
Beacham, James	Ella Kintzing	1823	Sharp Blt Schooner	1	2	65.00	22.58	9.58	148.07	James Frazier
Beacham, James	Tom	1823	Full Blt Schooner	1	2	48.58	19.75	6.42	64.83	Hugh McElderry/Himself
Despaux, Anthony	Wall	1823	Schooner	1	2	45.33	18.21	6.83	55.25	Samuel Wall
Dunham, Jacob	Rock Point	1823	Ful Built Schooner	1	2	45.50	16.75	5.46	43.83	Thomas Raven
Gardner, George	Racer	1823	Rnd Tk Pil Blt Sch	1	2	52.54	19.38	7.81	83.72	Cary Southcomb
Gardner, George	Yellott	1823	Rnd Tk Pil Blt Sch	1	2	78.25	21.25	9.33	146.66	Isaac McKim
Gardner, George	Noel	1823	Rnd Tk Pil Blt Sch	1	2	51.75	18.00	7.08	69.45	James Bosley
Price, William	Ann Francis	1823	Rnd Tk Schooner	1	2	66.25	22.42	10.00	156.35	Himself/Sold to: John Repeto
Price, William	Blue-Eyed Mary	1823	Rnd Tk Schooner	1	2	63.17	22.42	10.00	149.25	Capt Daniel Gardner
Price, William	Sophia	1823	Rnd Tk Schooner	1	2	54.97	19.08	8.58	94.78	Msrs. Baric & Lagueronne of Phila
Price, William	Elizabeth	1823	Round Tuck Brig	1	2	70.00	26.66		260.51	Himself/Sold to: Capt Baptiste Mezick
Price, William	Herald	1823	Rnd Tk Schooner	1	2	58.00	19.33	8.66	102.51	Mr. Walter Price
Turner, Joseph	Mary Olivia	1823	Schooner	1	2	44.00	18.50	7.58	64.95	
15			Averages			58.55	20.64	8.43	118.49	
Beacham, James	Nonpareil	1824	Sharp Blt Schooner	1	2	63.25	21.33	9.00	197.83	John G. Chappell
Beacham, James	Ella	1824	Sharp Blt Schooner	1	2	70.50	21.54	7.79	123.73	Buck/Hendrick/Himself
Beacham, James	Peruvian	1824	Full Built	2	3	92.00	28.00		379.62	E Tyson/Charles Malloy/Matthew Kelly

*Master Carpenter Certificates (see endnote.)

APPENDIX 1   COMMERCIAL VESSELS BUILT IN BALTIMORE 1795-1835*

Builder/#Built	Vessel Name	Date	Style	Decks	Masts	KeelLng	BrdthBeam	HoldDpth	Tonnage	Built For:
Culley, Langley B	Harriet	1824	Schooner			40.00	19.00	7.00	48.00	Benjamin A. Ferguson
Flannigan, Andrew	General Winder	1824	Sharp Blt Schooner	1	2	65.33	21.33	9.33	137.00	William Parish
Gardner, George	George Gardner	1824	Rnd Tk FBlt Brig/fhd	2	2	79.83	26.92	13.42	301.96	James Johnson/Joshua Mezick/BMezick
Gardner, George	Alisanna	1824	Rnd Tk Pil Blt Sch	1	2	65.42	20.66	8.18	98.47	Cary Southcomb
Gardner, George	Joanna	1824	Rnd Tk Pil Blt Sch	1	2	68.92	21.92	9.00	143.48	Robert Mandisville Hamilton
Gardner, George	George & Henry	1824	Rnd Tk FBlt Brig/bhd	2	2	73.67	26.92	13.42	281.14	1/2 Wm Patterson&Sons/1/2Henry Patterson
Leaf & Goodwin	Leaf	1824	Sharp Blt Schooner	1	2	53.00	21.25	9.50	125.00	John Powell
Leaf & Goodwin	General Lafayette	1824	Full Built Sloop	1	1	47.00	19.75	6.33	63.21	Robert Constable
Price, William	Black-Eyed Susan	1824	Rnd Tk Schooner	1	2	66.67	22.83	10.25	164.36	Himself
Price, William	Iris	1824	Rnd Tk Schooner	1	2	60.75	20.08	9.00	115.86	Himself
Price, William	Elizabeth	1824	Schooner		2	55.75	19.08	8.18	91.22	
Price, William	General Pulaski	1824	Round Tuck Sloop	Q	1	48.42	18.75	8.00	75.59	McFaden & Harris
Price, William	William Price	1824	Rnd Tk Schooner	1	2	42.00	17.00	6.50	48.85	Lewis Shallford/Joseph H Rowe/Jas Rare
Riggin, Levi&Israel	Eliza & Mary	1824	Schooner		2	40.00	19.00	6.75	54.00	Thomas Coward
Turner, Joseph	Colonel Tennant	1824				51.50	18.92	8.50	87.56	George Bier
18			Averages			66.94	21.35	8.83	141.02	
Bailey & Dorgin	Grace Ann	1825	Sharp Blt Schooner	1	2	68.00	21.25	8.00	122.64	John G Chappell/R Douglass
Beacham, James	Lady Adams	1825	Full Built Brig	2	2	78.00	24.33	12.18	241.28	Thomas Tenant
Etienne Benillant	James Monroe	1825	Sharp Blt Schooner	1	2	62.00	22.50	10.18	149.39	VonKapff & Brun

*Master Carpenter Certificates (see endnote.)

APPENDIX 1 COMMERCIAL VESSELS BUILT IN BALTIMORE 1795-1835*

Builder/#Built	Vessel Name	Date	Style	Decks	Masts	KeelLng	BrdthBeam	HoldDpth	Tonnage	Built For:
Flannigan, Andrew	Union	1825	Full Built Sloop	1	1	58.00	18.66	6.00	55.97	
Flannigan, Andrew	Elizabeth Jane	1825	Sharp Blt Schooner	1	2	62.67	18.58	6.88	69.27	William C Tilden
Flannigan, Andrew	Saravac	1825	Sharp Blt Schooner	1	2	83.50	21.75	10.00	159.96	William Tilden
Gardner, George	Covington	1825	Rnd Tk FBlt Ship	2	3	82.50	27.12	13.56	319.50	William Wilson & Sons
Gardner, George	Diana	1825	Rnd Tk Pli Blt Sch	1	2	46.25	16.92	6.66	55.15	Francisco Domingo
Kinnard, Samuel	Montezuma	1825	Sharp Blt Brig	2	2	86.00	24.33	11.50	223.21	William Patterson
Leaf & Goodwin	Constancy	1825	Sharp Blt Schooner	1	2	62.50	22.00	9.50	158.47	Capt William Kennedy
Leaf & Goodwin	Baltimore	1825	Sharp Blt Schooner	1	2	65.17	21.50	8.75	129.04	Themslvs ("non de property" of R Hamilton)
Price, William	Gen R(V?)ives	1825	Round Tuck Sloop	Q	1	48.42	18.75	7.92	75.59	McFadon & Harris
Price, William	Betsy	1825	Sharp Schooner	1		56.00	20.00	8.50	94.61	Richard H. Johns
Riggin, Levi&Israel	Mary Hobin	1825	Schooner	1		57.58	21.50	9.50	123.90	ThomasWHobin/AaronWills/ThomasWilson
Turner, Joseph	Chasseur	1825	Sharp Blt Schooner	1	2	51.50	19.33	8.82	92.58	Thomas Boyle
15			Averages			64.54	21.24	9.2	138.04	
Bailey & Dorgin	Star	1826	Sharp Blt Schooner	1	2	43.42	18.00	6.50	56.85	JacobReese/WmPate/JnHayne/WmFiscoe
Bailey & Dorgin	Two Sons	1826	Sharp Blt Schooner	1	2	33.50	15.21	5.50	31.00	Samuel Wall
Beacham, James	Baltimore	1826	Ship	4	3	166.42	45.58	35.42	2028.71	Henry Eckford
Beacham, James	Greyhound	1826	Sharp Blt Schooner	1	2	62.00	20.33	8.07	107.26	WmLawman/Ag. Perkins/Cushing/Cabots
Culley, Robert	Felicity	1826	Sharp Blt Schooner	1	2	43.00	19.25	7.00	63.83	Benjamin Ferguson
Gardner, George	Chimborazo	1826	Rnd Tk Pli Blt Brig	1	2	70.00	21.75	9.60	153.94	Capt Archibald Kerr

*Master Carpenter Certificates (see endnote.)

APPENDIX 1 COMMERCIAL VESSELS BUILT IN BALTIMORE 1795-1835*

Builder/#Built	Vessel Name	Date	Style	Decks	Masts	KeelLng	BrdthBeam	HoldDpth	Tonnage	Built For:
Harrison, William	Mathilda	1826	Sharp Blt Schooner			51.75	19.75	7.82	83.02	T B Saporteux of New Orleans
Price, William	Jefferson	1826	Round Tuck Ship	2		85.75	28.50		366.86	Rbt Leslie (25%) Chas Karthaus (75%)
Price, William	Louisa	1826	Herm Rnd Tk Brig	1		71.92	22.25	10.66	179.61	Thomas Tenant for L R P Desbarreaux
Turner, Joseph	Sylph	1826	Brig	1	2	78.00	25.83	10.17	215.42	John W Olgood/Robert Olgood
10			Averages			70.58	23.65	11.20	328.65	
Bailey & Dorgin	Messenger	1827	Sharp Blt Schooner	1	2	54.54	20.42	7.92	92.74	Louis Cherteau [Messanger?]
Beacham, James	Thomas Jefferson	1827	Full Blt Steamboat	1	1	122.00	27.50	9.50	335.50	Benjamin Ferguson
Dunkin, Levin H	Melville	1827	Rnd Tk Sh Blt Brig	2	2	75.17	23.50	11.75	218.47	William Wilson & Sons/Thomas Baker
Flannigain, Wm	Correo	1827	Sharp Blt Schooner	1	2	68.50	22.25	8.00	127.41	William Tucker
Flannigain, Wm	Henrietta	1827	Sharp Built	1	2	65.42	19.34	9.17	119.55	Hugh McElderry
Flannigain, Wm	Patuxent	1827	Full Blt Steamboat	1		107.00	24.33	7.83	214.68	Hugh McElderry/James Corner
Gardner, George	Courier	1827	Rnd Tk Pil Bt Brig	1	2	71.08	22.17	9.59	159.52	John B Lasala of New York
Gardner, George	Rosa	1827	Rnd Tk Pil Blt Sch	1	2	57.66	20.33	5.75	70.84	Colonel Thomas Tenant
Gardner, George	Ch Carroll/Carriltn	1827	Rnd Tk Pilot Bt Brig	1	2	70.00	21.58	10.04	153.94	Capt Joel Aicken/James Frazier
Gardner, George	Celeno	1827	Rnd Tk Pilot Bt Brig	1	2	70.17	21.58	10.50	160.00	Capt A Kerr
Gardner, George	Nine	1827	Rnd Tk Pilot Bt Brig	1	2	69.75	22.00	8.15	160.00	Edmond Didier/Capt Edmund Gardner
Leaf & Goodwin	Julia Ann	1827	Sharp Blt Schooner	1		47.00	18.25	7.25	72.00	Himslef and Johnrey Leaf
Leaf & Goodwin	Oscar	1827	Sharp Blt Schooner	1	2	50.00	19.25	7.08	77.72	Thomas Byrn
Turner, Joseph	Shillelah	1827	Schooner	1	2	56.00	20.50	9.00	108.76	John Odom "on the city block"

*Master Carpenter Certificates (see endnote.)

APPENDIX 1   COMMERCIAL VESSELS BUILT IN BALTIMORE 1795-1835*

Builder/#Built	Vessel Name	Date	Style	Decks	Masts	KeelLng	BrdthBeam	HoldDpth	Tonnage	Built For:
Turner, Joseph	Della Costa	1827	Schooner	1	2	52.00	20.00	7.92	86.65	James Corner/Frances Gallega
Turner, Joseph	Dola Costa	1827	Schooner	1	2	52.00	20.00	7.92	86.63	James Corner, Francis Gallega
16			Averages			68.02	21.44	8.59	140.28	
Auld, Hugh	Mary Jane	1828	Full built Sloop	1	1	40.42	18.00	5.50	42.12	William Kirby, Queen Ann Co. MD
Bailey, Thomas	Eagle	1828	Pilot Boat Schooner	1	2	38.50	16.75	9.17	45.00	WmBucoi/JReese/JnHamel/WmPate
Bailey, Thomas	Spark	1828	Brig	1	2	77.50	23.00	10.17	191.56	John S Smith/John Dorgin/Himself
Beacham, James	Baptist Mezick	1828	Full Blt Brig	2	2	90.00	27.00	13.50	345.32	Frederick Dawson
Beacham, James	James Beacham	1828	Full Blt Brig/Ship	2	2	92.75	27.66	?	373.72	B Mezick/CFSingleton/TSchlozsk/WTuckr
Culley, LB & R	Benjamin Ferguson	1828	Sharp Blt Schooner	1	2	60.50	19.50	7.50	66.10	William Owen, John Ferguson
Dorgin, John	Journl of Commerce	1828	Schooner	1	2	54.00	16.25	6.08	46.04	John G. Chappell
Dunkin, Levin H	Amelia	1828	Rnd Tk Sh Blt Schnr	1	2	65.75	21.42	9.58	142.66	Joseph [T] Beeman
Dunkin, Levin H	Fourth of July	1828	Rnd Tk Sh Blt Schnr	1	2	46.00	17.50	6.50	55.04	James Griggs
Flannigain, Andrew	Columbia	1828	Steamboat	1	2	116.54	30.38	10.50	389.81	Baltimore & Potomac Steam Packet Co
Flannigain, Andrew	Colonel Howard	1828	Brig	2	2	90.08	25.46	12.73	310.81	Hugh MacElderry
Gardner, George	Herald	1828	Rnd Tk Pil Bt Brig	1	2	70.75	22.25	9.75	161.13	John B Lasala of New York
Gardner, George	Triton	1828	Rnd Tk Pil Bt Brig	1	2	61.25	20.29	8.25	107.89	Nathaniel Webber
Gardner, George	Eclipse	1828	Rnd Tk Pil Bt Brig	1	2	71.00	22.25	10.00	166.28	Capt P Baldwin
Gardner, George	El Ora	1828	Rnd Tk Pil Blt Sch	1	2	64.58	21.08	11.75	105.83	Capt Henry Hall
Gardner, George	Union	1828	RndTuckPilBltBng	1	2	76.00	24.92	10.83	215.82	Capt Wm Kennedy

*Master Carpenter Certificates (see endnote.)

143

APPENDIX 1   COMMERCIAL VESSELS BUILT IN BALTIMORE 1795-1835*

Builder/#Built	Vessel Name	Date	Style	Decks	Masts	KeelLng	BrdthBeam	HoldDpth	Tonnage	Built For:
Harrison, Edward	Ann Elizabeth	1828	Full built Sloop	1	1	40.00	18.00	5.25	40.00	Valentine Wareham, Queen Ann, MD
Price, William	Jane	1828	Sharp Blt Schooner		2	60.50	20.17	8.21	105.34	Franklin Chase
Skinner, William	Corinthian	1828	Full Built Schooner	1	2	40.00	19.33	5.66	51.98	Thomas Cannon
Skinner, William	Experiment	1828	Steamboat			70.00	18.00	3.50	46.45	General Charles Ridgely
See Note*	SW	1828	Sharp Blt Schooner	1	2	45.33	18.21	6.83	49.37	Saml Wall (blt by Hardy & Anthony Despaux)
21			Averages			65.28	21.26	8.36	145.64	
Bailey & Dorgon	Mary Louisa	1829	Brig	1	2	67.00	21.66	9.00	145.37	John G Chappell
Beacham, James	Carroll of Carrollton	1829	Sharp Blt Steamboat	1	0	132.33	29.33	9.00	408.88	PA,DE,MD Navigation Company
Beacham, James	Pocahontas	1829	Steamboat	1	1	116.50	30.42	11.00	410.31	Maryland & Virginia Steam Navigation Co
Beacham, James	Seraphim	1829	Brig	1	2	75.00	22.33	9.00	158.65	Henry Thompson
Beacham, James	Carroll of Carrollton	1829	Full Built Ship	2	3	175.00	33.00	17.00	685.87	James Beacham
Culley, LB & R	Conception	1829	Sharp Blt Schooner	1	2	56.00	20.58	8.08	98.06	Thomas Wilson
Dorgin, John	Laura & Mary	1829	Schooner	1	2	60.04	20.08	8.83	112.92	Thomas Bailey
Dorgin, John	Two Marys	1829	Schooner	1	2	74.92	22.42	8.33	147.28	R H Douglas
Dorgin, John	Selim	1829	PilBoatBltSchooner	1	2	45.33	17.75	6.58	55.80	James Greggs
Dunkin, Levin H	Splendid	1829	BlltetHdRndTkShBrig	1	2	75.00	24.08	11.50	219.56	Buck & Hednick
Dunkin, Levin H	Murdock	1829	ShBltRndTkSchoon	1	2	67.42	22.25	9.58	151.51	Joseph I Beaman
Flannigain, Andrew	Celestine	1829	Sharp Blt Schooner	1	2	68.75	21.54	8.08	136.00	Richard H Douglas & Co
Gardner, George	Superior	1829	RndTkPilBt Brig	1	2	73.50	22.92	10.50	177.25	Capt P Baldwin

*Master Carpenter Certificates (see endnote.)

APPENDIX 1   COMMERCIAL VESSELS BUILT IN BALTIMORE 1795-1835*

Builder/#Built	Vessel Name	Date	Style	Decks	Masts	KeelLng	BrdthBeam	HoldDpth	Tonnage	Built For:
Gardner, George	Columbus	1829	FullBltRndTkSteamb	1	1	117.66	25.42	11.00	413.79	Maryland & Virginia Steamboat Company
Gardner, George	LaZona	1829	RndTkPilBtSchoon	1	2	65.00	21.21	8.00	112.11	Capt Henry Hull
Gardner, George	Count Villanueva	1829	PilBltRndTkBrig	1	2	71.42	22.29	9.71	162.55	John B LaSalle
Gardner, George	William Gardner	1829	RndTkPilotBoat	1	2	68.42	21.75	9.50	148.73	Capt Henry Hull
Leaf & Goodwin	Rebecca	1829	Brig	1	2	52.00	19.00	7.83	89.86	William Fisher
Robb&Donaldson	Firm	1829	Schooner			54.00	18.75	7.00	73.52	Jacob B Donaldson, John A Robb
Skinner, William	Atlantic	1829	Sharp Blt Schooner	1	2	49.00	21.17	7.66	90.00	James Hooper
20			Averages			78.22	22.9	9.36	199.90	
Bailey & Dorgin	Evan T Ellicott	1830	Schooner	1	2	75.83	21.25	8.00	112.88	William Mason
Bailey & Dorgin	Trimmer	1830	Sharp Blt Schooner	1	2	38.00	15.75	5.83	42.28	Harry Curtis/James Coyle
Bailey & Dorgin	Tybee	1830	Schooner	1	2	56.00	17.50	6.58	54.50	Charles Gwinn,Agent for Wm Crabtree etal
Bailey & Dorgin	Laura & Mary	1830	Schooner	1	2	60.50	20.08	8.83	112.97	Himself & Thomas Bailey
Bates, John	Beoary	1830	Schooner	1/2	2	75.33	20.58	3.92	53.47	John Bates
Beacham, James	Timbactoo	1830	Sharp Blt Brig	1	2	64.00	22.25	8.00	119.92	James Corner, James I. Corner
Beacham, James	Salem	1830	Full Blt Steamboat	1	0	75.00	21.00	7.00	110.05	PA,Del,MD Steam Navigation Company
Beacham, James	Carroll of Carrollm	1830	Full Blt Ship	2	3	117.00	33.42	16.71	685.28	Himself
Beacham, James	Serene	1830	Full Blt Brig	2	2	84.75	25.50	12.75	190.00	James Frazier
Culley, LB & R	Volador	1830	Sharp Blt Brig	1	2	91.58	22.25	10.08	184.83	John G. Chappell
Culley, LB & R	Mary Ann	1830	Full Built Sloop	1	1	49.50	18.92	5.50	53.82	Samuel Meeteer/William Meeteer/Baltimore

*Master Carpenter Certificates (see endnote.)

APPENDIX 1 COMMERCIAL VESSELS BUILT IN BALTIMORE 1795-1835*

Builder/#Built	Vessel Name	Date	Style	Decks	Masts	KeelLng	BrdthBeam	HoldDpth	Tonnage	Built For:
Dunkin, Levin H	Constitution	1830	Rnd Tk Sh Blt Schnr	1	2	44.08	17.08	6.50	50.86	HBuckless/HBailey/JasCole/JasWarrett
Gardner, George	Emily	1830	Rnd Tk FBlt Schnr	1	2	60.25	21.25	5.50	74.12	Capt Williams/WM Furlong
Gardner, George	Mary Clare	1830	Rnd Tk Pil Blt Schnr	1	2	47.00	20.25	4.58	45.87	Francis Brooks
Kinard, Samuel	James Ramsey	1830	Brig w/bullethead	1	2	76.00	21.58	9.38	134.67	Capt Joseph Drew
Robb&Donaldson	Rappahanock	1830	Steamboat			115.00	26.00	9.33	293.76	Baltimore&Rappahanock Steam Packet Co
Robb, John	Ohio	1830	Brig			76.50	23.67	15.00	225.53	William H Conking/James Corner
Skinner, William	Catherine Jane	1830	Schooner			45.00	19.00	5.50	49.00	John Edmondson
Skinner, William	Sterett	1830	Sharp Blt Schooner	1	2	72.33	22.33	10.42	193.52	Dugan/Lane/Hardesty/Hooper/Edwards.Balt
Skinner, William	William	1830	Full Built Schooner	1	2	48.00	19.33	5.71	55.51	Capt Thomas Cannon
Stephens, Alexndr	Mary	1830	Schooner	1	2	42.00	18.25	6.00	48.38	Samuel Wall
21			Averages			67.32	21.30	8.15	137.68	
Auld & Harrison	John Hutson	1831	Schooner	1	2	48.58	19.83	58.69	57.97	Samuel Wall
Bailey & Dorgin	Liberty	1831	Schooner	1	2	47.75	18.25	6.71	61.48	Reese, Pate, Jonathan Samner
Bailey & Dorgin	Tallyho	1831	Schooner	1	2	44.00	17.50	6.50	52.91	Louis Ford/John Sword/TGLClark/GeoBean
Beacham, James	Joseph Maxwell	1831	Ship	2	3	85.50	25.50	12.75	292.61	GTyson, WmTHawes/BRussell/NBedfdMA
Culley, LB & R	William	1831	Sharp Blt Brig	1	2	67.25	21.33	9.33	140.92	R L Bailey, Agent for P Pingner/Salem, MA
Culley, LB & R	Edward Beck	1831	Full Built Sloop	1	1	41.50	19.66	6.82	52.95	Luther J Cox/James Moir
Culley, LB & R	Phantom	1831	Sharp Blt Schooner	1	2	53.00	19.50	7.92	85.12	John Hugg
Dunkin, Levin H	Eagle	1831	Rnd Tk Sh Blt Schnr	1	2	53.66	18.33	7.17	48.55	Singleton/Mezick/Baptiste Mezick

*Master Carpenter Certificates (see endnote.)

APPENDIX 1   COMMERCIAL VESSELS BUILT IN BALTIMORE 1795-1835*

Builder/#Built	Vessel Name	Date	Style	Decks	Masts	KeelLng	BrdthBeam	HoldDpth	Tonnage	Built For:
Dunkin, Levin H	Central America	1831	Sharp Blt Brig	1	2	76.17	24.42	11.17	218.60	CaptLouisAChasteau/JasFisher/B Moxley
Dunkin, Levin H	Margaret Mercer	1831	Sharp Blt Schooner	1	2	46.66	17.75	6.58	57.90	American Colonization Society
Gardner, George	Patrickson	1831	Pilot Bt Rnd Tk Brig	1	2	68.66	21.92	9.71	153.76	Singleton/Mezick/Baptiste Mezick
Gardner, George	Joppa	1831	Rnd Tk FBlt Schnr	1	2	63.17	19.75	3.92	51.21	Msrs J M & E Patterson
Leaf & Goodwin	Belrdmas	1831	Sharp Blt Sloop	1	1	46.42	18.50	5.83	52.77	William P Mathers/William C Frieman
Leef, Henry	Kate	1831	Schooner	1	2	54.00	23.25	8.00	98.91	BenjHardester/WmHooper/OKellogg/JClark
Miles, Isaac H	Florida	1831	Brig	1	2	60.00	21.58	8.00	120.03	Benjamin Buck/Fredk Mason/Wm Mason
Miles, Isaac H	Henry Clay	1831	Brig	1	2	85.00	22.00	10.00	160.57	TisdalePaul,Tapphnck,VA/ZachJellison/Bos
Price, Wm & Son	Argyle	1831	Round Tuck Brig	1	2	71.00	25.50		242.92	J Huson/D R Wilson
Price, Wm & Son	Erie	1831	Round Tuck Brig	1	2	67.50	22.54		150.44	James Corner/James I Corner/C G Snow
Skinner, William	Chaptico	1831	Full Built Schooner	1	2	47.00	19.50	10.08	58.91	James J Gough Esq/St. Mary's County
Stephens, Alexndr	Bonita	1831	Schooner	1	2	41.00	18.75	6.00	48.55	JChappell/JKingJr/WmTucker/RoswellPFish
20			Averages			58.39	20.77	7.90	111.62	
Auld & Harrison	Salm	1832	Sq Stern Schooner	1	2	28.00	14.00	5.50	23.00	John Wallace, Charles Hanson
Auld/Harrison	Mexico	1832	Schooner	1	2	57.50	20.75	7.17	88.00	Themselves
Bailey & Dorgan	Superior	1832	Barque	1	2	85.00	24.38	12.19	265.80	Hims/f/ThosBailey/Smith/Wilson/Peterkins
Bailey & Dorgan	Amazon	1832	Brig	1	2	89.83	23.50	12.75	236.50	Jacob W Hugg/Hugh Jenkins
Beacham, James	Medora	1832	Full Blt Ship	2	3	106.33	28.92	14.46	267.96	Luke&ChasTiernan/WmGraham/DGriffith
Beacham, James	Raritan	1832	Sharp Blt Schooner	1	2	57.00	20.25	7.50	91.12	Andrew Patrullo of New York

*Master Carpenter Certificates (see endnote.)

147

APPENDIX 1 COMMERCIAL VESSELS BUILT IN BALTIMORE 1795-1835*

Builder/#Built	Vessel Name	Date	Style	Decks	Masts	KeelLng	BrdthBeam	HoldDpth	Tonnage	Built For:
Beacham, James	Engineer	1832	Full Blt Schooner	1	3	96.75	30.33	9.00	270.14	Andrew Patrullo of New York
Beacham, James	Chesapeake	1832	Sharp Blt Schooner	1	2	57.00	20.25	7.50	91.12	Andrew Patrullo of New York
Beacham, James	Mezelle	1832	Sharp Blt Schooner	1	2	63.50	20.25	7.75	104.90	Eugene Marchand
Beacham, James	Susquehanna	1832	Sharp Blt Schooner	1	2	57.00	20.25	7.50	91.12	Andrew Patrullo of New York
Beacham, James	Delaware	1832	Sharp Blt Schooner	1	2	57.00	20.25	7.50	91.12	Andrew Patrullo of New York
Beacham, James	Beacham	1832	Sharp Blt Schooner	1	2	58.33	18.66	7.00	80.16	Andrew Patrullo of New York
C Goodwin & Co	Frances Jane	1832	Schooner	1	2	71.50	21.71	10.17	166.11	Themselves1/8each+Balt & NY owners
Culley, LB & R	Hortensia	1832	Full Built Barque	2	3	81.33	24.33	12.83	253.51	Captain William Massicott
Dunkin, Levin H	Averick Heineken	1832	Full Blt Rnd Tk Ship	2	3	100.00	29.50	14.75	458.02	JnAParker&Sons/JosDunbore/CAHeineken
Gardner, George	Hermann	1832	Full Built Rnd Tuck	2	3	114.83	28.66	20.50	410.16	CWKarthaus/RbtLeslie/EdwVuntz/BHauxnal
George Gardner	Gazelle	1832	Rnd Tk Pil Bt Schnr	1	2	44.75	19.25	5.63	51.21	John Chauncey/John Cowan
Kinard, Samuel	Pennsylvania	1832	Full Built Schooner	1	2	61.25	19.66	5.38	54.00	Himself & James Williamson
Miles, Isaac H	Harriett of Baltimre	1832	Schooner	1	2	70.00	23.00	10.00	174.27	Mathws/Hopkins/Hardester/Hooper/Gibbs
Miles, Isaac H	Frederickburg	1832	Schooner	1	2	48.00	19.25	6.92	69.37	James Hooper Jr.
Miles, Isaac H	Napoleon	1832	Brig	1	2	94.75	22.66	11.33	222.32	Zachariah Jellison of Boston, MA
Miles, Isaac H	John H Holland	1832	Schooner	1	2	44.00	18.50	6.75	62.00	J W Zacharie of New Orleans
Price, Wm & Son	Caroline	1832	Round Tuck Brig	1	2	62.17	20.25	8.92	118.47	Jos P Burnett/Thoms Wilson/Geo W ???
Price, Wm & Son	Canada	1832	Round Tuck Brig	1	2	86.50	24.12	12.25	269.17	Bapt Mezick/Th J Mezick/C Singleton
Riggin, Levi&Israel	Hope	1832	Schooner	1	2	55.00	20.50	8.47	96.47	JnBeatty/GeoJohnson/JnDouglas,AlexVA
Riggin, Levi&Israel	Mary & Francis	1832	Schooner	1	2	74.00	22.00	8.50	145.66	Henry Spearing of New Orleans

*Master Carpenter Certificates (see endnote.)

APPENDIX 1 COMMERCIAL VESSELS BUILT IN BALTIMORE 1795-1835*

Builder/#Built	Vessel Name	Date	Style	Decks	Masts	KeelLng	BrdthBeam	HoldDpth	Tonnage	Built For:
Robb&Donaldson	Splendid	1832	Full Built Sloop	2	3	106.66	27.66	19.42	458.65	Joseph King Jr/William Tucker/R P Fish
Robb&Donaldson	Baltimore	1832	Brig			82.50	24.08	15.50	251.21	William H Conkling/James Corner
Robb, John	Bazil Lamar	1832	Flat Bottom Stmbt		2	105.00	27.50	7.38	223.61	SavGA:Long/Glaghorn/Wood/Gaudroy/etal
Skinner, William	Kentucky	1832	Steamnboat	1		169.00	25.33	9.00	400.00	The Peoples Steam Navigation Co
Skinner, William	Indies	1832	Full Built Brig	1	2	68.00	22.00	8.66	132.00	Washington B Jones
Stephens, Alexndr	Gratitude of Mobile	1832	Schooner	1	2	63.00	18.25	6.66	60.19	Andrew Dorgan of Mobile
Stephens, Alexndr	Rosina	1832	Schooner	1	2	53.00	21.00	8.75	102.00	Himself
33			Averages			74.84	22.46	9.81	184.22	
Auld & Goodland	Mexicana	1833	Schooner	1	2	58.33	20.38	7.48	90.11	John H. Love
Auld & Goodland	Alexander	1833	Sharp Blt Schooner	1	2	45.42	17.63	6.38	53.39	Cooper, Roll, Roberts, Singleton
Bailey & Dorgin	Boston	1833	Sharp Blt Schooner	1	2	42.50	16.25	6.00	13.62	John Oliver/Jonathan Bruce of Boston
Bailey & Dorgin	Stag	1833	Brig	1	2	72.79	22.92	10.08	177.02	Henry H. Williams
Beacham, James	Harkaway	1833	Full Blt Ship	2	3	117.33	29.83	14.92	549.62	JBrander,PetersbugVA/RFisher,NorfolkVA
Dunkin, Levin H	General Marion	1833	Rnd Tk. Sh Blt Brig	1	2	82.75	23.00	10.00	200.34	Msssrs Buck/Hendrick; Capt H D Delano
Dunkin, Levin H	Creole	1833	Rnd Tk Sh Blt Schnr	1	2	64.58	21.92	8.08	120.43	Capt Lewis Carnier
Gardner, George	Gossamer	1833	Rnd Tk Pil Blt Schnr	1	2	36.00	15.75	5.66	33.82	Daniel Proctor
Gardner, George	Napier	1833	Full Blt Rnd Tk Ship	2	3	105.79	28.88	14.44	464.24	Capt Robert Hancock/Thomas Lucas
Gardner, George	Liberty	1833	Rnd Tk Pil Blt Schnr	1	2	51.00	17.75	6.58	62.19	Rees/Pate/Sarnnia/Garner
Gardner, George	Dido	1833	Rnd Tk Pil Bt Brig	1	2	72.25	22.92	10.00	174.26	James Corner/Solomon Corner

*Master Carpenter Certificates (see endnote.)

APPENDIX 1   COMMERCIAL VESSELS BUILT IN BALTIMORE 1795-1835*

Builder/#Built	Vessel Name	Date	Style	Decks	Masts	KeelLng	BrdthBeam	HoldDpth	Tonnage	Built For:
Jones, Washgtn B	Augusta	1833	Full Blt Schooner	1	2	43.00	20.00	4.00	36.00	? Buck
Kinard&Williamson	Ann McKim	1833	Ship	2	3	109.58	27.00	13.5	420.37	Isaac McKim (with James Williamson)
Miles, Isaac H	Shamrock	1833	Schooner	1	2	68.00	21.50	9.00	126.63	Saml & Alexander Phillips/Fredericksburg VA
Miles, Isaac H	Patapsco	1833	Schooner	1	2	54.00	19.83	6.92	75.00	Baltimore Chemical Manufacturing Co
Price, Wm & Son	Troubadour	1833	Round Tuck Brig	1	2	72.88	23.21	10.92	188.34	J Hutson/Ringburn/Jenkins
Price, Wm & Son	William Price	1833	Round Tuck Brig	1	2	82.00	23.21	?	232.67	J Hutson
Riggin, Levi&Israel	Silas E Burrows	1833	Barque	1	3	98.00	23.66	12.00	235.00	William H Trott
Robb, John	Louisa	1833	Barque		3	78.50	24.66	13.00	264.97	Bevn/Humphreys/Frazier of Philadelphia
Skinner, Zachariah	J G Tomkins	1833	Sharp Blt Schooner	1	2	65.75	21.33	7.54	89.00	Capt Thomas Taylor
20			Averages			71.02	22.08	9.29	181.87	
Abraham&Cooper	Cayuga	1834	Brig	1	2	97.50	24.17	11.66	239.00	ThosWilson/GWPeterkin/WMason/WFrisbie
Bates, John	Beauty	1834	Sharp Blt Schooner	1/2	2	75.33	20.58	3.92	53.50	Himself
Beacham, Jas, Est	Ann Louisa	1834	Full Blt Barque	2	3	85.33	25.38	12.66	289.27	HoratoGWard,NY/JohnLand,Ipswich, MA
Bissett, Owen	E. Dorsey	1834	Schooner	1	2	53.00	20.50	7.50	88.00	Himself
Dunkin, Levin H	Eliza B Hallet	1834	Rnd Tk Sh Blt Schnr	1	2	72.17	23.75	8.00	144.33	Capt John Frazier
Dunkin, Levin H	Palmira	1834	Rnd Tk Sh Blt Schnr	1	2	78.66	24.42	11.50	232.51	Capt Thomas Baker
Dunkin, Levin H	Nymph	1834	Rnd Tk Sh Blt Schnr	1	2	67.66	22.25	7.75	122.51	Mssrs Birckhead & Pearce
Lawrence, R D	Matilda	1834	Sloop	1	1	31.66	16.00	3.83	20.36	H Linthicum of Ann Arundel Co
Miles, Isaac H	Mary Bernard	1834	Brig	1	2	88.00	22.66	8.92	151.20	JBeetly/GJohnson/JDouglass:Alexnd/DC

*Master Carpenter Certificates (see endnote.)

APPENDIX 1 — COMMERCIAL VESSELS BUILT IN BALTIMORE 1795-1835*

Builder/#Built	Vessel Name	Date	Style	Decks	Masts	KeelLng	BrdthBeam	HoldDpth	Tonnage	Built For:
Price, Wm & Son	Falcon	1834	Round Tuck Brig	1		73.58	23.33	9.00	155.68	Wilson & Peterkin/William Mason
Riggin, Levi&Israel	Isaac Clason	1834	Brig	1	2	92.39	24.88	10.29	206.60	William H Trott
Riggin, Levi&Israel	Chanticleer	1834	Brig	Poop	2	76.00	23.33	11.00	205.34	William H Trott
Robb, John	Alcipe	1834	Schooner	1	2	60.75	20.75	7.17	94.00	Richard Wells of New York
Robb, John	Rockhall	1834				37.25	17.17	6.00	40.38	Thomas Harris
Robb, John	Superb	1834	Full Built Ship	2	3	111.75	29.50	14.75	507.83	Joseph King/William Tucker/R P Fish
Stephens, Alexndr	Morris (Gross?)	1834	Schooner	1	2	37.00	17.00	5.33	37.00	Himself
16			Averages			71.12	22.23	8.71	161.75	
Abraham&Cooper	Jacob Heald	1835	Schooner	1	2	68.00	18.33	6.79	69.73	J D Turner
Bailey, Thomas	Rebecca Frances	1835	Schooner	1	2	52.50	16.75	5.83	43.64	Rebecca Knap
Bailey, Thomas	Conchita	1835	Sq Stern Schooner			74.00	19.00	7.71	99.61	William Pate
Brown, John S	Souviner	1835	Brig	1	2	77.00	20.50	8.17	115.00	Themselves
Culley & Rogers	Merchant	1835	Steamboat	1	2	150.00	25.00	8.33	306.44	William G Harrison/Gorham Brooks
Culley, Langley	Oglethorpe	1835	Hermaphrodite Brig	1	2	69.75	21.33	9.25	144.76	William Bennett/Chas Gwinn/S Philbrick
Dunkin, Levin H	Falcon	1835	Rnd Tk Sh Blt Schnr	1	2	51.33	17.83	6.50	62.63	Mr. Lewis Ford
Dunkin, Levin H	Isaac Franklin	1835	Full Blt Rnd Tk Brig	1	2	73.17	22.66	10.75	187.66	John Ormfield Esq.
Gardner, Wm & Geo	Caroline	1835	Rnd Tk Pil Blt Schnr	1	2	46.00	17.75	9.17	41.32	Capt A Williams
Gardner, Wm&Geo	Canton	1835	Full Blt Rnd Tk Barq	2	3	86.08	24.42	12.21	272.85	Conkling/Frazier/Shephenson
Jones, Washngtn B	Nelson Clark	1835	Round Tk Brig		2	78.00	23.00	9.75	180.00	JClark/WHooper/JHenderson/ZKinner/Hms

*Master Carpenter Certificates (see endnote.)

151

APPENDIX 1 COMMERCIAL VESSELS BUILT IN BALTIMORE 1795-1835*

Builder/#Built	Vessel Name	Date	Style	Decks	Masts	KeelLng	BrdthBeam	HoldDpth	Tonnage	Built For:
Jones, Washngtn B	Sarah	1835	Schooner			60.00	20.75	10.00	60.00	Himself and Zachariah Skinner
Kinard, Samuel	W Robbins	1835	Schooner	1	2	51.00	18.00	5.50	53.15	Himself
Moss, David	General Tacon	1835	Schooner	1	2	66.00	20.50	9.00	129.39	Capt Matthew Kelly
Moss, David	Galgo	1835	Brig	1	2	80.50	22.83	10.00	193.47	Capt Matthew Kelly
Price, Wm & Son	Greyhound	1835	Round Tuck Schnr	1	2	70.50	22.00	10.17	166.01	Mssrs William Honelt & Son
Price, Wm & Son	Inca	1835	Round Tuck Brig	1		71.25	24.00	11.75	211.50	Abijah Fisk of New Orleans
Robb, John	Invincible	1835	Schooner			66.25	21.00	7.83	114.72	Richard Wells
Robb, John	SouthCarolina	1835	Steam Packet			148.00	22.75	12.17	461.56	Atlantic Steam Packet Co
Robb, John	Hector	1835	Brig			74.66	22.25	11.08	193.83	Farrow:Balt/Prescott/Chapin/Kettel:Boston
Robertson, John M	Eliza Ann	1835	Ship	2	3	102.00	26.83	13.42	386.54	August Newman
Samuel Kinard	Gunpowder	1835	Full Blt Rnd Tk Schnr	1	2	66.00	21.75	5.00	75.55	Mssrs W & E Patterson
22			Averages			76.45	21.33	9.11	162.24	
			Overall Average							

Carpenter Certificates, see Chapter 1 footnotes for full description.
Carpenter names in italics indicate that these records were found in the Brewington Index, MHS original records not being available.
fjvessan2

*Master Carpenter Certificates (see endnote.)

State of Maryland
Baltimore City & County viz

I Wm Price of the City and County of Baltimore, Master Ship builder, do Cetify that the Schooner Named ~~Eliza~~ was built by me or under my direction in the City of Baltimore for Mr Walter Price in the Months of Jan.y Feb.y and March 1822. That the Said Schooner is round Tucked flush deck and has two masts is Sixty three feet four inches Straight Rabbit. Breadth of Beam twenty two feet four Inches debth of Hold Nine feet four inches & one half. And is one Hundred thirty Nine 5/95 Tons Carpenters Measurement as Witness my hand this ~~fifteenth day~~ of April 1822.

William Price

APPENDIX 2 Shipbuilder Production 1795-1835

Shipbuilder	Year	No. Carp Cert Issued	Total Tons	Average Tonnage
Hugh Auld etal	1805	1	105	105.00
Hugh Auld etal	1828	1	42	42.00
Hugh Auld etal	1831	1	58	58.00
Hugh Auld etal	1832	2	111	55.50
Hugh Auld etal	1833	2	143	71.50
Hugh Auld		7	459	65.57
Bailey & Dorgin	1825	1	123	123.00
Bailey & Dorgin	1826	2	87	43.50
Bailey & Dorgin	1827	1	93	93.00
Thomas Bailey	1828	2	237	118.50
Bailey & Dorgin	1829	4	461	115.25
Bailey & Dorgin	1830	4	323	80.75
Bailey & Dorgin	1831	2	114	57.00
Bailey & Dorgin	1832	2	502	251.00
Bailey & Dorgin	1833	2	190	95.00
Thomas Bailey	1835	2	143	71.50
Bailey & Dorgin		22	2273	103.32
James Beacham	1820	2	292	146.00
James Beacham	1822	2	541	270.50
James Beacham	1823	4	543	135.75
James Beacham	1824	3	701	233.67
James Beacham	1825	1	241	241.00
James Beacham	1826	2	2059	1029.50
James Beacham	1827	2	336	168.00
James Beacham	1828	2	719	359.50
James Beacham	1829	4	1664	416.00
James Beacham	1830	4	1104	276.00
James Beacham	1831	1	293	293.00
James Beacham	1832	8	1088	136.00
James Beacham	1833	1	550	550.00
James Beacham	1834	1	289	289.00

APPENDIX 2   Shipbuilder Production   1795-1835

Shipbuilder	Year	No. Carp Cert Issued	Total Tons	Average Tonnage
James Beacham		37	10420	281.62
James Cordery	1803	1	66	66.00
James Cordery	1807	2	261	130.50
James Cordery	1808	2	158	79.00
James Cordery	1809	3	429	143.00
James Cordery	1812	3	599	199.67
James Cordery	1813	2	258	129.00
James Cordery	1814	1	134	134.00
James Cordery	1815	1	373	373.00
James Cordery		15	2278	151.87
L B & Robert Culley	1824	1	48	48.00
L B & Robert Culley	1826	1	64	64.00
L B & Robert Culley	1828	1	66	66.00
L B & Robert Culley	1829	1	98	98.00
L B & Robert Culley	1830	2	238	119.00
L B & Robert Culley	1831	3	278	92.67
L B & Robert Culley	1832	1	254	254.00
L B & Robert Culley	1835	2	451	225.50
L B & Robert Culley		12	1497	124.75
Lewis DeRochebrune	1797	1	89	89.00
Lewis DeRochebrune	1798	2	319	159.50
Lewis DeRochebrune	1799	1	380	380.00
Lewis DeRochebrune		4	788	197.00
Andrew Descande	1812	1	230	230.00
Andrew Descande	1813	3	507	169.00
Andrew Descande	1814	2	406	203.00
Andrew Descande	1815	1	148	148.00
Andrew Descande	1816	3	553	184.33
Andrew Descande		10	1844	184.40

APPENDIX 2   Shipbuilder Production   1795-1835

Shipbuilder	Year	No. Carp Cert Issued	Total Tons	Average Tonnage
Joseph Despaux	1810	1	302	302.00
Joseph Despaux	1813	1	242	242.00
Joseph Despaux	1817	1	194	194.00
Joseph Despaux	1819	1	152	152.00
Joseph Despaux		4	890	222.50
Levin H. Dunkin	1827	1	218	218.00
Levin H. Dunkin	1828	2	198	99.00
Levin H. Dunkin	1829	2	371	185.50
Levin H. Dunkin	1830	1	51	51.00
Levin H. Dunkin	1831	3	325	108.33
Levin H. Dunkin	1832	1	458	458.00
Levin H. Dunkin	1833	2	321	160.50
Levin H. Dunkin	1834	3	499	166.33
Levin H. Dunkin	1835	2	250	125.00
Levin H. Dunkin		17	2691	158.29
Andrew Flannigain	1824	1	137	137.00
Andrew Flannigain	1825	3	285	95.00
Andrew Flannigain	1828	2	701	350.50
Andrew Flannigain	1829	1	136	136.00
Andrew Flannigain		7	1259	179.86
Flannigain & Beacham	1817	1	242	242.00
[William Flannigain]	1818	1	304	304.00
Flannigain & Beacham	1819	4	484	121.00
Flannigain & Beacham		6	1030	171.67
William Flannigain	1804	3	213	71.00
William Flannigain	1805	4	455	113.75
William Flannigain	1806	3	113	37.67
William Flannigain	1807	2	484	242.00
William Flannigain	1808	3	261	87.00

APPENDIX 2   Shipbuilder Production   1795-1835

Shipbuilder	Year	No. Carp Cert Issued	Total Tons	Average Tonnage
William Flannigain	1811	1	291	291.00
William Flannigain	1813	2	248	124.00
William Flannigain	1814	1	269	269.00
William Flannigain	1815	1	53	53.00
William Flannigain	1816	3	373	124.33
William Flannigain	1818	1	48	48.00
William Flannigain	1827	3	462	154.00
William Flannigain		27	3270	121.11
George Gardner	1813	1	172	172.00
George Gardner	1815	1	172	172.00
George Gardner	1821	1	103	103.00
George Gardner	1822	2	244	122.00
George Gardner	1823	3	300	100.00
George Gardner	1824	4	825	206.25
George Gardner	1825	2	375	187.50
George Gardner	1826	1	154	154.00
George Gardner	1827	5	704	140.80
George Gardner	1828	5	757	151.40
George Gardner	1829	5	1014	202.80
George Gardner	1830	2	120	60.00
George Gardner	1831	2	205	102.50
George Gardner	1832	2	461	230.50
George Gardner	1833	4	733	183.25
Wm & George Gardner	1835	2	314	157.00
George Gardner		42	6653	158.40
Gardner & Robson	1817	3	350	116.67
Gardner & Robson	1818	7	685	97.86
Gardner & Robson	1819	2	185	92.50
Gardner & Robson	1820	3	546	182.00
Gardner & Robson	1822	1	423	423.00
Gardner & Robson		16	2189	136.81

157

APPENDIX 2   Shipbuilder Production   1795-1835

Shipbuilder	Year	No. Carp Cert Issued	Total Tons	Average Tonnage
Thomas Hall	1813	2	168	84.00
Thomas Hall	1814	2	94	47.00
Thomas Hall	1815	3	183	61.00
Thomas Hall	1816	3	281	93.67
Thomas Hall	1817	1	129	129.00
Thomas Hall		11	855	77.73
John Hutton	1806	2	287	143.50
John Hutton	1807	4	561	140.25
John Hutton	1808	4	546	136.50
John Hutton		10	1394	139.40
Kemp & Gardner	1815	3	454	151.33
Kemp & Gardner	1816	9	754	83.78
Kemp & Gardner		12	1208	100.67
Thomas Kemp	1804	1	110	110.00
Thomas Kemp	1805	4	425	106.25
Thomas Kemp	1806	5	502	100.40
Thomas Kemp	1807	7	947	135.29
Thomas Kemp	1808	2	287	143.50
Thomas Kemp	1809	4	439	109.75
Thomas Kemp	1810	2	219	109.50
Thomas Kemp	1811	11	1834	166.73
Thomas Kemp	1812	5	1003	200.60
Thomas Kemp	1813	6	1112	185.33
Thomas Kemp	1814	3	388	129.33
Thomas Kemp	1815	2	274	137.00
Thomas Kemp		52	7540	145.00
Samuel Kennard*	1815	2	74	37.00
Samuel Kennard	1818	1	232	232.00
Samuel Kennard	1825	1	135	135.00

APPENDIX 2   Shipbuilder Production 1795-1835

Shipbuilder	Year	No. Carp Cert Issued	Total Tons	Average Tonnage
Samuel Kennard	1830	1	135	135.00
Samuel Kennard	1832	1	54	54.00
Samuel Kennard	1833	1	420	420.00
Samuel Kennard	1835	1	76	76.00
Samuel Kennard		8	1126	140.75
Leaf & Goodwin	1824	2	187	93.50
Leaf & Goodwin	1825	2	288	144.00
Leaf & Goodwin	1827	2	150	75.00
Leaf & Goodwin	1829	1	90	90.00
Leaf & Goodwin	1831	2	152	76.00
Leaf & Goodwin		9	867	96.33
Isaac H. Miles	1831	2	281	140.50
Isaac H. Miles	1832	4	528	132.00
Isaac H. Miles	1833	2	201	100.50
Isaac H. Miles	1834	1	151	151.00
Isaac H. Miles		9	1161	129.00
William Parsons	1801	1	79	79.00
William Parsons	1803	2	40	20.00
William Parsons	1804	4	542	135.50
William Parsons	1805	3	486	162.00
William Parsons	1806	4	730	182.50
William Parsons	1807	2	187	93.50
William Parsons	1808	3	355	118.33
William Parsons	1811	3	370	123.33
William Parsons	1812	3	410	136.67
William Parsons	1813	5	850	170.00
William Parsons	1814	3	288	96.00
William Parsons	1815	3	614	204.67
William Parsons	1816	6	493	82.17
William Parsons		42	5444	129.62

APPENDIX 2   Shipbuilder Production 1795-1835

Shipbuilder	Year	No. Carp Cert Issued	Total Tons	Average Tonnage
Charles/Joseph Pearce	1798	1	25	25.00
Charles/Joseph Pearce	1803	1	53	53.00
Charles/Joseph Pearce	1815	1	33	33.00
Charles/Joseph Pearce	1819	1	17	17.00
Charles/Joseph Pearce		4	128	32.00
John Price	1809	1	198	198.00
John Price	1811	1	368	368.00
John Price	1812	6	1334	222.33
John Price	1813	2	143	71.50
John Price	1815	4	798	199.50
John Price	1816	1	70	70.00
John Price	1817	1	75	75.00
John Price	1820	2	120	60.00
John Price	1821	1	90	90.00
John Price		19	3196	168.21
William Price	1798	1	134	134.00
William Price	1803	1	126	126.00
William Price	1805	2	460	230.00
William Price	1806	1	318	318.00
William Price	1807	5	648	129.60
William Price	1808	1	236	236.00
William Price	1809	3	651	217.00
William Price	1810	1	338	338.00
William Price	1811	3	1619	539.67
William Price	1812	4	902	225.50
William Price	1813	4	727	181.75
William Price	1815	1	419	419.00
William Price	1816	2	685	342.50
William Price	1817	2	418	209.00
William Price	1819	3	375	125.00
William Price	1820	1	178	178.00

APPENDIX 2   Shipbuilder Production 1795-1835

Shipbuilder	Year	No. Carp Cert Issued	Total Tons	Average Tonnage
William Price	1821	1	129	129.00
William Price	1822	4	428	107.00
William Price	1823	5	763	152.60
William Price	1824	5	496	99.20
William Price	1825	2	170	85.00
William Price	1826	2	546	273.00
William Price	1828	1	105	105.00
William Price	1831	2	393	196.50
William Price		57	11264	197.61
William Price & Son	1832	2	388	194.00
William Price & Son	1833	2	421	210.50
William Price & Son	1834	1	156	156.00
William Price & Son	1835	2	378	189.00
William Price & Son		7	1343	191.86
Levi/Israel Riggin	1818	1	493	493.00
Levi/Israel Riggin	1819	1	54	54.00
Levi/Israel Riggin	1821	1	106	106.00
Levi/Israel Riggin	1822	1	39	39.00
Levi/Israel Riggin	1824	1	54	54.00
Levi/Israel Riggin	1825	1	124	124.00
Levi/Israel Riggin	1832	2	241	120.50
Levi/Israel Riggin	1833	1	235	235.00
Levi/Israel Riggin	1834	2	412	206.00
Levi/Israel Riggin		11	1758	159.82
Robb & Donaldson	1829	1	74	74.00
Robb & Donaldson	1830	2	518	259.00
Robb & Donaldson	1832	3	932	310.67
Robb & Donaldson	1833	1	265	265.00
John Robb	1834	3	641	213.67
John Robb	1835	3	770	256.67

APPENDIX 2   Shipbuilder Production   1795-1835

Shipbuilder	Year	No. Carp Cert Issued	Total Tons	Average Tonnage
Robb & Donaldson		13	3200	246.15
Robson & Denny	1814	1	143	143.00
Robson & Denny	1815	1	35	35.00
Robson & Denny	1816	1	152	152.00
Robson & Denny		3	330	110.00
Bernard Salenaves	1811	1	202	202.00
Bernard Salenaves	1812	2	504	252.00
Bernard Salenaves	1813	1	332	332.00
Bernard Salenaves	1814	1	241	241.00
Bernard Salenaves		5	1279	255.80
William Skinner	1828	2	96	48.00
William Skinner	1829	1	90	90.00
William Skinner	1830	3	299	99.67
William Skinner	1831	1	59	59.00
William Skinner	1832	2	532	266.00
Zachariah Skinner	1833	1	89	89.00
William & Zachariah Skinner		10	1165	116.50
Alexander Stephens	1830	1	48	48.00
Alexander Stephens	1831	1	49	49.00
Alexander Stephens	1832	2	162	81.00
Alexander Stephens	1834	1	37	37.00
Alexander Stephens		5	296	59.20
Joseph Turner	1812	1	111	111.00
Joseph Turner	1813	2	406	203.00
Joseph Turner	1815	1	94	94.00
Joseph Turner	1816	1	64	64.00
Joseph Turner	1817	2	136	68.00
Joseph Turner	1821	1	41	41.00

APPENDIX 2   Shipbuilder Production   1795-1835

Shipbuilder	Year	No. Carp Cert Issued	Total Tons	Average Tonnage
Joseph Turner	1822	2	183	91.50
Joseph Turner	1823	1	65	65.00
Joseph Turner	1824	1	88	88.00
Joseph Turner	1825	1	93	93.00
Joseph Turner	1826	1	215	215.00
Joseph Turner	1827	3	282	94.00
Joseph Turner		17	1778	104.59
Lemuel Taylor	1817	3	156	52.00
Turner & Taylor	1819	2	147	73.50
Lemuel Taylor	1821	3	362	120.67
Turner & Taylor		8	665	83.13
Joshua Wills	1805	2	195	97.50
Joshua Wills	1806	1	119	119.00
Joshua Wills	1807	1	126	126.00
Joshua Wills	1809	1	34	34.00
Joshua Wills		5	474	94.80
Miscellaneous Yards		42	4139	98.55
GRAND TOTAL		585	88151	150.69
shbuild.wk4				

APPENDIX 3
Documents Relating to the *Hannibal*

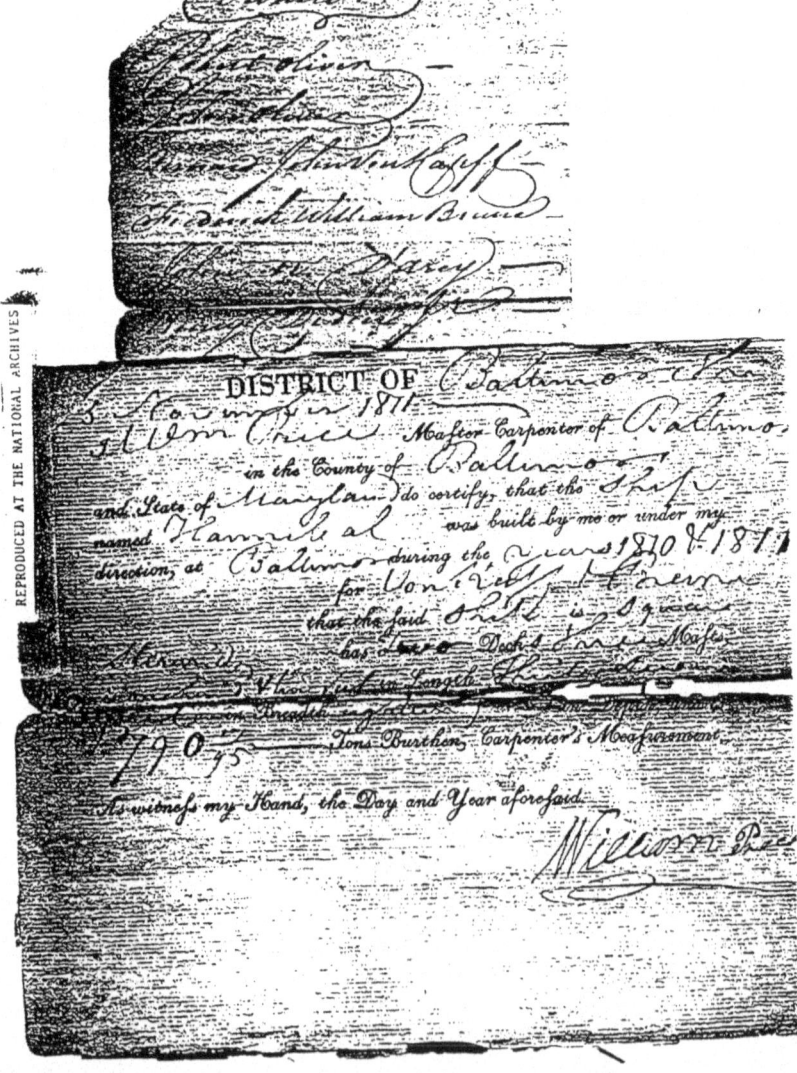

APPENDIX 3
Documents Relating to the *Hannibal*

[Newspaper clipping: Commercial Daily Advertiser, Baltimore, Saturday, July 6. Published daily by Chin & G. Dobbin & Murphy, No. 4, Harrison-Street.]

SALE BY AUCTION

THIS DAY

6 July inst. at 3 o'clock in the afternoon, at No. 95, North Howard st. will be sold by auction—by virtue of a Deed of trust, to satisfy the claims of creditors,

A variety of Groceries,

an extensive assortment of LIVERPOOL WARE.

W. G. HANDS & Co. Auct'rs

SALE BY AUCTION

The remarkably fine SHIP,

fit by Mr. Wm. Price, Fell's Point, that offered at auction the 21st instant, and is off to a gentleman, for the use of the rietors, or agents of the said ship, but instance no renders it necessary the of the said ship should take place, and THIS DAY, the 6th day of July, at clock, precisely, at Mr. Price's wharf Point

will positively be sold without reserve for the purpose of closing the concern. It is allowed by the best of judges to be a handsome and well finished ship, and her model. It is supposed will be a very sailer. She is corvette built, pierced 6 guns, burthen 850 tons, is 136 ft. 6 in. deck and 27 ft. 8 in. in breadth, is coppered fastened to the bends, and coppered to water line mark.

n inventory of her materials (which is complete) may be seen at the Vendue in Frederick street; and capt. Bess show the ship, now at Price's wharf, those who wish to view her previous to sale.

THOS. CHASE Auct'r

SALE BY AUCTION

Immediately after the sale of the large new ship at Mr. W. Price's wharf, F. Point,

THIS DAY at 11 o'clock

The Brig WANDERER,

with all her materials, will be offered at auction at said wharf—burthen about tons; a faithful built vessel and sails —Terms will be made known, and an

---

Just received and for Sale by

J. M. FISSOUX,

No. 5, Light st.

5000 pieces plain and Madras Bandana Ribbon, from No. 2 to No. 7.

100 lbs. sewing Silk, assorted

Plaid and black Mantua

Coloured hdkfs. and 6-4 silk Shawls

Black Florentine Canton Crape, Mens and Womens Gloves, Ladies black silk Stockings, Coloured Galoons, Silk Cords, White and coloured Satin, White Mantua figured Silk and Satin, two boxes cotton Laces, &c. and one box Platillas, one bale E. India Hhkfs. fit for the W. India Market. *also on hand*,

Black Crape, black & white Lace Veils, Hhkfs. &c. Madras do. Black Galloons, Shoe and Hat Bindings, &c.

June 13   d61 tothst21

TWO NEW COACHEES FOR SALE.

Enquire at Mr. John Finley's Paint shop, Frederick st. opposite Gen. Ridgely's dwelling.

June 27   thstnttf

Pocket Book Lost, or Stolen.

Yesterday morning about 6 o'clock, supposed to be in the Marsh Market, a red morocco Pocket Book, containing bank notes to the amount of about 225 dollars, one of them a fifty dollar note of the Bank of Lancaster, and some small notes of that and other Banks, not recollected; with sundry notes of hand, payable to the owner, one of which is drawn by James M'Ivey, for seven dollars and some cents, dated 4th April, $10, payable in six months after date. Also a note drawn by Patrick M'Gouldrick for 30 or thereabouts, and sundry other notes and papers, useful only to the owner.

Twenty five Dollars will be paid for the Pocket Book, Money & Papers, or a proportionable reward for whatever part may be restored. Apply at this office, or Hennaw's tavern, Old Town.

July 4   dtf

Cotton, Copper, Coffee, &c.

New Orleans Cotton
Flotant Indigo
Carthagena Bark
Cayenne Cocoa
300 boxes Raisins
7 by 9 & 8 by 10 Window Glass
Tin in Boxes
Sheathing Copper, &c

For Sale by   LUKE TIERNAN & Co.

Who will sell on a long credit

300,000 lbs. of COFFEE.

June 28   tmw10tf

JAMES & WILLIAM GLENN,

COMMERCIAL

BALT.

Capt. Tho's Par Sunday next, with Letter bag will be this day.

The brig Robert intended going to C Lord Wellington battle in Portugal was not given in the

On Tuesday last was presented by the President of the U credentials as Envoy ter Plenipotentiary States.

Mr. Monroe secretary of Legation, the Legation.

Orasco Pinson Delegate to Congress Territory by a law

The New York late English gazette minister to this country the most unlimited

An Error—Our last paper to prevent with these words Mr. Foster's arrival that the latter gent irritation" This inserted, being in ville Temple, whe Mr. Foster to the

The anniversary dence has been ce monstrations of jo ferent corps of vo on the morning of parties assembled the day in social aunally select a f ment

Seve At The new mean

Commodore Ro rels encircle the ces insults offered cheers.

The Americans their honourable Liberty and in rica.

A constitution

Notes to Introduction

1. Gary L. Browne. *Baltimore in the Nation*, 1789-1861. Chapel Hill, NC: University of North Carolina, 1980, 4.

2. Jerome R. Garitee. *The Republic's Private Navy*. Middletown, CN: Wesleyan University Press, 1977, 11.

3. Ibid., 19; Browne, 3; Robert G. Albion, *The Rise of New York Port (1815-1860)*. Newton Abbot, GB: David & Charles, 1970, 419.

4. Albion, 377-379.

5. Ibid., 37.

6. Ibid., 37-38.

7. George C. Rogers, Jr. *Charleston in the Age of the Pinckneys*. Columbia: University of South Carolina Press, 1980, 3.

8. Ibid., 138-139.

9. Norman K. Risjord. *Jefferson's America*, 1760-1815. Madison, WI: Madison House Publishers, Inc., 1991, 29.

10. Ibid., 34.

11. Thomas M. Doerflinger. *A Vigorous Spirit of Enterprise*. Chapel Hill: University of North Carolina Press, 1986, 5.

12. RG #41, Carpenter Certificates 1795-1835. National Archives. Ship Carpenter Certificates form the nucleus of original research for this thesis. *Acts of the Second Congress of the United States*, Statute 2, Chapter 1, 1792 established the form and procedure to be used by the Master Carpenters in charge of ship construction in all American shipyards. This record for the Baltimore jurisdiction has been preserved at the National Archives and throws great light on the shipbuilding industry in this period. it describes each ship by name, builder, tonnage, dimensions, style, and in addition, in many instances, lists the name of the person for whom the ship was built.

Notes to Chapter One

1. Warren D. Renninger, "Government Policy in Aid of American Shipbuilding," (Ph.D. dissertation, University of Pennsylvania, 1911), 22.

2. Manufacturers, Communicated to the House of Representitives, 11 April 1789, reprinted in vol 1, *American State Papers (ASP)*, Commerce & Navigation, Finance; reprint ed., (Washington, DC: Gales and Seaton, 1832), 5.

3. John J. McCusker, "The Rise of the Shipping Industry in Colonial America." *America's Maritime Legacy*, Robert A. Kilmarx, ed. (Boulder, CO: Westview Press, 1979), 4-5.

4. *ASP*, Commerce & Navigation, 1:5-6. Charleston's letter was dated April 13, New York's April 18, Philadelphia's May 25 and Boston's June 5, all 1789.

5. A G Kenwood & A. L. Lougheed, *The Growth of the International Economy 1820-1990*, 3rd ed., (New York: Routledge, 1992), 3.

6. Doerflinger, 265.

7. Renninger, 16.

8. Ibid., 20.

9. Ibid., 18.

10. Jerome R. Garitee, *The Republic's Private Navy*, (Middletown, CN: Wesleyan University Press, 1977), 20.

11. Risjord, 30.

Notes to Chapter One

12. Garret Power, "Parceling Out Land in Baltimore 1632-1815," *Maryland Historical Magazine*, 87(1992):453-66, 88(1993):151-80, 156, 162.

13. Risjord, 17-21.

14. McCusker, 11.

15. Ibid, 17; John G. B. Hutchins, *The American Maritime Industries and Public Policy, 1789-1914*, reissue. (New York: Russell & Russell, 1969), 171, 175, 177.

16. Mary Beth Norton and others. *A People & A Nation*, 3rd ed. Princeton, NJ: Houghton Mifflin Co., 1990, 1:195.

17. Hutchins, 248.

18. *ASP*, Finance 1:9.

19. *Public Statutes at Large of the United States of America, 1789-1845*, Richard Peters, ed. 1:24 (1789).

20. *Registry and Enrollment Act*, 1 STAT. 55 (1789).

21. 1 U. S. Statute 24 (1789); 1 U. S. Statute 27 (1789); 1 U. S. Statute 135 (1789); U. S. Statute 180 (1790).

22. Hutchins, 250, 254.

23. Session 2, Chapter 1, Section 8, December 31, 1792.

24. Hutchins, 185, 250.

25. McCusker, 4-5.

Notes to Chapter One

26. C. Joseph Pusateri, *A History of American Business*, (Arlington Heights, IL: Harlan Davidson, Inc., 1988), 97.

27. Norton, 195.

28. *Maryland State Government & Council* (Proceedings), August 6, 1793, Maryland State Archives: S 1071-28, MdHR:85L, 255.

29. William Stinchcombe, *The XYZ Affair*, (Westport, CN: Greenwood Press, 1980), 7.

30. Ibid, 14.

31. Alexander DeConde, *The Quasi-War*, (New York: Charles Scribner's Sons, 1966), 124.

32. Michael A. Palmer, *Stoddert's War: Naval Operations During the Quasi-War with France, 1798-1802*, (Columbia, SC: University of South Carolina Press, 1987), 53.

33. Ibid., 125.

34. Ibid., 53.

35. Ibid., 128.

36. Ibid., 239.

37. Howard I. Chapelle, *The History of the American Sailing Navy*, (New York: W. W. Norton & Co., 1949), 180.

38. Baltimore *Maryland Gazette*, 5 August 1784, 2:2.

39. Risjord, 251.

Notes to Chapter One

40. Although this was a minor incident, as wars go, it should have alerted Congress to the fact that a strong and diverse navy was a most vital component of America's foreign policy. The message went unheeded, however. Only seven years later, the American Navy was again to find itself drastically outgunned.

41. K. Jack Bauer, "The Golden Age," *America's Maritime Legacy*, ed. Robert A. Kilmarx, (Boulder, CO: Westview Press, 1979), 32.

42. Norton, 223.

43. *ASP*, Gales & Seaton, 623.

44. U.S. Bureau of the Census, *Historical Statistics of the United States, 1780-1945*, supplement, Washington, D.C., 1949, 211; Hutchins, 186. "[C]onstruction rose from 77,921 gross tons in 1799 to 124,755 gross tons in 1801, and then receded to 88,448 gross tons in 1803. Then it rose again, after the resumption of war, to 128,507 gross tons in 1805, and then collapsed to 31,755 gross tons in 1808, when the embargo seriously injured shipping. Output again revived after the resumption of commerce, reaching 146,691 gross tons in 1811, a particularly active year, but receded after the outbreak of war to 32, 583 gross tons in 1813."

45. Bauer, 33-4

46. *ASP*, Gales & Seaton, 727.

47. Ibid., 873.

48. Ibid., 744-5.

Notes to Chapter One

49. Bauer, 33-4.

50. Risjord, 265.

51. Norton, 38.

52. T. Harry Williams, *The History of American Wars from 1745 to 1918*, (New York: Alfred A. Knopf, 1981), 97.

53. Garitee, 239.

54. Ibid.

55. Ibid, 243-4.

56. *Maryland Gazette*, 25 December 1783, 1:1.

57. Albion, 38.

58. Ibid., 47.

59. Ibid.

60. Ibid., 53.

61. Ibid.

62. Ibid., 92.

63. Bruce Laurie, *Working People of Philadelphia, 1800-1850*, (Philadelphia: Temple University Press, 1980), 10.

64. Helen L. Sumner, *History of Women in Industry in the United States*, reprint, 1974, (New York: Orno Press, 1910), 50.

Notes to Chapter One

65. Victor S. Clark, *History of Manufactures in the United States*, 3 vols., (New York: McGraw-Hill Book Co., 1929), p. 276.

66. Ibid., 566.

67. Ibid., 560-567.

68. Norton, 235.

69. Hutchins, 253.

70. Richard L. Bushman, "Family Security in the Transition From Farm to City, 1750-1850." *Journal of Family History* (Fall, 1981): 238-245.

71. Doerflinger, 342.

72. Howard I. Chapelle, *The Baltimore Clipper*, reprint, (Mineola, NY: Dover Publications, Inc., 1988), 107.

Notes to Chapter Two

1. Laurie, 6.

2. Hamilton Owens, *Baltimore on the Chesapeake*. Garden City, (NY: Doubleday, Doran & Company, Inc., 1941), 128-129.

3. Garitee, *Republic's Private Navy*, 240.

4. Ibid., 241.

5. Ibid., 240-242. The quotes in this paragraph and the one above are both cited from this author's exhaustive and complete study of the period and the private armed vessel force.

6. Carpenter Certificates; Brewington File, Maritime Finding Aid; Maryland Historical Society. It must be noted that several factors impinge on the interpretation of the shipbuilding statistics, particularly these early years. For example, there are no Carpenter Certificates in these files for the years 1800 and 1829. To supplement this lack in these years, in fact several years, the Brewington Compilation has been used; on these records the shipbuiler's name appears in italics. It is also probable that between 1797 and 1807, the record-keeping improved thus influencing the number of ships recorded. However, since these records, imperfect as they may be, are all that have survived, this thesis will use them as general indicators of trends throughout the period 1795-1835, with the exception listed below, will accept these records as complete (see Appendix 1.2). Another factor that must be considered is that these records cover commercial vessels only, and that a decline in production in a war year may indicate that shipyards were turned to the production of naval vessels instead of their regular commercial production. For example, the period 1797-1801, there is record of at least three Baltimore shipyards involved in the war effort, with consequent reduction in manufacture of commercial vessel..

7. Doerflinger, 101.

8. Ibid., 117.

Notes to Chapter Two

9. Baltimore *American*, 3 June 1799.

10. Chapell, *American Sailing Navy*, 146, 188, 197, 205, 212.

11. Pusateri, 98.

12. J. Thomas Scharf, *History of Baltimore City and County, Maryland*, (Baltimore: Regional Publishing Company), 1:375-376.

13. Bauer, 32, 38.

14. Ibid., 55-57.

15. Browne, 70-89. Chapter IV of this book, "Economic Crisis & New Directions 1815-1831" is a thorough study of this postwar period, presenting a comprehensive overview of local and national economic problems in this period.

16. Doerflinger, 341.

17. James V. Crotty, *Baltimore Immigration 1790-1830: With Special Reference to Its German, Irish and French Phases*. (MA Thesis, Catholic University, Washington, D.C.,1951), 57.

18. Ibid., 1-3.

19. Ralph Clayton, *Slavery, Slaveholding, and the Free Black Population of Antebellum Baltimore*. (Bowie, MD: Heritage Books, Inc., 1993), 57.

20. Ibid., *Slavery*, 1-2, 209-250.

21. Ibid., 57-58.

22. Frederick Douglass, *Narrative of The Life of Frederick Douglass, An American Slave*. (New York: Penguin Books, reprint 1982), 71.

Notes to Chapter Two

23. Ibid., 75.

24. Ibid., 78.

25. Ibid., 79.

26. Ibid., 131-132.

27. Clayton, *Black Baltimore: 1820-1870*. (Bowie, MD: Heritage Books, 1987), 2.

28. U. S. Census Reports 1790-1840.

29. Eugene Fauntleroy Cordell, *The Medical Annals of Maryland: 1799-1899*. (Baltimore: The Medical & Chirurgical Faculty of the University of Maryland, 1903), 36, 64, 669, 694; J. Thomas Scharf, *History of Baltimore City and County*. (Baltimore: Regional Publishing Company, 1971), 187; Wilbur Franklin Coyle, *The Mayors of Baltimore*. (Baltimore: Baltimore Municipal Journal, 1919), 23-4.

30. Browne, p. 86.

Notes to Chapter Three

1. According to Quentin Snediker & Ann Jensen in *Chesapeake Bay Schooners* (Centreville, MD: Tidewater Publishers, 1992), 239-244, a brig is defined as a "two-masted, square-rigged vessel" and a schooner as a "fore- and aft-rigged vessel with two or more masts and gaffsails." A ship is a "type of large, oceangoing sailing vessel, square-rigged with three or more masts" and a sloop is a "single master fore- and aft-rigged vessel." The term rigging is a "collective term for masts, spars, sails, shrouds, stays, and other equipment." A mast is defined as a "wood or metal pole that supports booms, gaffs, yards, and gear for carrying sails." Although the Carpenter Certificates do include the number of masts on most vessels, the sail configuration is not specifically mentioned by the builder. Thus, if the carpenter says the vessel is a schooner, this thesis presumes that it has fore- and aft-rigging with tow or more masts and gaffsails.

2. Snediker & Jensen, 243.

3. Garitee, 119.

4. M. Florence Bourne, "Thomas Kemp, Shipbuilder, and His Home, Wades Point." *Maryland Historical Magazine*, 49, no. 3 (September 1954), 275.

5. Chapelle, for example in *The Baltimore Clipper* traces the history of the type, from its pre-revolutionary rise to its end, saying: "few of the type were left by 1860." (p. 142). According to the terminology of the carpenters who built these ships, they were schooners, maybe sharp, or pilot boat, or privateer fashion, but schooners, nevertheless. Thus, his study of individual vessels of the type enhances the more statistical and general information of this thesis. In fact, his description of the *Hannibal/Andromeda* has filled in the story after she left Baltimore laden with coffee; on the other hand, Jerome Garitee does state in *The Republic's Private Navy* that the term clipper was applied by merchants to schooners in 1812 (p. 115). However, the Oxford English Dictionary, 1971 ed., first cites the word usage in 1830.

Notes to Chapter Three

6. Chapelle, 36.

7. Garitee, 24.

8. Ibid., 129.

9. Ibid, 128.

10. Ibid., 115.

11. Ibid.

12. Ibid., 17; *Naval Documents Related to the Quasi-War between the United States and France, v. 2*, Dudley W.Knox, USN, Ret., ed. (Washington: United States Government Printing Office, 1936)1:181. The bond stipulations accompanying Letters Of Marque were variable. During the Revolution the requirements were $5,000 for vessels under one hundred tons and $10,000 for vessels exceeding this weight. On the other hand, in 1798 during the Quasi War, the requirements were $7,000, or "if such vessel be provided with more than one hundred fifty men, then in the penal sum of fourteen thousand dollars..." For the War of 1812, the bond requirement was adjusted again to five and ten thousand, reflecting the inconvenience that the larger sum would cause an owner of several smaller vessels.

13. Ibid., 91-92.

14. Frederick C. Leiner, "The Subscription Warships of 1798." *The American Neptune*, 1986. 46(3, 1986), 141-158.

15. Leiner, 145.

16. Baltimore *American*, 4 June 1799.

17. Knox, 377.

18. Ibid., 3:159.

Notes to Chapter Three

19. *Dictionary of American Fighting Ships*, v. 4, (Washington: Navy Department, 1969), 224.

20. Ibid., 256.

21. Quentin Snedeker & Ann Jensen, *Chesapeake Bay Schooners*, (Centreville, MD: Tidewater Publishers, 1992), 240.

22. Chapelle, *Baltimore Clipper*, 105.

23. Snedeker & Jensen, 241.

24. Ibid., 16-17.

25. Chapelle, *Baltimore Clipper*, 110, 111; Snediker & Jensen, 32, en., *234*.

26. Snediker & Jensen, 38; M. Florence Bourne, 272.

27. *American*, 20 July 1825.

28. Chapelle, 107-141; Garitee, 228-230.

29. Chapelle, 228.

30. Hutchins, 171-173.

31. Snediker & Jensen, 239.

32. Ibid., 243.

33. Ibid.

34. Baltimore *American & Commercial Daily Advertiser*, 6 July 1811.

35. Chapelle, *Baltimore Clipper*, 78. Also Chapelle has illustrations of the ship's lines, spar plan and hull, 79-81.

Notes to Chapter Three

36. Chancery Court (Chancery Papers) #5188; Thompson, John & James, Henry Davis vs. Bernard I. VonKapff, Frederick W. Brune, William Price, BA Contract to Ship Gunpowder to Santo Domingo, 1811 [MSA S512, MdHR 17,898-5188, 1/37/2/29]. Maryland State Archives.

37. Chapelle, *Baltimore Clipper*, 79-81.

38. Didier Collection: Letterbook; MS 295, Maryland Historic Society, 194-195.

39. Chapelle, *Baltimore Clipper*, 79.

40. Allen Johnson and Dumas Malone, ed. *Dictionary of American Biography.* (New York: Charles Scribner's Sons, 1931), 3:4.

41. Garitee, 235.

42. *Oxford English Dictionary*, 1971 ed., s. v. "Bark, barque"

43. "Petition of George Stiles to the Mayor & City Council of Baltimore," 9 June 1808.

44. Robert J. Brugger, Maryland: A Middle Temperament, (Baltimore: Johns Hopkins University Press, 1988), 144.

Notes to Chapter Four

1. Howard Rock, *Artisans of the New Republic,* (New York: New York University Press, 1979), 155, 158.

2. Browne, 74.

3. Scharf, *History of Baltimore City and County,* 456-457.

4. Ibid, 461.

5. Pusateri, 102.

6. Browne, 78.

7. Raymond A. Mohl, *Poverty in New York 1783-1825*, (New York: Oxford University Press, 1971), 140-141.

8. Scharf, 483.

9. Brugger, 146.

10. Scharf, 246-251.

11. Rock, 252.

12. Ibid., 253.

13. Browne, 49.

14. Mohl, 17.

15. Ibid., 22.

16. Ibid., 28-29.

17. Garitee, 113-114.

18. Scharf, 84, 826.

Notes to Chapter Four

19. Ralph J. Robinson. "Shipbuilding on the Patapsco: Part III - Shipbuilding Comes of Age." *Baltimore*, 50 (June, 1957), 33.

20. Garitee, 45, 200-201.

21. Bourne, 271-289.

22. M Allison Carll, "'Great Neatness of Finish:' Slave Carpenters in South Carolina's Charleston District, 1760-1800," *Southern Studies*, 26(2:1987) 89-100.

23. Ralph Clayton, *Slavery*, 209-250.

24. Baltimore County Registry of Wills (Wills) 14 October 1806, 8:101-102, [MSA WK 1002-3].

25. Ibid., 5 June 1802, 6:552, [MSA WK 1001-02:2].

26. George B. Wilson, *The Descendants of Dr. Lewis DeRochebrune of Queen Anne's County, Maryland.* (Baltimore: George B. Wilson, 1976), 27.

27. J. H. Powell, *Bring Out Your Dead: The Great Plague of Yellow Fever in Philadelphia in 1793*, reprint, (Philadelphia: University of Pennsylvania Press, 1993), 23, 48, 81, 92.

28. Cordell, 669.

29. Cordell, 36, 37, 64-66, 666, 694.

30. Richard Kelley, "A Step Backwards Into the Past", (Baltimore: Center for Urban Archaeology, 1969), 9.

31. Ralph Clayton. *Slavery*, 9.

32. *Baltimore City Directories*, 1796, 1799, 1800, 1810, 1814-15, 1816, 1817-18, 1819.

Sources Consulted

PRIMARY SOURCES

1. Published Documents

American State Papers, Commerce & Navigation, Finance, vols. 1 and 2. *Finance. Documents, Legislative and Executive, Congress.* Washington: Gales and Seaton, 1832.

Annals of Congress. Second Congress. (Debates and Proceedings) Washington D. C.: Gales and Seaton, 1849.

Bauer, K. Jack, ed. *New American State Papers.* Naval Affairs, vol. 1: General Naval Policy and Defense. Wilmington, DE: Scholarly Resources Inc., 1981.

Dictionary of American Fighting Ships, v. 4. Washington, DC: Navy Department, 1969.

Douglass, Frederick. *Life and Times of Frederick Douglass.* New York: Gramercy Books, 1993.

Heads of Families at the First Census of the United States, Maryland, 1790. Baltimore: Southern Book Company, 1952.

Historical Statistics of the United States, 1780-1945, supplement. U. S. Bureau of the Census. Washington, D. C., 1949.

Historical Statistics of the United States, Colonial Times to 1957. U. S. Bureau of the Census. Washington, D. C., 1960.

Historical Statistics of the United States, Colonial Times to 1970, Bicentennial Edition, Parts 1 and 2. U. S. Bureau of the Census. Washington, D.C., 1975.

Hyman, Harold, intro. *The New American State Papers: Labor & Slavery,* v.1. Wilmington, DE: Scholarly Resources Inc., 1973.

Kilty, William, ed. *The Laws of Maryland with Index,* v. 2. Annapolis: Frederick Green, 1800.

Knox, Dudley W., USN Ret., ed. *Naval Documents Related to the Quasi-War between the United States and France,* vol. 2. Washington, D. C.: United States Government Printing Office, 1936.

Lowrie, Walter and Clarke, Matthew St. Clair, eds. *Documents, Legislative and Executive of the Congress of the United States, 1789-1815,* v.7. Washington: Gales and Seaton, 1832.

Matchetts *Baltimore Directory,* 1798-1835. Baltimore: Pratt Library, Maryland Reading Room.

Peters, Richard, ed. *The Public Statutes at Large of the United States of America, 1789-1845,* 4 vols. *Acts of the Second Congress of the United States.* Statute II, Chapter I, 1792. Boston: Little, Brown & company, 1861.

Proceedings & Acts of the General Assembly of Maryland, v 30. Baltimore: Maryland Historical Society, 1910.

Richard Walsh, ed. *Journal and Correspondence of the Council of Maryland* v 10, Journal of the Council 1789-1793. Baltimore: Maryland Historical Society, 1972.

U. S. Congress, Senate. Bureau of Labor's Report on condition of Woman and Child Wage Earners in the U. S.., and, in series, Document #645, 61st Congress, 2nd Session, vol. 9 of 19. "History of Women in Industry in the United States," by Helen L. Sumner. Washington, D.C.: GPO, 1910. New York: Orno Press, 1910.

2. Government Documents and Correspondence

United States National Archives. Washington, DC.
    "Index to Letters from Collectors of Customs 1812-1815", Entry 389, 4, 590-688.
    Bureau of Navigation Files, RG 41. "Master Carpenter Certificates 1790-1835."
    Registry and Enrollment Act, 1 STAT, 55 (1789).

Maryland State Archives. Annapolis, Maryland
    "Communication from Secretary of War Henry Knox," 6 August 1793.
    "Contract to Ship Gunpowder to Santo Domingo." Chancery Court (Chancery Papers) #5188.
    Maryland State Government and Council (Proceedings) 1791-1793.
    Baltimore County Court (Land Records).
    Baltimore County Register of Wills (Wills)
    Baltimore County Register of Wills (Inventory)

Baltimore City Hall Records. Baltimore, Maryland.
    Tax Records, 1798. City Archives.
    Small, Jacob. "Survey & Chart of that part of the Harbour....," 18 February 1828. Baltimore City: Planning & Records Department.
    Stiles, George. Petition "To the Mayor & City Council of Baltimore," 9 June 1808. Baltimore City: Planning & Records Department.

3. Manuscript Collections

Maryland Historical Society. Baltimore, Maryland.
    Baltimore Port Entries 1784, 1799, 1804, 1809, 1815, 1819, MS 2301.
    "Bill of Sale for Schooner 'Infant Patriot'," 12 September 1794. MS 1809.

Bureau of Customs. Record of the Collector of Customs at Baltimore: Entrances and Clearances, 1799; MS 2301.
Census of the United States, 1790, 1800, 1810, 1820, 1830, 1840, 1850.
Didier Collection: "Letterbook." MS 295.
Diehlman-Hayward File.
Registered Tonnage 1789-1810, MS 2301.
Registry of Vessels/Port of Baltimore 1799-1811, MS 2301.
St. Paul's P.E. Church Records, Norris Harris Church Register File #27.
Wilkens File. Archives of Baltimore City: Burial Records.

Center for Urban Archaeology
Kelley, Richard. "A Step Backwards into the Past." Baltimore: Center for Urban Archaeology (18BC2), 1969.

4. *Newspapers*
Baltimore *American.*
Baltimore *American & Commercial Daily Advertiser.*
Baltimore *Federal Gazette & Baltimore Daily Advertiser.*
Baltimore *Maryland Gazette.*

5. *Miscellaneous*
Dictionary of American Fighting Ships, v. 4. Washington: Navy Department, 1969.
Johnson, Allen and Malone, Dumas, eds. *Dictionary of American Biography.* New York: Charles Scribner's Sons, 1931.
Oxford English Dictionary. 1979 ed.

SECONDARY SOURCES

1. Books

Albion, Robert Greenhalgh. *Square-Riggers on Schedule*, reprint. London: Oxford University Press, 1938. Hamden, CN: Archon Books, 1965.
??????. *The Rise of New York Port (1815-1860)*. New York: Charles Scribner's Sons, 1939; reprint ed., Newton Abbott, GB: David & Charles, 1970.

Arnold, Joseph L. *Maryland: Old Line to New Prosperity*. Northridge, CA: Windsor Publications, 1985.

Beirne, Francis F. *The Amiable Baltimoreans*. Baltimore: The Johns Hopkins University Press, 1951.

Bishop, J. Leander. *A History of Manufactures from 1608-1860*. Philadelphia: Edward Young & Co., 1868.

Blackmar, Elizabeth. *Manhattan for Rent 1785-1850*. Ithaca, NY: Cornell University, 1989.

Briggs, L. Vernon. *History of Shipbuilding on North River*. Boston: Coburn Brothers, 1889. New York: Research Reprints Inc., 1970, reprint.

Browne, Gary Lawson. *Baltimore in the Nation 1789-1861*. Chapel Hill: University of North Carolina Press, 1980.

Brugger, Robert J. *Maryland, A Middle Temperment, 1634-1980*. Baltimore: The Johns Hopkins University Press, 1988.

Chapelle, Howard I. *The History of the American Sailing Navy: The Ships and Their Development*. New York: W. W. Norton & Company, 1949.
??????. *The History of American Sailing Ships*. New York: W. W. Norton & Co., Inc., 1935.

_____. *The Baltimore Clipper*. Salem, Mass: Marine Research Society, 1930. Mineola, NY: Dover Publications, Inc., 1988, reprint.

Clayton, Ralph. *Slavery, Slaveholding, and the Free Black Population of Antebellum Baltimore*. Bowie, Maryland: Heritage Books, Inc., 1993.
_____. *Black Baltimore: 1820-1870*. Bowie, MD: Heritage Books, 1987.

Cordell, Eugene Fauntleroy, preparer. *The Medical Annals of Maryland, 1799-1899*. Baltimore: The Medical & Chirurgical Faculty of the University of Maryland, 1903.

Coyle, William Franklin. *The Mayors of Baltimore*. Baltimore: Baltimore Municipal Journal, 1919.

Crotty, James V. *Baltimore Immigration 1790-1830: With Special Reference to Its German, Irish and French Phases*. Washington, D. C.: Catholic University, MA Thesis, 1951.

Davis, David Brion. *Revolutions: Reflections on American Equality and Foreign Liberations*. Cambridge, MA: Harvard University Press, 1990.

DeConde, Alexander. *The Quasi-War*. New York: Charles Scribner's Sons, 1966.

Doerflinger, Thomas M. *A Vigorous Spirit of Enterprise*. Chapel Hill: University of North Carolina Press, 1986.

Garitee, Jerome R. "Private Enterprise and Public Spirit". Washington: The American University, Doctoral Dissertation, 1973.
_____. *The Republic's Private Navy*. Middletown, CN: Wesleyan University Press, 1977.

Goldin, Claudia Dale. *Urban Slavery in the American South 1820-1860*. Chicago: University of Chicago Press, 1976.

Hahn, Harold M. *The Colonial Schooner 1763-1775*. Annapolis, MD: Naval Institute Press, 1981.

Hall, Clayton Colman. *Baltimore: Its History and Its People*. New York: Lewis Historical Publishing Company, 1912.

Hutchins, John G. B. *The American Maritime Industries and Public Policy, 1789-1914*, reissue. New York: Russell & Russell, 1969.

Jordan, Winthrop D. *White Over Black*. Chapel Hill: University of North Carolina, 1968.

Kenwood, A. G. & A. L Lougheed. *The Growth of the International Economy 1820-1990*, 3rd ed. New York: Routledge, 1992.

Laurie, Bruce. *Working People of Philadelphia, 1800-1850*. Philadelphia: Temple University Press, 1980.

Lord, Walter. *The Dawn's Early Light*. New York: W.W. Norton & Company, Inc., 1972.

MacGregor, David R. *Schooners in Four Centuries*. Annapolis, MD: Naval Institute Press, 1982.

McKay, Richard C. *South Street: A Maritime History of New York*. New York: G. P. Putnam's Sons, 1934.

Mayer, Henry. *A Son of Thunder*. Charlottesville: University Press of Virginia, 1991.

Mohl, Raymond A. *Poverty in New York 1783-1825*. New York: Oxford University Press, 1971.

Monkkonen, Eric H. *America Becomes Urban: The Development of U.S. Cities & Towns 1780-1980.* Berkeley: University of California Press, 1988.

Nettels, Curtis P. *The Emergence of a National Economy 1775-1815*, v.2, (The Economic History of the U. S.). New York: Holt, Rinehart and Winston, 1962.

Norton, Mary Beth, et al. *A People and A Nation*, 3rd ed., vol. 1. Boston: Houghton Mifflin Company, 1990.

Owens, Hamilton. *Baltimore on the Chesapeake.* Garden City, NY: Doubleday, Doran & Company, Inc., 1941.

Palmer, Michael J. *Stoddert's War.* Columbia: University of North Carolina Press, 1987.

Powell, J. H. *Bring Out Your Dead: The Great Plague of Yellow Fever in Philadelphia in 1793.* Philadelphia, University of Pennsylvania Press, 1949. Philadelphia: University of Pennsylvania Press, 1993, reprint.

Pusateri, C. Joseph. *A History of American Business.* Arlington Heights, IL: Harlan Davidson, Inc., 1988.

Renninger, Warren D. "Government Policy in Aid of American Shipbuilding." Doctoral Thesis, University of Pennsylvania, 1991.

Risjord, Norman K. *Jefferson's America 1760-1815.* Madison, WI: Madison House Publishers, Inc., 1991.

Rock, Howard. *Artisans of the New Republic.* New York: New York University Press, 1979.

Rogers, George C., Jr. *Charleston in the Age of the Pinckneys.* Columbia: University of South Carolina Press, 1980.

Rothman, David J. *The Discovery of the Asylum: Social Order and Disorder in the New Republic.* Boston: Little, Brown and Company, 1971.

Rubin, Lester. *The Racial Policies of American Industry, Report #17: The Negro in the Shipbuilding Industry.* Philadelphia: University of Pennsylvania Press, 1970.

Rukert, Norman G. *Federal Hill, a Baltimore National Historic District.* Baltimore: Bodine & Associates, Inc., 1980.

Scharf, J. Thomas. *History of Baltimore City and County, Maryland.* Baltimore: Regional Publishing Company, 1971.
_____. *History of Philadelphia, 1609-1884.* Philadelphia: L.H. Everts & Co., 1884.

Snediker, Quentin & Ann Jensen. *Chesapeake Bay Schooners.* Centreville, Maryland: Tidewater Publishers, 1992.

Stinchcombe, William. *The XYZ Affair.* Westport, Connecticut: Greenwood Press, 1980.

Stoddard, T. Lothrop. *The French Revolution in San Domingo.* New York: Houghton & Mifflin Company, 1914.

Stone, Lawrence. *The Past and the Present.* Boston: Routledge & Kegan Paul, 1981.

Tryon, Rolla Milton. *Household Manufactures in the United States, 1640-1860.* New York: Sentry Press, 1917. New York: Augustus M. Kelley - Publishers, 1966, reprint.

Wade, Richard C., ed. *The Negro in American Life.* Boston: Houghton Mifflin Company, 1965.
_____. *Slavery in the Cities: The South 1820-1860.* New York: Oxford University Press, 1964.

Warner, Sam Bass. *Streetcar Suburbs, The Process of Growth in Boston (1870-1900).* Cambridge: Harvard University Press, 1978.

Warren, Marion E. *Baltimore: When She Was What She Used to Be, 1850-1930.* Baltimore: The Johns Hopkins University Press, 1983.

Weinberg, Meyer. *America's Economic Heritage.* Westport, CN: Greenwood Press, 1983.

Williams, T. Harry. *The History of American Wars from 1745 to 1918.* New York: Alfred A. Knopf, 1981.

Wills, Garry. *Cincinnatus: George Washington and the Enlightenment.* Garden City, NY: Doubleday & Company, Inc., 1984.

2. *Journals*

Maryland Historical Magazine

Bourne, M. Florence. "Thomas Kemp, Shipbuilder, and His Home, Wades Point." v. 49, no. 3 (September 1954).

Gilbert Geoffrey. "The Ships of Federalist Baltimore: A Statistical Profile." v 79, no. 4, Winter, 1984, 314-318.

Hartridge, Walter Charleton. "The Refugees from the Island of St. Domingo in Maryland," v. 38 (June, 1943) 2:103-122.

Kilbourne, John D. "The Society of the Cincinnati of Maryland: Its First One Hundred Years, 1783-1883," v. 78, (Fall,1983), 3:169-185.

McGrain, John W. "English Consul and the Labyrinth of Local Record," v. 84, Spring, 1989, 57-72.

Power, Garret. "Parceling Out Land in Baltimore 1632-1815." v. 87(1992):453-66, 88(1993):151-80, 156, 162.

Roberts, Emerson B. "Among the Meeters at the Bayside," v.39, Winter, 1944, 335-344.

_____. "A Visitation of Western Talbot," v. 41, Fall, 1946, 235-245.

Sharrer, G. Terry. "Flour Milling in the Growth of Baltimore, 1750-1830," v. 71 (Fall, 1976) 3:322-333.

Sheads, Scott S. "Defending Baltimore in the War of 1812: Two Sidelights," v. 84, (Fall 1989), 252-258.

3. *Miscellaneous Journals*

Abbott, Carl. "The Neighborhoods of New York, 1760-1775." *New York History* 55 (January 1974).

Bauer, K. Jack. "The Golden Age." *America's Maritime Legacy: A History of the U. S. Merchant Marine and Shipbuilding Industry Since Colonial Times*, Robert A. Kilmarx, ed. Boulder, CO: Westview Press, 1979, 27-63.

Bushman, Richard L. "Family Security in the Transition from Farm to City, 1750-1850." *Journal of Family History*, Fall, 1981, 238-245.

Carll, M. Allison. "Great Neatness of Finish: Slave Carpenters in South Carolina's Charleston District, 1760-1800." *Southern Studies*, v 26(2), 1987, 89-100.

Clark, Victor S. "Textiles." *History of Manufactures in the U. S*, v. 3. New York: McGraw-Hill Book Company, 1929.

Gilbert, Geoffrey. "Baltimore's Flour Trade to the Caribbean, 1750-1815." *Journal of Economic History*, v. 37, 1977: 249-251.

Leiner, Frederick C. "The Subscription Warships of 1798." American Neptune, 46 (Summer, 1986), 141-158.

McCusker, John J. "The Rise of the Shipping Industry in Colonial America." *America's Maritime Legacy: A History of the U. S. Merchant Marine and Shipbuilding Industry Since Colonial Times*, Robert A. Kilmarx, ed. Boulder, CO: Westview Press, 1979, pp. 1-25.

Montgomery, David. "The Working Classes of the Pre-Industrial American City, 1780-1830." *Labor History*, 9 (Winter 1968):3-22.

Robinson, Ralph J. "Shipbuilding on the Patapsco: Part 3 — Shipbuilding Comes of Age." *Baltimore*, 50 (June, 1957).

Sharrer, G. Terry. "The Merchant Millers: Baltimore's Flour Milling Industry, 1783-1860. *Agricultural History Journal,* 56 (1982), 138-150.

Index

ACT, Embargo 22 Non-importation 22 Non-intercourse (1808) 23 Navigation (1817) 34 Reciprocity 34
ADAMS, 19 John 16 115 President 76
ADMIRALTY, Court 72
AGRICULTURE, Subsistence 6
ALABAMA, Westward Movement Of Cotton To 31
ALBEMARLE, Street 101
ALICEANNA, Street 101
ALLENDER, Dr 108-109 Dr Joseph 63 Eliza Ann 108 Joseph 98 108
ALLIANCE, French-American [1778] 15
ALLISANNA, Street East 78
AMERICA, 2
AMERICAN, Colonies 7 Congress 9 Navy 8 Revolution 39 72
"ANDROMEDA", Vessels 86-87
"ANN LOUISA", Vessels 89
"ANN MCKIM", Vessels 86-88
ANN, Street 62-63 113
ANNAPOLIS, 40 102 113
ANNE ARUNDEL, County 78 102
"ANTELOPE" (registered as "SURPRISE") 88 Steamboat 88 103
APPRENTICESHIP, 13
ARMY, American 33
ARTICLES OF CONFEDERATION, 3
ARTISAN, Slaves 93
ARTISANS, 93 97 115 Free Black 108 New 93
ASSISTANCE SOCIETY, 97
ATHENIAN SOCIETY, 96
AULD, 60 Household 59 Hugh 58 105 107 111-112 Sophie 58
BAILEY, & Dorgin 66 82
BALL, James 107
"BALTIMORE", Vessels 83 88
"BALTIMORE AMERICAN", Newspaper 56
BALTIMORE CITY, 1 3 53 58 72 77 86 88 100 Baltimore Town And Fells Point Became 40
BALTIMORE CLIPPERS, 48 69 89
BALTIMORE, Defense Of 99 Immigration 56 Insurance Company 98 Merchants Of 7 Petitioners 2 Port Of 47 Principio Iron Works 6 Schooner 73 Shipbuilding Industry In 37 Shipment Of Grain 8 Shippers 5 Town 40 53
BALTIMORE'S, Population 54

BALTIMORE'S (Cont.)
  Total Output 48
BALTIMORE CITY COTTON,
  Factory 64
BALTIMORE TOWN, 2
  Establishment As a City In
  1795 8
BANK, Franklin 96 Mechanics' 96
  National Marine 96 Of
  Baltimore 95 Of Baltimore
  Mechanics 96 Of Maryland 94
  Of The United States 95-97
BANKRUPTCIES, 33
BARGEMEN, 100
BARQUES, 65 89
BAY, Chesapeake 27
"BAZIL LAMAR", Vessels 89
BEACHAM, 83 87 James 66 78
  82-83 88-89 94 103
BELT, Ann 62 James Jr 62
BERLIN, Decree 22
BEVIN, Mr 89
BIAYS, James 98 102 James [Ship
  Joiner] 63 Joseph 96
BLACK BALL LINE, 28
BLACKS, Free 56 Slaves 56
BLOCKADE, Britain's 14
BOISLANDRY, R C 102
BORDEAUX, 86
BOSTON, 3 5 30 73 97 113
BOTTLERS, 63
BOTTOMS, Sailing Out Of
  Liverpool And London 12
BOUNTIES, Production Of Naval
  Stores 4
BOYLE, Thomas 104
BREMEN, Direct Trade With 35
BRICKLAYERS, 110
BRITAIN, France Declared War
  On 15
BRITISH, Captains 26
  Commercial Fleet 7

BRITISH (Cont.)
  Deserters 26 Mercantile
  Policies 5 Naval Vessels 37
  Navy 71 Order In Council
  [1783] 4 Royal Navy 27-28 86
  Ban On West Indian Trade 5
  West Indies 3-6
BROADWAY STREET, 96 98
BROOKLYN, Navy Yard 88
BRUNE, 83
BUCHANAN, 70 Francis 108
  James 75 82 102 Philip 108
BURKE STREET, 101
CALHOUN FAMILY, 40
CALIFORNIA, 53
CALVERT STREET, 96
CALVERTON MILLS, 96
CAMPBELL, Archibald 95
CANAL, Erie 31
CAPE OF GOOD HOPE, 53
CAPTAINS, Sea 63
CARGOES, American Capture
  And Sale Of 16
"CAROLINE", Schooner 104
CARPENTER, Certificates 11 44-
  45 65 74 80 Certificates [1807]
  43 Master 48 Master Certificate
  Filed At Customs Office 11
CARPENTERS, 110 Master 80
  101 Ship 59 100
CARTERS, 106
CAULKERS, 100
CAULKING, Ship 59
CENSUS, 1832 Baltimore
  Directory 57 US [1790] 55
CENTRAL AMERICA, Trade
  With 82
CERTIFICATES, Carpenter 65 74
CHAPELLE, 77 86 Howard 76
CHARLES COUNTY, 107
CHARLESTON, 3 30-31
CHASE, Thorndike 96 98 102

"CHASSEUR", 72 104 Schooner 104 116
"CHESAPEAKE", Vessels 74
CHESAPEAKE, Affair 26 Bay 27 45 54
CHRISTOPHE, Henry Ruler Of The New Haitian Republic 83 84
CINCINNATI OHIO, 79 102
CLIPPERS, Baltimore 48 89
CLOTH MILLS, 53
COAST GUARD CUTTERS, 45
COFFEE, Transshipment To European Ports 12
COLE, Thomas 62 98 Thomas [Ship Chandler] 98
COLLINS, Edward [Innkeeper] 62 Peter 62
COLONIES, American 72
COLUMBIA, Direct Trade With 35
COMMERCE, American 34 West Indian 9
"COMMERCIAL DAILY ADVERTISER" 56
COMMERCIAL, Tonnage 42
COMMITTEE, Of Commerce And Manufactures Of PA 22
CONFEDERATION, Articles Of, 1
CONGRESS, 1-3 Of Vienna 45
CONGRESSIONAL, Act Of March 3 1803 19
CONNECTICUT, Mills In 34 Shippers And Shipyards In 4
CONSPIRACY, Unlawful 15
"CONSTELLATION", 73-74 76 87 Vessels 106
CONSTITUTION, 1 39 New 9
CONSUMPTION, 2
COPE, Thomas P 30

CORDERY, James 63 66 78 James [Shipbuilder] 63 Maria 78
CORNER, James 88 103
COTTON, Preferred Material For American Sails 69
COULTER, John 96
COURT OF EQUITY, Baltimore County 79
CROOK, Charles 101 Charles Jr 64
CROTTY, 56
CRUISER, Barbary 20
CUBA, 88
CULLEY & ROGERS, 88
CURACAO, 75-76
CUTTERS, Coast Guard 45 Revenue Marine 18 73 U S Navy 45
D'ARCY, Courtney 84 Mr 86
"DART", Schooner 101
DAVIS, Henry 84 Peter 107
DAWSON, John [Congressman] 76
DECATUR, Stephen 20
DECKER, George 96
DECREE, Berlin 22 Milan 22
DELAWARE, Movement Of Grain 8 River 4
DEPRESSION, Of 1819 95 Postwar 100
DEROCHEBRUNE, 44 107 Louis 45 74 76 83 106-107 Louis [Shipbuilder] 63 Thomas 107
DESCANDE, Andrew 78
DESHON, Christopher 113
DESPAUX, Joseph 104
DIDIER, Edmond 103 Henry 84 Henry Jr 84
DISASTER, Natural 100
DOCK WORKERS, 100
DODGE, Mr 86 Samuel 62

DOUGLASS, Frederick 57-60 105 108 111-112
DRAYMEN, 106
DUKE STREET, 101
DUNAN, L M 101
DUNKIN, Levi 82 Levin H 66
DUTIES, Fixed Rigging 4 Foreign Carpentry Works 4 Import 11 Ready-make Sail 4 Tarred Cordage 4 Tea Shipped From Europe 11 White Rope 4 Yarn 4
EASTERN SHORE, Maryland 54
ECKFORD, Henry 87
ECONOMIC, Policies Napoleon's 16
ECONOMY, American 33
ELLICOTT, Andrew 47 Family 40 John 47 Joseph 47
EMBARGO,
EMBARGO, 23-26 53 55 97 100 Act 22 33 Of 1809 115
ENGLAND, 2-3 42 Iron Ore Demand In 5-6 Rum Shipped 6
ENGLISH, Commericial Interests 4 Navy 6 Seamen 6
ENGLISHMEN, 2
ENOCH PRATT FREE LIBRARY, 56
EPIDEMICS, Yellow Fever 100 109
ERIE CANAL, 31
"EXPERIMENT", Steamboat 88
EXPORTS, Increase Of 37
FARM, Wade's Point 104
FAYETTE STREET, 96
FEDERAL HILL, 102
FEDERALIST PERIOD, 96
FELL, Ann 40 Edward 40 47
FELL STREET, 105
FELLS POINT, 44 53-54 60 62 90 105 107 Fire Companies 98

FELLS POINT (Cont.) First Bank In 96 Growth Of After 1800 60 Harbor At 40 Homes In 109 Real Estate 104 Shipbuilders 46 Shipbuilders In 108 Shipbuilders Of 64 Shipyards Of 64 93 Vessels In 79
FIRE COMPANY, Columbian 98 Deptford 98
FLANNIGAIN, 83 Andrew 78 101-102 William 66 78 82 88 94 96 101-103
FLEET STREET 63 98 105
FLOUR-MILLS, Baltimore 47 53
FORT MCHENRY, 99
FOUNTAIN STREET, 63 105
FOWLER, Margaret 102
FRANCE, 45 Quasi-War With 73
FRANCO-AMERICAN, Relations 14
FRANKLIN BANK, 96
FRAZIER, Mr 89
FREEBLACK, Population 57
FREE BLACKS, 112
FREEBLACKS OCCUPATIONS, Blacksmith 57 Brickmaker 57 Caulker 57 Drayman 57 Laborer 57 Laundress 57 Mariner 57 Porter 57 Sawyer 57 Waiter 57 Washer 57
FREEMEN, 59
FRENCH AND INDIAN WAR, 27
FRENCH, Atlantic Fleet 17 Navigation Act Of 1793 9 Navy 44 Revolution In 1789 39 West Indies 17 West Indies Restricted Trade 15
FRIENDS, Meeting House 102
FROLIC CLASS SHIP-SLOOPS, 87
GALLEGA, Francis 113

GANTEAUME, James 113 Julie Claire 113
GARDNER, 83 104 & Robson 66 George 66 69 82 88 94 103-105 Mr 60 William 103 107 William Shipbuilder 59
GARDNER'S, Yard 112
GARITEE, 94 Jerome R 27
GAUDROY, 89
GAY, Street 96
GEDDES, Captain Henry 74
GENERAL, Assembly Maryland's 97-98
GENET, Citizen 15 Citizen Edmond 14
GEORGE, & Wolfe Streets Intersection Of 79 Street 62-63 113
GLAGHORN, 88
GOODS, American 34 American-made 32 European-made 32
GOVERNOR, Of Maryland 14-15
GRAIN, And Cotton Markets For 30 Increased Production In Pennsylvania 12 Increased Production In Western Maryland 12 Maryland Export Of 12
GREAT, Britain Britain Britain
GREAT BRITAIN, 2-3 6 32 44 71 84 Competition With 33 Treaty With 34
GREEN, Tom 108
GUESTIER, G A Ship Broker 78
GUIANA, French 76
GUNBOATS, Jeffersonian 70
GWYNN, William 96
HAITI, Guns And Munitions Shipped To 84
HALL, Thomas 78 107
HAMBURG, Direct Trade With 35

"HANNIBAL", 83-84 86-87 Vessels Exceptionally Large 83
HANOVER, Street 102
HARFORD, County 102 107
HAVRE DE GRACE, France 76
HERRING, Elizabeth 101
HOLLAND, France Declared War On 15
HOLLIN, Family 40
HOLLINGSWORTH, Family 40 Levi 102 Samuel 95
HOLLINS, John 63
"HOPE", Vessels 84
HOUSE OF REPRESENTATIVES, 3
HUGHES, Victor 16
HUMPHREYS, Mr 89
IMMIGRANTS, European 30
IMMIGRATION, 100 Baltimore 55 To Baltimore 56
IMPORT, Tax 24
IMPORTS, America's 8 Cheap Cotton Cloth 5 Coffee 12 Foreign 37 Household Goods 5 Raw Hemp 4 Spices 5 Sugar 12 Tea 5 Tools 5
INDEPENDENCE, America's 9
INDIES, West Trade With The 82
INDUSTRIAL REVOLUTION, 36 45
INVESTORS, Maryland 41
IPSWICH, Massachusetts 89
IRELAND, 42
IRON, Bar 6 Deposits 5 Local Production 6 Maryland Export Of 12 Ore 5 Ore Demand In England 5-6 Pig 6 Semi-processed Ore 5 Workers British 6
ISLAND, Conflict 14 Dutch 9 French 9 Spanish 9

ISLAND (Cont.)
    Trade 4 9 13 42 Traders 43
    Transport Goods To And From 7
JAMES, 87
"JAMES BEACHAM", Vessels 68
JAY, John 15 Treaty 16 Treaty Of 1795 16
JAY'S, Treaty 21
JEFFERSON, 20 22
    Administration 21 President 20 26 Thomas 19 115
JEFFERSONIAN, Gunboats 70
JESSOP, George 96
JOURNEYMEN, 99 Carpenters 99 Masons 99
KAPFF, Abraham Von 84
KARTHAUS, C W 103 Peter 78
KEMP, 83 105 & Gardner 66 Joseph 104 Thomas 63 66 69 78 80 82 94 101 103-104 115 Thomas [Shipbuilder] 63
KERR, Archibald 96
KILTY, John 15
KINARD, [Kennard] & Williamson 88
KING GEORGE, Street 113
KNOX, Henry 15 Henry Secretary Of War 14
LABORERS, 13 22 63 99 100 105 106 110
LAKE, Ontario 87-88
LAMAR, 88
LAND, John 89
LAW, British 2
LAWS, Navigation 2
LEE, John 96
LETTERS, Of Marque 8 14 Of Reprisal 8
LEWIS, Negroe 106
LIBERIA, Black Baltimoreans Who Migrated To 108

LIVERPOOL, 30 Merchants Of 7
LLOYD, Col 58
LONDON, Complaining Shipbuilders 6 Merchants Of 7
LONG, 88
LOUISA, Vessels 89
LUBECK, Direct Trade With 35
MANUFACTURES, Domestic 21 Maritime 4 Textile 33 Woolen Goods 34
MANUMISSION, Documents In Maryland 108
MARKET, Street 98
MARPLE, Mr 86
MARYLAND, 4 47
"MARYLAND", Vessels 75-76
MARYLAND, Archives 56 Bank Of 94 Border State 13 Eastern Shore 47 Eastern Shore Of 42
"MARYLAND GAZETTE", 20 28
MARYLAND, Eastern Shore 54 Grain Export Of 12 Historical Society 56 Import And Export Duties 4 Iron Export Of 12 Movement Of Grain 8 Shippers 5 St Michaels 47 Tobacco 5
MASSACHUSETTS, Shippers And Shipyards In 4 Waltham 33
MASTER, Carpenters 80 101
MASTERS, [Artisans] 94
MCELDERRY, Hugh 88
MCKENZIE, & Thomas Blacksmith Shop 62
MCKIM, Family 40 Isaac 63 88 103
MECHANICS', Bank Of Baltimore 95-96
MERCANTILE, System 6-7 9 12
MERCANTILISM, 2 12 Colonial 9
MERCANTILIST, 7 Period 2

MERCHANT, Community
  Baltimore 42 Fleet America's
  26 System Early 97
MERCHANT MARINE, 37
  American 6 28 English 6
MERCHANTS, American 2 13 72
  And Financiers New York's 45
  And Shippers Fells Point 53
  Baltimore's 44 46 Philadelphia
  8
"MERRIMACK", 75
MERRYMAN, Mary 102
MEZICK, Baptiste 96 98 108
MILAN, Decree 22
MILES, Isaac H 82
MILLS, 89 Cloth 53 Flour 53
MISSISSIPPI, Steamboats 31
  Cotton Production 31
MITCHELL, Ann Maria 79
  Francis J 79
MONROE DOCTRINE, 35
"MONTAZUME", Vessels 78
MOORE, William 47
MOSHER, James 96
NAPOLEON, 21-22
NAPOLEONIC, Wars 80
NATIONAL, Bank Of Baltimore
  95 Marine Bank 96
NAVAL, Act Of 1 July 1797 18
NAVIGATION, Act Of 1817 34
  Acts 9
NAVY, American 33 44 74
  American Lack Of Professional
  8 British 21 71 British Royal
  20 27-28 72 86 Department 18-
  19 French 44 Napoleon's 20
  Royal 21 70 Secretary Of The
  17
NEWBURYPORT, Massachusetts
  73
NEGRO, Charles 107 Harry 107

NEGRO (Cont.)
  Jack 107 Law 106 Leon 107
  Stephen 107 Will 107
NETHERLANDS, 75 Direct Trade
  With 35
NEW ORLEANS, 88
NEW YORK, 30-31 41 45 64 73
  88-89 97 99-100 103 113
  Artisans Of 94 City 87
  Construction Trade In 99
"NILES WEEKLY REGISTER",
  56
OCCUPATIONS, 106
OHIO, Steamboat Construction In
  103
OLIVER, John 84 Mr 86 Robert 84
ORIENT, Trade With 88
PA DE MD, Navigation Company
  63
PANIC Of 1819 88 96
PARSONS, 83 William 66 69 78
  88 102
"PATAPSCO", Vessels 76 83
"PATAPSCO/CHESAPEAKE",
  Vessels 75
PATTERSON, 88
"PATUXENT", Vessels 88
PENNSYLVANIA, Movement Of
  Grain 8 Shippers And
  Shipyards In 4
PHILADELPHIA, 3-5 8 31 42 73
  89 97 113 18th Century
  Shipping In 42 Yellow Fever
  Epedemic 109
PHILADELPHIA, Population Of
  54
PHILPOT, Street Fells Point 78
PICKERING, Timothy Secretary
  Of State 75
PILCH, James Tallow Chandler 62
PINCKNEY, Treaty 76

PITT, Street 62-63 96 98 113
PLYMOUTH [ENGLAND], Yard 86
POOR, Relief 97 Urban 100 Working 100
POPULATION, Baltimore's 54 Free Black 57 Philadelphia's 54
PORT, American 11 Dues 11 Wardens Appointed 40
PORTERS, 106
PORTS, American 72 Atlantic 9 North American 82
PRICE, 83 108 111 Family 105 Home Still Standing In Fells Point 110 John 66 79-80 94 111 Shipyard 74 82 105 Walter 60 66 105 107 111 William 44-45 62-63 66 69 74 79-80 83 94 96 98 103-105 107-110 113 William & Son 105
PRIDE II, Schooner 115
PRINCIPIO IRON WORKS, 6
PRIVATEER, 41 System Revolutionary 73
PRIVATEERING, 41 Vessels 94
PRIVATEERS, 14 36 American 44 Baltimore Haven For 40 French 14 44 Out Of Baltimore 71
PRODUCTION, 2 American 33 American Colonial 5 Pitch 4 Sail 4 Tar 4 Turpentine 4 Wool 33
PRUSSIA, Direct Trade With 35
QUASI-WAR, 17 19 44-45 76 With France 73
QUEEN ANNE'S COUNTY, 107
RAILROADS, 31
RAWLINGS, Ann 102
RECIPROCITY, Act 34
RE-EXPORTS, From United States 13

REGISTRY, Act Of 1789 10 American Vessels 11
REGULATION, Of Commerce 9
REPUBLICANS, 113
"REVENGE", Schooner 104
REVENUE, Marine 74
REVOLUTION, 6 115 American 1-2 8 39-40 72 French 13 16 39 Industrial 36 45 Privateering During 8 San Domingo 109
RHODE ISLAND, Shippers And Shipyards In 4
RIDGLEY, Charles 88
RIGAUD, And Toussaint Two Rebels 14
RIGGERS, 63 100
RIGGIN, Israel 88 Levi 88
RIGGING AND RAKE, 68
RIVER, Boatmen 100 Mississippi 31 Patapsco 40 Susquehanna 54
ROBB, & Donaldson 83 88 John 88-89
ROBBS, John 89
ROBERT FULTON, Steamboat 88
ROBSON, Joseph 66 94 103
RODGERS, Captain John 74
ROYAL NAVY, 70
RUM, 6
RUSSIA, Direct Trade With 35
SAIL-MAKERS, 63
SAILORS, British 26 English 21
SAN DOMINGO, Rebelled Against France [1791] 15 Rebelling Colonies 13 Rebels Of 15 Revolution 14 109
SANDY HOOK, 30
SARDINIA, Direct Trade With 35
SAVANNAH, Georgia 89
SAWYERS, 106
SCHOONERS, 3 12 36-37 66 68

SCHOONERS (Cont.)
77 82 102 105 116 American 28 80 "Ann Of Baltimore" 63 Baltimore's 28 68-69 71 76 80 "Baltimore" 73 "Caroline" 104 "Chasseur" 104 116 "Dart" 101 101 "Maryland" 63 Most Popular Vessel 65 "Paragon" 63 "Pride II" 116 Privateer 104 "Revenge" 104 Sharp-built 69 78 Shipbuilders 80 Speed Of Baltimore's 70 Total Tonnage 69

SEAMEN, Baltimore 70 British 26 Naturalized Citizens Registered As 26

SEAMSTRESSES, 63

SEAPORTS, Atlantic 7

SECOND, Street 96

SEGRIEL, 89

SHIP, Of War "Constellation" 87

SHIP-SLOOPS, "Frolic" Class 87

SHIPBUILDERS, 2-3 American 2 11 81 American Great Prosperity 13 Baltimore 35 39 48 77 79 82 89 Baltimore Town's 9 British 7 Fells Point 46 102 106 Master 93 Number Of 42 Schooners 80

SHIPBUILDING, Fells Point 103 Nationwide Decline In 1797 And 1798 11-12

SHIPMENT, Of Goods In American Bottoms 7

SHIPPERS, Local 4

SHIPPING, American 4 British Regulation Of 2 Colonial 2

SHIPS, 68 American 34 American Capture And Sale Of 16 British 4 8 26 34 English 2 Exceptionally Large "Hannibal" 83

SHIPS (Cont.)
"Hannibal" 84 86 Largest Class Of Vessels in Baltimore 83 Sales 9 Subscription 18 Subscription "Maryland" 74 Subscription "Patapsco" 19 74

SHIPYARD,

SHIPYARDS, American 2 American Employers Of Artisans 13 American Employers Of Skilled Craftsmen 13 Annual Production 66 Baltimore's 53 78 93-94 Colonial 7 Fells Point 102 Fells Point Slave Labor 13 Gardner 60 Local 4 Number Of 42 Price 60 63 74 82-83

SHOP SYSTEM, 94

SINCLAIR, Rebecca 102

SKINNER, William 88

SLAVE, Frank 111 Harris 111 Labor In Shipyards Fells Point 13 Laborers 13 Lewis Dixson 106 Major 111 Plantation 58-59 Trade 77 Trading 37 Urban 58

SLAVEHOLDERS OCCUPATIONS, 57 59 Butchers 57 Carpenters 57 Clerks 57 Grocers 57 Hotel Keepers 57 Lawyers 57 Merchants 57 Physicians 57 Shoemakers 57 Tavern Keepers 57

SLAVERY, Urban 60

SLAVES, 59 105-106 113 Freed 57 West Indies 4

SLOOPS, 65 82 "Patapsco" 83 Sharp 78 "Splendid" 83

SMITH, Family 40 Joseph 62 Robert [2nd Secretary Of The Navy] 20 S 70 Samuel 95

SMUGGLED PRODUCE, West Indies 5
SMUGGLING, North American Colonies 72
SOCIETY, Assistance 97 Athenian 96
SOUTH, America Trade With 82 88 Productivity Of The 31
SPAIN, France Declared War On 15
"SPLENDID", Vessels 83
ST MICHAELS, 78
STATES, Barbary 20
STEAM, Propulsion Rotary Engine 103
STEAMBOATS, "Antelope" 88 103 "Experiment" 88 "Robert Fulton" 88
STEEL, John 63 107 Mr 63
STILES, George 63 88 101-103 113 George Mayor 63 John S 113 Major 113
STODDER, David 106-107
STODDERT, 18-19 Benjamin 17 David 73
STRAWBERRY, Street 103
SUGAR, 6 Distillers 6 Transshipment To European Ports 12
SUPPLIES, Hard Pine 81 Oak Planking 81 Oak Timber 81 Pine Masts 81
SURINAM, 75
SUSQUEHANNA, River 54
SWEDISH, And Danish Vice Consul 62
SYSTEM, Continental 22
TAILORS, 63
TALBOT, County 80 107
TARIFF, Of 1816 34 Protective Act In 1783 4
TARIFFS, 1 32 Import 8

TAX, Import 24
TAYLOR, Catherine Eliza 102 James 101 Lemuel 96 102
TEA, Duties 11
TENANT, Family 40 Thomas 63 78 98 102-103
THAMES, Street 63
THOMPSON, James 84 John 84
TIERNAN, Luke 102
TOBACCO, 7
TONNAGE, American 11
TRADE, Coastal 7 Colonial 2 English 2 Island 7 Restrictions British 35
TRADERS, 63 Baltimore 47 Island 43
TRADESMEN, 97
TRAFALGAR, 20 Battle At 21
TREATY, Of Alliance Of 1778 15-16 Of Ghent 28
TRIPOLI, Harbor 20
TURNER, Joseph 66 102 107 Rebecca 102
UNION, Line Steamboats 63
UNITED STATES, 1 3 BANK OF THE 96
US NAVY, 44 74 Cutters 45
VAGRANTS, 99
VANBIBBER, Isaac 95
VESSEL, American Definition Of 10 Increase Of Capacity 43 Sizes Philadelphia 43
VESSELS, American 7 13 20 26 34 37 American Cost Of Transport In 12 American Merchant 32 American Private Armed 71 American Tea Duties Baltimore Built And Crewed In 40 "Andromeda" 86 Baltimore's 64 "Ann Louisa" 89 "Ann McKim" 86 88 "Baltimore" 88

VESSELS (Cont.)
Baltimore-built 41 "Bazil Lamar" 89 British 28 41 British "Leopard" 26 British Naval 37 "Chasseur" 72 "Chesapeake" 26 "Constellation" 18 73 76 106 "Constitution" 18 Construction Of Coastal 7 "Croyable" 18 "Dart" 101 "Delaware" 18 European 41 81 Exceptionally Large "Hannibal" 83 Fore And Aft Rigged 65 Foreign 34 Foreign Built And Owned 11 Foreign Built Surcharge 10 French 14 16 French Duty Placed On 35 "Hannibal" 84 86 "Hope" 84 "Louisa" 89 Merchant 44 "James Beacham" 68 Joiners 63 "Maryland" 75-76 "Montazume" 78 Need For Speed 17 Newfoundland Fishing 28 "Patapsco" 45 76 83 "Patuxent" 88 Privateering 94 Sailing Construction Of 43 Seizing American 22 "Splendid" 83 Subscription "Maryland" 74 Subscription "Patapsco" 19 74 "United States" 63 "United States" 18 United States 47 US Naval 70
VIRGINIA, Shippers And Shipyards In 4 Tobacco 5
VONBIBBER, Abraham 108
VONKAPFF, 83 & Brune 84
VOYAGES, Transatlantic 7

WADE'S, Point Farm 104
WAITERS, 106
WAR, Civil 47 French And Indian 27
WAR OF 1812, 20 25 33 36 41 45 55 69 71-72 77 79-80 95 97 99-100 104 113 Of 1812 Privateering In 27
WARD, Horatio G 89
WARS, Napoleonic 80
WARSHIPS, Baltimore-built 74
WASHINGTON, 16 George 115 President 14 18
WATERS, Hezekiah 63 96 98 102 108 Wharf 98
WEARY, Peter 63
WELLS, CD 13
WEST INDIES, 8 11 16 40 42-43 47 British 35 French 17 Markets In 7 Starvation Of Thousands Of Slaves In 14 Trade With 88
WEST INDIAN, Carrying Trade 7
WHARF, Price's 79
WHETSTONE POINT, 6
WILSON, Henry 78 William 98 William & Sons 103
WOLFE, Street 79-80 101 103
WOOD, 89
XYZ AFFAIR 16 20
YELLOTT, Jeremiah 108
YELLOW, Fever 63 Fever Epidemics 100 Fever Outbreaks 63 Fever St Domingan Refugees Brought 109
ZACHARIE, Peter 90

205

www.ingramcontent.com/pod-product-compliance
Lightning Source LLC
Chambersburg PA
CBHW071228170426
43191CB00032B/1133